A YACHTSMAN'S FIJI

A YACHTSMAN'S FIJI

A Navigator's Notebook

Michael Calder

The Cruising Classroom
SYDNEY

Published by
The Cruising Classroom
20 Milham Crescent, Forestville, NSW 2087, AUSTRALIA

Typeset by The Cruising Classroom

Printed in Singapore by
Kyodo Printing

National Library of Australia
Cataloguing-in-Publication entry

Calder, Michael, 1931- .
A Yachtsman's Fiji : a navigator's notebook.

2nd ed.
Includes index.
ISBN 0 646 14682 3.

1. Pilot guides - Fiji. 2. Yachts and yachting - Fiji.
I. Title.

623.89299611

First Published in 1987
2nd Edition - 1993

Preface

In July of 1984, I arrived in Fiji from Vanuatu in my yacht 'Eureka', and after clearing customs at Lautoka, set off to cruise in the Yasawas. Charts were non-existent, but I was able to obtain some second-hand copies of 'Pickmere's' from a fellow yachtie who was moving on to Vanuatu. Until that time I had no knowledge of their existence and had already found that, except for the Pacific Islands Pilot Vol.II, published by The Hydrographer of the Navy, there was no information of any sort on the waters of Fiji, particularly those areas of interest to a yachtsman.

Undaunted, I set off in typical yachtie fashion, and in the traditions of the early navigators, to eyeball my way through some of the most beautiful cruising grounds of the South Pacific.

I had one advantage. I had visited the area out of Lautoka aboard the 'Matthew Flinders' some 6 years earlier and knew that there were some safe anchorages, and that when I arrived I could safely anchor at Sawa-I-Lau and 'Blue Lagoon'. Word of mouth from other yachties made up the remainder of my knowledge.

Within 24 hours I had experienced my first 'near miss'. The sight of a beautiful coral head, the position of which you have been unable to see, suddenly passing under the bow at 5 knots, tends to leave one a little weak. Charted as 'drying', I can safely say that the particular reef has at least two metres at low water!

Nevertheless, 30 years as a naval hydrographer had left its mark, and I placed my first bit of information on my chart and into the log for future reference - I did not realise it at the time, but this book had just been born.

Within weeks the need for a guide to these waters had become patently obvious and I set about collecting data in earnest. My holiday in Fiji had become work! But a better place to labour would be hard to find.

Many people fail to appreciate the size of Fiji. From the Yasawas in the west to Taveuni and Budd Reef in the east the islands cover a cruising ground that, in Australia, would stretch from Rockhampton to Townsville, in Europe would cover the Greek Islands, and in the West Indies would stretch from the Virgin Islands to Guadeloupe.

Fiji is not the place you go to for a couple of weeks. It is a place to which you can return often, and many yachts do just that.

In gathering the data for this book I have concentrated on the most popular areas. I have not visited the northern coasts of either Viti Levu or Vanua Levu. These I will keep for another time. Except in a very few instances, and these I have specifically noted, I have visited all the places mentioned. 'Eureka' cruised Fiji from July to November 1984, and from May to October 1985. And even that was a quick trip. In many places that I spent days, I could have spent weeks; in the few where I spent weeks, I could have spent months. That is except Suva. Only the British could have selected a capital in one of the wettest parts of Fiji. Maybe 1985 was a bad year?

What This Book Is:

My objective in writing this book is to give the cruising yachtsman the information needed to plan a cruise in Fiji; to enable that cruise to run more smoothly and safely through the benefit of prior knowledge of the ever-present bureaucratic processes with which a foreigner becomes involved; to briefly highlight some of the more important customs of the country and, most importantly, where it is safe to take a boat. One of the major worries that I experienced before moving to a new location in Fiji was whether I would be able to anchor safely and check out an area before nightfall. If this book enables the cruising yacht to move more freely and see parts of Fiji that, through a natural sense of caution, have so far been out of consideration, it will have achieved its aim.

What This Book Is Not:

The book is not a substitute for the navigational chart, the Pilot, books on meteorology, the history and culture of Fiji, and the prudent practice of navigation in uncharted waters.

The descriptions and chartlets given within are not the results of detailed hydrographic surveys. They have resulted from a sketch survey at best, and usually from an aerial photograph supplemented by a field inspection with a few lines of soundings made with a recording echo sounder, and a very thorough use of the 'MkI eyeball'.

I am always amazed at the number of yachts that still sail the world with inadequate chart coverage. I appreciate the cost of charts, and I am well aware that our forebears had nothing. I accept that for many on a restricted budget there is a great saving to be made by having only the minimum of charts. I have quoted chart numbers and referred to the Pilot whenever it is necessary. For this I make no apology; I see no reason to reinvent the wheel. For those with limited charts, I am sure this book will be of great assistance, but I would recommend that you at least borrow and study the correct chart before you set off for some delightful anchorage that is but a speck on the 1:800,000-BA2691, FIJI ISLANDS.

Anyone who has the complete chart coverage of Fiji will realise the shortcomings of the set. For them, and the many who have 'just enough', I am sure you will find this book a timely addition.

I wish you good cruising in 'A Yachtsman's FIJI'.

Preface to the 2nd. Edition.

Little changes quickly in Fiji, and mostly, any changes are of a minor nature. As I had promised myself at the end of my 1985 season in these delightful islands, I returned seven years later; landfall Suva, 20 May 1992.

EUREKA had spent the cyclone season in Auckland after having "closed the loop" to complete a world cruise on arriving there in September of 1991.

There had been, however, one major change in the intervening period. Fiji had become a republic. It was about to embark on the first democratic elections under a new electoral system, and it had a new constitution. The elections passed quietly, the new government was installed, and life resumed the previous leisurely pace to which I had been accustomed. It was almost as if I had never been away.

One conclusion, reached as EUREKA's bows pressed ever westward during the four years of her circumnavigation, I found fully substantiated. There are no more peaceful cruising grounds than those of the South-west Pacific, and those of Fiji are second to none.

I immediately set about my primary task of revision of this book. First, I voyaged north about the main island of Viti Levu to complete my coverage of that island, then I turned my attention to the north coast of Vanua Levu, circumnavigating that island in a clockwise direction. Whenever I came upon areas already covered by the book I checked out my previous instructions. As I have said, little had changed. But there were some changes.

The state of the top marks on the beacons was not good. Most of the beacons, or their remains, were in place, but many top marks were missing. The "Mk I. Eyeball" was now even more important as a navigation aid.

Possibly memories are deceptive, but the weather did not seem as benign as in earlier years. "Reinforced Trades" seemed to be the catch cry of the locals. Although there was drought in the Western Division and in the north of Vanua Levu, many days were overcast and reef spotting was difficult. Only the west lived up to its reputation for sunshine.

And the fishing was not what I remembered. Fijians had several theories; sea temperature too warm, the drought, and others, but all agreed the fish were not biting. Some were caught but not many. I even considered revising the section on "FISHING in FIJI" but, with the typical optimism of the angler, have decided that it will be better next year.

Last, but not least, more yachts are now visiting Fiji. There were 87 yachts at Musket Cove during Regatta Week 1992. The Yasawas and Mamanucas are as popular as ever, but the greater number of yachts and a heightened awareness by the local villagers of possibility of directly extracting some of the "tourist" dollars has seen some villages imposing charges for anchoring off. It is up to the individual to assess the worth of the impost. Most of Fiji has not yet been tainted by commercialism. Kadavu has been "discovered" but remains as friendly as ever, the Eastern Division is still relatively untouched but, with possible further development at Savusavu, is unlikely to remain so. Hopefully it will still be many years, if ever, before Fiji suffers the commercialism that is the West Indies or the Med.

As I cruised Fiji I met many yachts and received valuable feed back on the use, suggested improvements, and even errors that they had found in the first edition. These have been taken onboard and, in most cases, incorporated into this second edition.

While cruising in the West Indies, I found the oblique aerial photographs, included in many of the guides of great value in getting a feel for an anchorage before actually arriving there. In this edition I have obtained as many as possible, particularly of the more popular areas, and I know that this will not only assist in navigation but make the book a better souvenir of your Fiji cruise.

The advent of GPS, with its constant update of position, and the continuing reduction of costs of the equipment, has seen many cruising yachts using it as a primary method of navigation. Suggestions were often made that I should give "GPS Coordinates" of entrances or approaches to the anchorages. Not only am I not prepared to accept responsibility for the accuracy of such "information", but I would go further and enjoin all yachts to be singularly careful of such completely misplaced reliance on GPS. The charts of Fiji are on differing geographical datums many of which are not even programmable into GPS processors. The chartlets that I have drawn are illustrative, positions given are approximate and are there only to enable correlation with the same feature on the published chart. Further, I have met several yachts whose skippers have no idea of what datum shifts are all about. I do not wish to think I contributed to any "GPS assisted" groundings.

Acknowledgements

Much of the information in this book has its origin in original research, and I must primarily acknowledge the Government of Fiji, through the Permanent Secretary For Home Affairs and Immigration, for permission to undertake that research during 1984 and 1985. I would also like to thank the Prime Minister's Office for permission to visit Vanuabalavu and Gau, and the Ministry of Fijian Affairs for permission to visit the many other out islands.

My special thanks go to the Surveyor General, whose department lies within the Ministry of Lands, Energy and Mineral Resources. Within that department, Mr Hannif Khan of the Aerial Mapping Section, was most co-operative in assisting me to obtain aerial photographs, often at very short notice.

That I am able to convey my thanks to the foregoing is in no small way due to the invaluable assistance of Commander Stan Brown OBE, of the Naval Division of the Royal Fijian Military Forces. Without Stan's knowledge of Fiji and 'the where, the why, and the who', the project would never have seen the light of day.

There were many others with whom I came in contact; in the islands over a bowl of grog, in the towns over a beer. All were eager to further my knowledge of their vanua and their nation overall. I well remember their friendliness even if I cannot remember their names. I hope they will recall the visits of 'EUREKA' and accept my thanks.

There are some whose help was particularly significant. 'Rocky' Moody and the Committee of the Royal Suva Yacht Club; Joe and Lomani and all the staff members of the RSYC; Don Taylor; David Ives and the staff of the Fiji Hydrographic Unit; John and Margery Williams; Ned Fisher; Noel and Flora Douglas; Frank and Jo Kloss; June Elms; Mosese Tui Dama; The Fiji Visitors Bureau.

Then there are those who sailed with me from time to time aboard 'EUREKA'. Without their help and company life would have been far from pleasant. My wife Rosemary, our son Sam; Mike Fisher; Rosemary Pearce; George and Eva; Callum and Steve; Ann Hurrell; Siteri, Sue and Howard; Ike, Andrew, Laurie, Don, Ian, and Bruce; Bill, Des, Joe and Lennie.

On my return to Australia, Ken Morley of John Sands Electronics, in translating my computer tapes to disk saved weeks of work, and together with equipment loaned by Geoff Kennedy and Dan Fitzhenry enabled the timely production of the manuscript.

Finally, the book would never have been readable but for the diligent proof-reading of Margaret Davis. To her a special thanks.

2nd. Edition - 1993.

As the second edition of this book is really only an expanded version of the original, the foregoing acknowledgements are not to be forgotten. In some places the names have changed.

In the Aerial Mapping Section of the Lands and Survey Department, Mr Fauro, Principal Photogrammetrist, assisted with aerial photographs.

The Royal Suva Yacht Club has a new Commodore and some new staff members but most of the old faces are still around.

Stan Brown has now retired, with the rank of Captain, but was as willing as ever to lend a hand, and his influence, if required.

Bill Whiting of the Fiji Visitors Bureau must be thanked, not only for his own personal assistance, but also for putting me in touch with Jim Seirs ("THE best photographer in Fiji") whose photography has contributed so much to the value of this edition.

To the many yachts that passed comments to me over a beer or two or over the radio, and particularly Barry and Suzanne of the New Zealand yacht "Orca" and Stewart and Ann of the US yacht "Annie's Song" who took time to write or phone me in Australia, special thanks.

Some of my old crew members came back for a second "Fijian experience". My wife Rosemary, who, although she cannot understand why anybody would wish to forsake the pleasures of the hearth for life in a yacht, still managed to spend nine weeks onboard and made sure that I did not lose sight of the real task in hand - this revision. It is to her, for allowing me to pursue the cruising life, that I am, as ever, most deeply indebted.

Again, Margaret Davis proof-read the new chapters, while Alan Champion made a further check of "Fijian" details. Alan lived in Fiji for many years, and crewed with me from New Zealand on the last trip.

Photography:

All photographs used in the book and on the cover are by Jim Seirs. For the technically minded Jim used two Minolta DYNAX cameras. One an 8000i with a 28mm f2.8 wide angle lens, and the other a 9xi with a 35mm f1.4 wide angle lens. In both the metering mode used was the 14 segment honeycomb setting. The film used was Fuji 100 ISO Reversal. Flying was undertaken in a Cessna 172 at between 1000 and 1500 feet.

Jim has also published some excellent photographic records of life in Fiji. Amongst the titles are:- Fiji in Colour (1970), Fiji Celebration and Fiji Experience (1985), and The Mamanucas---Islands in the Sun.

Orthography

Throughout this book I have endeavoured to use the Fijian method of spelling, particularly regarding place names. Unfortunately many of the names that appear on the published charts have been spelt phonetically. For example, on chart BA2691 - FIJI ISLANDS, which will most probably be used for planning your cruise, you will find the islands of BEQA and KADAVU spelt as MBENGGA and KANDAVU, which is of course how they are pronounced!

In the briefest possible way, the following are the five rules that apply to Fijian pronunciation:

b is pronounced as mb in number.
c is pronounced as th in that.
d is pronounced as nd in end.
g is pronounced as ng in singer.
q is pronounced as ng+g in finger.

There is an additional section in the index at the end of the book where the English equivalent found on the chart is listed with the Fijian spelling used in this book.
The British Admiralty chart provides the primary coverage of FIJI. As this series is revised, and generally metricated, the Fijian spelling is replacing English. If you cannot find NGGAMEA under 'N' use the above rules and look under 'Q'.
I have also omitted the suffix 'Island' when naming islands and have only used the Fijian name.

Contents at a glance

Contents

Part One - Introduction

Part Two - Suva, The Central and Eastern Division

Part Three - Savusavu and The Northern Division

Part Four - The Western Division

List of Chartlets

List of Coloured Plates

The camera symbol 📷 is inserted in the text where the plates below are particularly relevent.

PART ONE

Introduction

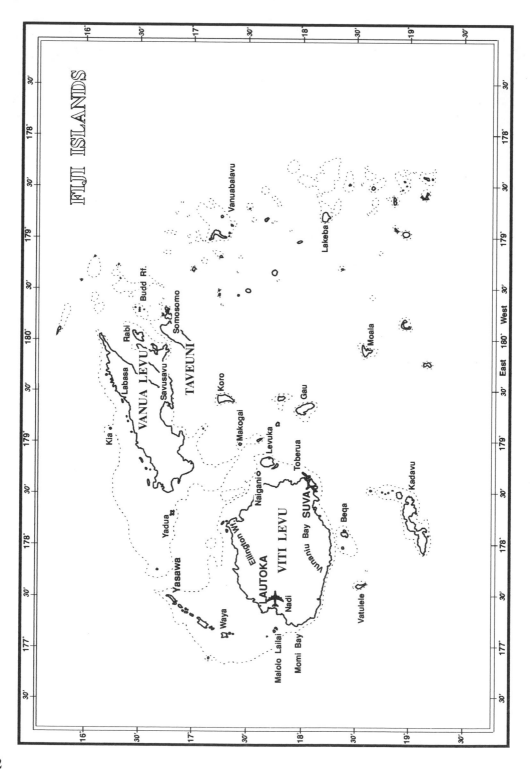

Fiji

The island nation of Fiji, made up of more than 300 islands dotted across some 200,000 square miles of sea, lies between 15 degrees and 22 degrees south of the equator and straddles the 180th meridian. In Fiji the new day begins, and a better place to start the new day would be hard to find!

Situated at the hub of the South-west Pacific, Fiji has become the crossroads of air and shipping services between North America and Australia-New Zealand. This, together with its position in relation to the other major island groups of the Pacific, makes it a natural port of call during any passage of the South-west Pacific. Not only does geographical location lend attraction to the yachtsman but in addition the port of Suva has a capable shipbuilding and repair industry, while Lautoka has a marina with a 63 tonne marine hoist and hardstand for 30 yachts, with either on site or access to full repair facilities. Suva and the other major ports have excellent provisioning facilities.

Magnificent cruising grounds abound in the waters of Fiji, and the yachtsman can seek out either developed resort areas or, if desired, total isolation.

The Land and it's People:

The total land area of Fiji is 18,333 square kilometres; of more than 300 islands at least 100 are inhabited. The largest island is Viti Levu, which contains the nation's capital, Suva, and is 10,429 square kilometres in area. Vanua Levu is next with 5,556 square kilometres, followed by the other main islands of Taveuni (470), Kadavu (411), Gau (140), Ovalau (101), Rabi (69), Rotuma (47), and Beqa (36).

The four biggest islands are volcanic in origin, as are many of the others. The summits of many mountains have distinct craters, but their activity has long since ceased. Hot springs are to be found, the most notable being those at Savusavu; though they are hardly in the spectacular category. Most of the high peaks on the main islands are basaltic, and the high rugged interior of most islands is uninhabited.

The coastal plains and river flats carry most of the country's agriculture. The most important are those formed by the major rivers; the Rewa, Navua, Sigatoka, Nadi, and Ba. The plains and lowlands of the north-west of Viti Levu contain the country's main sugar-growing area, together with parts of the north coast of Vanua Levu. Sugar is the main export of Fiji.

Fiji has accepted many nationalities to its shores and today is rich in diverse cultural backgrounds. The population, now approaching 730,000, comprises two major ethnic groups: native Fijians, about 49%, and Fijians of Indian descent, about 46%. Other groups to be found are part-Europeans, Europeans, Rotumans, Chinese and other Pacific Islanders. Most of the Europeans are from Australia and New Zealand.

More than 80% of the land in Fiji is owned by the native Fijians, approximately 12% by the Crown, and the rest is freehold.

The land owned by the Fijians is not however owned by individuals. It is held under customary tenure in the name of small tribal units, the most important of which is the mataqali. The subject and complexity of the ownership and use of 'native lands' is worthy of a book of its own. The guardian of the land owned by the Fijian people is the Native Land Trust Board (NLTB).

However, for the yachtsman it is only necessary to remember one rule: ALL land is owned by SOMEONE!!

The Shortest of Histories:

Archaeological research has shown that the Fiji Islands were populated at least 3,000 years ago, although there are some researchers who claim that original settlement was made as far back as 8,000 years.

According to Fijian legend, the great chief Lutunasobasoba led his people across the seas to the new land of Fiji. Most authorities agree that people came into the Pacific from south-east Asia by way of the Indonesian archipelago. Later, voyagers from Polynesia mixed freely with the Melanesians to create a highly developed society long before the arrival of the Europeans.

European discovery of the islands was made by Abel Tasman, who sighted islands and reefs north-east of Taveuni on 6 February 1643. Captain Cook visited the islands in 1774, but they were not recorded in detail until 1789 when, having been cast adrift by the mutineers of HMS BOUNTY, Captain Bligh sailed through them during his epic voyage in the longboat. Bligh did not set foot on the islands, doubtless due to the reputation 'Feegee men' had as cannibals, and his being chased out of the Yasawas by two war canoes.

The first Europeans to land and live among the Fijians were shipwrecked sailors or runaway convicts from Australian penal settlements. In 1805, sandalwood was discovered on Vanua Levu, and this led to a third group of immigrants, the traders. With these people also came muskets. The Fijian way of life - savage by any standard - turned into an era of even bloodier warfare. Although treachery, killing, and cannibalism was normal; the beachcombers added a new dimension by lending their talents as marksmen to the various warring chiefs.

The first Christian missionaries, two Protestant Tahitians, arrived in Lakeba in 1830. In 1835 two Wesleyan Europeans followed and it was one of these, David Cargill, who was responsible for the orthography of the present day Fijian language.

In time the beachcombers and mercenaries gave way to the planters and missionaries. The transition was greatly accelerated when Ratu Seru Cakobau, the chief of Bau, who was accepted by many Europeans as the 'Tui Viti', embraced Christianity in 1854. The rest of the country soon followed. Much of the old fierce fighting ceased and cannibalism was abandoned.

Cakobau faced debts arising from claims by a former American consul, John B. Williams. When W.T. Pritchard arrived in Fiji as the first British Consul in 1858, Cakobau offered to cede his islands to Britain if Britain would pay his debts. Pritchard took the offer to the Government in London and two investigators were sent out to examine the country's potential. Rumours that Fiji would become a British colony brought many settlers from Australia and New Zealand but the cession did not eventuate.

For several more years the settlers made various attempts to establish a stable government under Cakobau's authority but all ended in failure. Finally, on 10 October 1874, Britain accepted a second offer of cession and Fiji became a Crown Colony, with its capital at Levuka.

When the first British governor, Sir Arthur Gordon, arrived, the economy was stagnant. He considered that the best way to revive it was to greatly expand the growing of sugar, but he feared that large scale employment of Fijians as plantation labourers would disrupt their traditional way of life. He therefore authorised that labourers be imported from India to work on the sugar plantations.

The first Indians arrived in 1879 under an indenture system that lasted until 1916. In all more than 60,000 of these indentured labourers were to come to Fiji. When the system was abolished many of those under current contracts stayed on. There was already a large Indian population in Fiji made up of those who had made a similar decision on the completion of earlier contracts. These people became the independent farmers and businessmen who are now the backbone of Fijian commerce.

Although Fiji did not gain independence from Britain until 1970, a membership system of government was first introduced in 1964. Some elected members of the Legislative Council were given specific portfolios.

In 1965, a constitutional conference was held in London to discuss changes in the constitution to make further progress towards self government. A ministerial system of government was introduced in Fiji in 1967.

Discussions with Britain continued. In April 1970, Fiji's Legislative Council, led by the Chief Minister, Ratu Sir Kamisese Mara met in London to discuss framing a constitution and the move towards independence.

Five months later the nation gained independence on 10 October 1970 - 96 years to the day when Fijian chiefs ceded the islands to Queen Victoria. Fiji adopted a democratic system of constitutional government based on the British Westminster model. Independence Day was celebrated in an atmosphere of harmony, tolerance and co-operation.

1987 Coups:

Until 1987, Fiji was a member of the (British) Commonwealth of Nations. She maintained close ties with Great Britain and paid homage to Queen Elizabeth II, who was also proclaimed Queen of Fiji.

On the morning of 14 May 1987, in a bloodless coup led by Lieutenant Colonel Sitiveni Rabuka, the newly elected coalition government of Timoci Bavadra was overthrown. Without going into the details of situation it is sufficient to say that, in spite of Bavadra and the majority of his cabinet being ethnic Fijians and non-Indians, the coalition was considered to be "Indian dominated".

The long simmering fear that the major ethnic group in Fiji , the Indians, who already dominated the Fijian economy, would also gain political power was openly expressed. Ethnic Fijians feared loss of control over the Fijian lands and the slow disintegration of their culture.

Tension between the two races heightened. There was a degree of violence in the urban areas and, having handed back power to the civilian government, Rabuka found it necessary to stage a second coup four months later on 25 September.

On 7 October 1987, Fiji was declared a republic and the 113 year long close association with Great Britain was ended. Work began on the drafting of a new constitution that would ensure the ethnic Fijian remained master in his own land.

In May 1992 the first elections under the revised electoral system were held and the government of Fiji returned to an elected parliament.

In spite of the formal severance of ties with Great Britain and the Queen, many Fijians would still like their country to be readmitted to the Commonwealth. There is a strong attachment to the Royal Family and the concept of Royalty fits well into the Fijian system of heredity chiefs.

At present the government and constitution are seen by many outsiders as being less than fully democratic, and until this is resolved there is little hope that Fiji will return to the Commonwealth.

Nevertheless the ways of the Fijian people have changed little. They are still as delightfully hospitable as ever. And the beauty of the islands has not dimmed.

Climate:

Fiji enjoys a tropical maritime climate without great extremes of heat or cold. It lies in the area affected by tropical cyclones, which are mostly confined to the period from November to April, with the greatest frequency around January and February. On average some 10 to 12 cyclones per decade affect some part of Fiji, and two to three do severe damage.

At all seasons the predominant winds over Fiji are the trade winds from the east to south-east. On the western and the eastern sides of Viti Levu and Vanua Levu, day-time sea breezes blow in across the coast.

Temperatures at sea level are usually fairly uniform. Because of the influence of the surrounding oceans the changes from day to day and season to season are relatively small. Sunshine is relatively high in the north-western areas, especially in winter. South-eastern coastal areas and the high interior often experience persistent cloudy humid weather.

Rainfall is highly variable. It is usually abundant in summer, especially over the larger islands, but in winter and 'spring' it is often deficient, particularly in the dry zone on the western and northern sides of the main islands.

In the dry season, from May to October, the heaviest rainfall occurs on the windward (south-east) side of the larger mountainous islands.

Daily Averages.	January.		July.	
	Suva	Nadi	Suva	Nadi
Max C°	30	31	26	28
Min C°	24	23	20	18
Sun Hr/Day.	5.8	6.7	4.3	7.0
Rain mm.	310	280	160	50
Rain Days	22	17	17	4

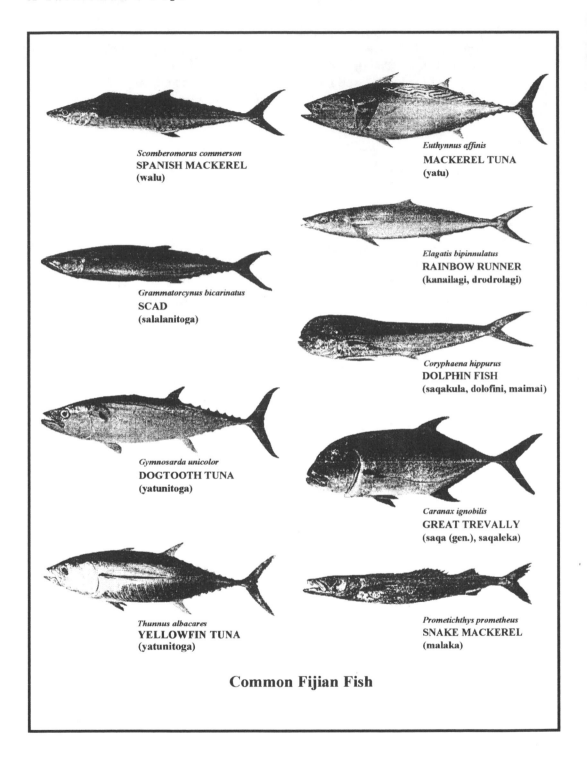

Scomberomorus commerson
SPANISH MACKEREL
(walu)

Euthynnus affinis
MACKEREL TUNA
(yatu)

Grammatorcynus bicarinatus
SCAD
(salalanitoga)

Elagatis bipinnulatus
RAINBOW RUNNER
(kanailagi, drodrolagi)

Coryphaena hippurus
DOLPHIN FISH
(saqakula, dolofini, maimai)

Gymnosarda unicolor
DOGTOOTH TUNA
(yatunitoga)

Caranax ignobilis
GREAT TREVALLY
(saqa (gen.), saqaleka)

Thunnus albacares
YELLOWFIN TUNA
(yatunitoga)

Prometichthys prometheus
SNAKE MACKEREL
(malaka)

Common Fijian Fish

Fishing in Fiji:

The knowledge of the author regarding the art of fishing can be written on the back of a postage stamp, but nevertheless the few words and the pictures that accompany them may assist others of similar levels of expertise.

Fishing, 'EUREKA Style', generally is carried out by trailing a line of indeterminate breaking strain (the heavier the better) from the back stay immediately on clearing a harbour and finally pulling it in before entering the next port of call (if I remember). With luck, some hapless fish of suicidal bent and of unknown species may impale itself upon the lure at some time between these two events. Providing that the flesh of the poor creature is not too dark, as with most tuna, fresh fish is immediately placed on the menu. That which cannot be readily eaten or frozen is thinly sliced and marinaded to make kakoda, the Fijian equivalent of sashimi and the many other raw fish dishes.

I should state here and now that I love eating fish, it is just that I do not have the patience required of the consummate angler.

As will be appreciated, such an unprofessional approach to the subject does not result in my table being heavily laden with piscatorial delights. In fact, until I reached Fiji, the strike rate was something of the order of one fish per one THOUSAND miles! In Fiji that all changed.

There, with little change in methodology, I could almost guarantee to catch at least one fish, of sufficient size to feed four, every time I set the line. If proceeding to a new area or village I would sometimes leave the line out for a second strike to provide an additional 'sevusevu' for my future host .

Those who know fishing will have favourite lures for special fish, and extra special (and expensive) ones for extra special fish. The lure used aboard EUREKA is the most common available: red plastic, about 12 cm. long, two hooks at one end and a brass ring at the other. A wire trace attaches the lure to the line, and a couple of trolling sinkers, the long thin kind, are threaded onto the line where it joins the trace to keep the lure just below the surface, and the whole lot has swivels inserted at strategic intervals to prevent the line twisting. The line is then attached to the backstay with a piece of rubber inner tube to provide a little 'give' when the fish hits.

Doubtless the type of fish caught bears some relationship to the area in which the fishing is done. All the fish listed here have been caught almost anywhere in Fiji. I have found, however that strikes generally occur more often going in and out of reef entrances, and the predominant fish is the magnificently succulent walu.

During my period in Fiji, the following found their way on to my table. For that reason alone I would assume that they are the most likely to be caught by others:-

Spanish mackerel	-	WALU.
Scad.	-	SALALANITOGA.
Dogtooth tuna	-	YATUNITONA.
Yellowfin tuna.	-	YATUNITOGA.
Mackerel tuna.	-	YATU.
Rainbow runner.	-	KANAILAGI
Dolphin fish.	-	SAQAKULA.
Great trevally.	-	SAQALEKA.
Snake mackerel.	-	MALAKA.

In truth, the last named never made the table. It looks so uninviting and full of bones as to be not worth the bother.

For those who are interested in game fishing, Fiji has all the facilities and many of the fish. Apart from your own boat, most of the resorts run charter trips daily. The Royal Suva Yacht Club also has its own Game Fishing Association. Amongst the fish to be found are black Pacific sailfish, black marlin, jack fish, barred mackerel, barracuda, and shark.

If you are of contemplative mood do not try the relaxation of hand line fishing from the cockpit of your boat. There are just too many fish and they will worry you to distraction. In common with most coral waters they range from the ubiquitous parrot fish to the delicious coral trout and cod.

One final word on fishing in Fiji. Having removed your choice fillets from the fish you have just caught, do not throw away the head and bones; the Fijian loves them and often considers them the best of the eating. Offer them to a passing canoe.

If you are interested in a fine pictorial record of the Food Fishes of Fiji, there are two excellent posters available from the Fisheries Division of the Ministry of Primary Industries for a very modest sum.

Good fishing.

2

Rules, Regulations and Customs

Ports of Entry:

There are three ports of entry into Fiji - Suva, Lautoka or Levuka. The latter has little to recommend its use as it is a relatively small town with limited provisioning facilities and is less than one full day's sail from Suva. The choice between the remaining two will probably be dictated by the direction of a yacht's approach to Fiji; Lautoka being ideal for those arriving from Vanuatu or New Caledonia.

If entering at Suva it may be necessary to sail for up to two or three days after making the first landfall. The importance of not going ashore before completing entry formalities at a port of entry cannot be too highly stressed. The Fiji Maritime Surveillance Centre is situated in Suva and a well developed reporting system is in operation.

Almost all inhabited islands in Fiji are connected to Suva by VHF radio telephone and the presence of a yacht in the outer islands will not go unnoticed. Disregard for the entry formalities may result in heavy fines, or difficulties later in your stay, and will reflect adversely on other yachts.

Should it be necessary for a yacht to seek shelter or respite for reasons beyond her control she should inform the customs authorities through SUVA Radio (3DP) on 2182 Khz., VHF Channel 16, or by telephone. Contact with the shore should be minimised.

Entry Procedures:

Immediately on arrival at the chosen port of entry the yacht, if free from disease, should hoist the Q flag requesting pratique; if available she should also hoist the Fijian flag as an act of courtesy, and proceed to the appropriate quarantine anchorage to await further instructions on VHF. Although the health official should board the yacht without further action, the practice in 1992 was for the yacht to go alongside either the main wharf in Suva, or to the Marina in Lautoka, for formalities to be carried out.

"PORT CONTROL" will issue the necessary instructions on VHF. If a VHF radio is not carried it may be necessary for the skipper to go ashore and report to customs, who will then initiate further action. The skipper ALONE should land under these circumstances.

It should be noted that customs and other formalities MUST begin within 24 hours of arrival. The practice of arriving on a Friday and not clearing until Monday is not acceptable. If arrival is made out of working hours, a charge of $60 (for a 3 hour minimum period) will be levied by the Customs Authorities for overtime.

Normal working hours are as follows:

Mon to Thur.........	0730-1300. 1400-1630.
Fri......................	0730-1300. 1400-1600.

Procedures must be completed by these times, and it must be realised that clearance procedures carried out on first arrival in the country are somewhat protracted. At least 3 hours to complete them is not unusual.

You must accept that your last port was a foreign country where agricultural and health standards may have been different to those in Fiji. Remember, here you are the foreigner! The Fijians welcome you to their land but they wish to ensure that you do not inadvertently bring with you unwanted pests, or through ignorance break the law; they also wish to ensure that when your time is up you are able to leave their country.

Pets are not allowed ashore and a bond may be required if you have one on board. Import duty may be payable on liquor supplies or they may be bonded. All arms and ammunition must be declared and surrendered to the Customs Officer for safe keeping by the Fiji Police; they may be collected immediately before departure.

All crew members must possess passports and they must be valid for six months after the date of entry. A visa is not required for a stay of up to one month. Visas, valid for up to four months, will be issued on arrival. They may be extended for up to a maximum of six months. The fee for such an extension is $50 (1992). Yacht owners and their crews are required to have evidence of funds to support themselves while in Fiji. I have always found that access to credit card facilities is acceptable. Anyone wishing to sign off is required to have an onward air ticket and documentation to enter another country or an air ticket to their country of origin.

Security:

Once the Health Officer has issued a certificate of Pratique, a yacht will normally be boarded and searched by the Port Security Unit and further formalities will not be undertaken until a security clearance has been issued by the PSU.

For the purpose of such clearance, vessels shall be required to furnish:-

a full list of all persons onboard.

a signed declaration of all arms, drugs and contraband cargo onboard

a proper manifest of cargoes to be loaded or discharged with destination ports clearly indicated. (Generally not applicable to yachts.)

Security clearance Certificates will be issued by Port Security Unit after searching the vessel.

All detained items (usually guns) will be documented and a copy of the document handed to the owner.

Collection of detained items will only be released upon production of the copy of the detention documents.

Any undeclared arms, drugs or contraband cargo will be confiscated and handed to the Security Forces and owners of the vessel reported to the Police for prosecution. Several such prosecutions were made during the 1992 season.

No vessel shall ply freely in Fiji waters unless given a security clearance from a declared port of entry. Security Clearance Certificates must be produced by vessels on demand.

Security Clearance Certificates will have to be endorsed by Port Security Unit before departure of all vessels.

A fee is levied for the security clearance. The minimum charge is $20. EUREKA was charged $37.50 in 1992.

Documentation Required on Arrival:

Although the relevant departmental officers will provide their own copious quantities of forms to be completed, the following should be readily to hand to speed procedures:

Customs:

Clearance from last port.
Ship's Papers.
Description of Yacht (see pro forma below.)
List of places to be visited.
All firearms.
Stowage list of all dutiable goods.
Crew List.

Immigration:

Crew list to include date of birth, nationality, passport number.

List of islands or Locations to be visited (this may be amended later if required).

Onward air tickets for any crew leaving or bond monies if required.

Financial status statement for owners may be required but this is usually given verbally.

Proforma of HM Customs Supplementary Information:

1. Vessel's Name.
2. Register No.
3. Home Port Vessel.
4. Owner's Name.
5. Owner's Address.
6. Master's Name.
7. Hull Colour.
8. Deck Colour.
9. Length.
10. Beam.
11. Type.
12. Rig.
13. Cabin Colour.
14. Sail Colour.
15. Type of Mast/Colour
16. Type of Navigational Equipment.
17. Type of Radio Equipment.
18. Radio Call Sign.
19. Type of Engine.
20. Distinguishing Marks(Structure, Location of Cabin and Boat, Colours, etc.).
21. List Names, Passport Nos., Nationality and ages of All Person/s on Board.
22. How long intend to be in Fiji.
23. Other places intended to visit.

The following is a copy of the notice given to owners of overseas yachts on arrival in Fiji. You will be required to sign a declaration of understanding and agreement to comply with these conditions.

CUSTOMS & EXCISE DEPARTMENT FIJI   Rotn No:.......
H.O.Y.R.No :....

NOTICE TO OWNERS/MASTERS OF OVERSEAS YACHTS.
CONDITIONS OF TEMPORARY ENTRY INTO FIJI
CUSTOMS REQUIREMENTS:

1. Visiting yachts may enter and be kept in Fiji without the payment of Customs dues provided:

a. The yacht is the sole property of the bona fide tourist.
b. The yacht is on a bona fide cruise or participating in a yacht race.
c. The yacht is solely for personal use of the owner.
d. The yacht shall remain in Fiji for a period not exceeding 6 months of its arrival. (Periods of extension beyond 6 months are available by application.)
e. The owner shall retain his/her immigration status as a bona fide tourist whilst in Fiji.

2. You must report your yacht inwards at a Customs Port on arrival in Fiji and must clear outwards at a Customs Port before leaving Fiji. If you wish to visit another Customs Port or cruise within Fiji waters, you must clear outwards at the Customs Port where you have last entered your yacht inward. After completion of your visit/cruise you must immediately report your yacht inwards at a Customs Port.

3. Your yacht will become liable to duty if:
it is in any way disposed of in Fiji (ie. sold, abandoned or given as a gift).
it is put into commercial use or for other consideration whilst in Fiji waters (ie. taken for commercial charters, hired or leased cruises, etc.).
the owner/master is associated with any entity in Fiji as an employee or employer, either upon arrival or subsequently.
the owner/master is holder of a Fiji Immigration Permit to Enter and Reside in Fiji either on arrival or subsequently.
the yacht is not exported within 6 months of the date of the yacht's arrival in Fiji. (unless extensions have been approved.)

4. Upon initial arrival you will be allowed landing passenger's allowances regarding high duty goods such as liquor, beer or wine and tobacco (or cigarettes), per each adult person over 17 years of age. All high duty goods in excess will have to be duty paid.

5. On arrival all arms and ammunition must be declared and surrendered to the Customs Office for safe keeping by the Fiji Police. These may by timely arrangement with the Police (48 hours at least) be collected before leaving Fiji.

6. No live animals, reptiles or birds of any kind, or fresh meat, fruit and vegetables on board the yacht may be landed or taken ashore. Some restriction whether such goods will be permitted to remain on board after your first arrival at a Customs Port may be enforced by officers of the Department of Agriculture.

7. No high duty goods such as liquor, beer, tobacco and cigarettes or other bonded or drawback goods may be shipped duty free as stores for yachts of less than 100 nett tonnes.

8. You will be asked to sign a copy of this Notice saying that you understand and accept the above conditions. Please ask the Customs Officer if you do not understand the Notice as failure to comply with any of the conditions may render you liable to penalties under the Customs laws.

Immigration Requirements:

Yachtsmen require permits from an Immigration Officer before they disembark in Fiji. If an Immigration Officer does not meet the yacht on its arrival a message should be sent through the Customs Officer to the Immigration Office, or a telephone call (312622 - Suva, 661706 - Lautoka, and 444148 - Levuka) made to that office requesting the attendance of an Immigration Officer. He will need to be provided by the person in charge of the yacht with two copies of a manifest listing all persons aboard, and will need to see every person, every person's passport and receive from all concerned a correctly completed passenger arrival card. As an alternative to an Immigration Officer visiting the yacht, the skipper may be required to carry out the necessary formalities at the Immigration Office.

Responsibilities Of The Skipper:

To expand a little on the foregoing.

The skipper of the yacht is considered in the same light as the master of any visiting ship, and you will note in all the forms that are filled in and signed you will be signing as Master. You are thus not only responsible for your yacht but also for all crew members that you bring into the country.

Crew Changes:

Generally the arrangements between skipper and crew are fairly loose, to say the least, but it is essential that, should any members of the crew wish to leave the yacht to 'do their own thing', they be formally 'signed off' at the nearest Immigration Office. A "Form A" will be filled in by the skipper and signed, and the Immigration Officer will amend the crew list accordingly. You will have to produce the crew member's passport and onward ticket to their next destination; in some instances the final destination of the ticket may have to be the country of nationality

If a new crew member joins, the skipper will have to complete a "Form B" and produce the member's passport at the Immigration Office, again the crew list will be amended.

If crews are exchanging between yachts, both skippers will need to attend the Immigration Office, with the relevant passport(s).

In none of the foregoing is the crew member required to attend.

Guns:

In 1992 there were several occasions when guns that had not been declared were found onboard yachts. They were confiscated and heavy fines imposed.

In another case, a yacht that landed a gun at one port of entry (Levuka), was unable to have it returned at another (Lautoka), even though it was said that this had already been agreed when landed. I understand that difficulty was also encountered even having weapons transferred between Suva and Lautoka.

Itinerary:

On entry you will have informed Customs and Immigration of your proposed itinerary and this should be adhered to.

Probably, after the first month or so, you will wish to change your original "best guess". The authorities will need to be advised. This will be done at your next 'internal' clearance from one of the major ports as described in the next section.

It is appreciated that yachts are at the mercy of wind and weather and reasonable changes to timing, and failure to visit a particular place will not cause any problems, but, with the exception of making passages along the coasts of the main islands of Viti Levu, Vanua Levu, Ovalau or Taveuni, visits to places not on the itinerary should be avoided.

Movement Within Fiji Waters:

It is a requirement whenever a yacht wishes to cruise Fiji waters outside the port limits of the port of entry she has to clear Customs outward and, on completion of the cruise, again clear inwards. This is theoretically true even if the boat is visiting NUKULAU a popular Suva yachties' weekend anchorage only about 7 miles from Suva, and from which Suva is clearly visible!

These 'internal' clearances are, however, far less time consuming than that carried out on first arrival. There are no requirements to go through any medical, quarantine, or immigration procedures and the visit to the Customs Office can be made up to 24 hours before sailing. If a visit to outer islands is intended, you must complete customs clearance first, then take your clearance to the relevant authority to obtain your permit (see later).

You will have to fill in a form almost identical to the one filled in on arrival. This you will consider to be a complete waste of time, particularly as 90% of the form is a repetition of the yacht's particulars. Of course, when you arrive at your next port of entry, even if it is the same one you left, you will again clear in and fill in yet another identical form.

But that is the Fijian Way. So much for the British- based bureaucracy! And surely to savour such 'charms' is the reason that you are visiting Fiji.

Actually these procedures are a form of compulsory movement reporting and are most useful in a Search and Rescue operation should you be so unfortunate as to need one.

Permits:

For yachts intending to visit the outer islands, those other than Viti Levu, Vanua Levu, Ovalau, and Taveuni; or any native village in the Fiji Group, you will need to obtain a permit. Permits should be obtained from the following authorities: In Suva, from the Ministry of Fijian Affairs; in Levuka, from the Commissioner Eastern Division; in Lautoka, from the Commissioner Western Division. It should be noted that a permit to visit the Yasawas can only be obtained at Lautoka. Further, in 1992, subsequent to an earlier Provincial Council Meeting, visits to the Lau Group were temporarily suspended.

The reason for this permit system is to restrict the influx of tourists into areas where there may be little or no facilities for them and to avoid unacceptable interaction between the western lifestyle and that of the Fijians in the less developed areas.

The Fijian and his land are indivisible. The Fijian word VANUA means not only the land on which the Fijian lives, the vegetation, animals, and other objects upon it, but it also includes his whole social and cultural system. There is great respect for the old ways in Fiji and a large degree of autonomy in the day-to-day running of the outer island communities. Many of these communities do not want visitors. They like their quiet, easy-going, undemanding life style and do not want it disrupted by foreign ways. If this is their wish it should be respected. Surely it was your wish to escape from the demands of your previous lifestyle that drew you to Fiji?

The permit that you do receive may be in either English or the Fijian language (Page 19 and 20). It will be seen it is not only a permit but also a letter of introduction to the 'turaga ni koro' (the village head), the 'Buli' (head of the provincial subdivision), or the 'Roko Tui' (provincial head). On arrival at an island the skipper should make a courtesy call on the appropriate personage, show him (or her) the letter, make a small gesture of respect by presentation of 'yaqona', and explain what you and your crew would like to see and do.

P/NO: Doz 133/92.

OFFICE OF THE DISTRICT OFFICER
LAUTOKA/YASAWA

PERMIT TO VISIT YASAWAS AND OTHER
NEIGHBOURING ISLANDS

This is to advise that permission has been granted to:

.....Michael Colder......HO34476......(SKIPPER)......

....

....

....

....

....

To visit Yasawas and other neighboruing islands in their yatch

the ....EUREKA...................... or by private

arrangement between ....30/8/92 – 30/10/92.......... provided:

1. That the (a) person named above has/have cleared by the
   Fiji Customs and Immigration authorities at a Port of
   entry into Fiji.

2. That he/she/they shall not enter any village or other
   premises unless invited or prior permission has been
   obtained from the head of the village to do so.

3. That he/she/they hold(s) valid visas into Fiji covering
   the period of the stay in Yasawas or ther neighbouring islands.

4. That he/she/they shall not behave in a manner prejudicial
   to the peace and good order of the villagers.

5. That no person other than those already named on the
   permit and who is not a Fiji Citizen shall be authorised
   to travel on their yacth (if applicable without obtaining
   prior permission from this office.

6. That this permit does not cover the village of Kese on the
   island of Naviti in Yasawa.

.............................(District Officer Lautoka/Yasawa)

cc: Roko Tui Ba
    The DPC/Western
    Forward Base(West) C/- 5th Battalion,FMF,Lautoka

English Language Permit

Ref.: No.68/8/4

Vale ni Tabaoakaoaka I Taukei
Government Buildings
SUVA

12 Okosita, 972

Kivei Kemuni na Turaga ni Vanua
Mata ki na Bose ni Yasana
Turaga ni Koro kei Kemuni na Turaga kei na
Marama lewe ni vanua ena ~~Yacana~~/Yanuyanu/Koro ko:

MALOLOLO, MANA KEI YANUYA

I'saka

VULAGI SARAVANUA KI NA VEIYANUYANU KEI NA VEIKORO

E rau/~~ratou~~ kauta tiko yani na i vola oqo
ko. M. CALDER .... kei ~~iratou~~
ko. MRS. CALDER .... ka rau/~~ratou~~
sokotaka tiko na ~~nona~~/nodrau/~~nodratou~~ i "YOTA" roka
VUNIVULA ... ka yacana EUREKA ....". E
rau/~~ratou~~ gole tiko mai vakagade mai OSTERELIA... ka
rau/~~ratou~~ via sarava eso na noda veiyanuyanu. Sa solia oti
~~vua~~/vei rau/~~vei iratou~~ na galala ni Tabana ni Kasitaba (H M
Customs & Excise) ka sa tiko vei M/CALDER... na
~~nona~~/nodrau/~~nodratou~~ i vola tara

Na i naki ni vola oqo moni vakasalataki ka kerei na Turaga
kei na Marama ena veivanua ka cavuti e cake, me
vakarawarawataka na ~~nona~~/nodrau/~~nodratou~~ i lakolako. Sa
vakamacalataki ~~vua~~/vei rau/~~vei iratou~~ na veika e vakatabui
ena ~~nona~~/nodrau/~~nodratou~~ i lakolako vakasarasara, ka me
rau~~rau~~/~~ratou~~ rokova na noda i tovo vakavanua na i Taukei.

Sa vakaraitaki oti ~~vua~~/vei rau/~~vei iratou~~ me kakua ni dua na
ka me rau/~~ratou~~ vakacolata vei kemuni, ka dodonu me
rau/ratou kerea se sauma na veika e rau/~~ratou~~ gadreva. Sa
vakasalataki talega na kena vakatabui ni tarai vakaveitalia
na kau, vuata, manumanu vuka, yava i va se dolo ka wili tu
vakaiyau vakamareqeti ni Matanitu se lewe ni vanua.

Sa nutaki ni na vakarawarawataki na ~~nona~~/nodrau/~~nodratou~~
sarasara wavoki, kei na taqomaki ni ~~nona~~/nodrau/~~nodratou~~ i
yau era kauta voli me tarova na kena tauri vakatawa dodonu
~~me~~ vakarogocataka na kena i rogorogo ki vanua tani.

E kerei vakabibi na nomuni veitokoni e na tikina oqo.

Me qai dau tukuni talega mai kevaka eso na Valagi Saravanua
era vakavagora na i tovo tawa kilikili eso, veisaqasaqa kei
na lawa se i tovo vakavanua ena gauna e kunei kina.

ENA VUKUNA NA VUNIVOLA TUDEI
NI VEIKA VAKAITAUKEI KEI NA
VEIVAKATOROCAKETAKI VAKAIWASEJASE

Fijian Language Permit

Remember; although you may be used to the idea that a man's property ends at his front gate and that the land outside private boundaries is public land this is not the custom in Fiji. The anchorage off the village, the beach, and the land surrounding the village and off into the hills all belongs to someone.

Anchoring off a village or an island is akin to pitching a tent in someone's front garden; you ask permission and then behave accordingly. It is not legally so in the strictest sense, but it is customary and the Fijian customs are to be respected.

The following is an approximate translation of the Fijian Language permit shown on Page 20:-

Ministry of Fijian Affairs.
Government Buildings.
SUVA.

The Representative of the Provincial Council,
Village headmen,
Villagers (ladies and gentleman of)
MALOLOLO, MANA KEI YANUYA

Sir,
TOURISTS VISITING ISLANDS AND VILLAGES.
Mr Calder and Mrs Calder are carrying this letter and are visiting in the yacht EUREKA, and are from AUSTRALIA.
Mr Calder has the Customs and Excise's permission to travel and have a clearance for that purpose. The person / people carrying this letter have been briefed on Fijian traditions and customs and is/are expected to observe them. He/they have been advised not to put any burdens on any of the villagers and are expected to purchase any requirements needed during their stay.
He/they/..... have been briefed on protected species.
Every assistance is requested to make the visit pleasant and memorable.
Villagers are requested to inform the Ministry of Fijian Affairs if any of the conditions laid down are not met.
(Signed)
for Permanent Secretary for Fijian Affairs.

Besides receiving the relevant permit, you will be briefed on the protocol to be observed when visiting the outer islands. It may be verbal, however in Suva in 1992 a single sheet handout was attached to the permit. In this way nobody could deny having been properly briefed.

This briefing contained a preamble and addressed several major aspects as quoted below.

"Preamble: In spite of many signs of modern developed society that are evident in the major cities of Suva and Lautoka, the way of life in the outer islands is still very much traditional. You will see few signs of the affluence that has modified city life. You will see many signs of adherence to traditional ways and of the acceptance and practice of Christian religious principles. The two most prominent denominations are the Methodist (Wesleyan) and Roman Catholic. Non believers are virtually non-existent as few will ever admit to being so.

Visitors: Casual visits between friends in Fiji are usually accompanied by the proffering of gifts, particularly yaqona. That is why you will see so many "pyramids" of kava on display in the markets. These "pyramids" are of course for more formal occasions. For a visiting yacht, the presentation of about half a kilogram of yaqona root to the turaga ni koro is the correct way to commence your visit. Visitors are not encouraged to give any other form of gifts during this formal occasion except for kava but thank you tokens could be given to villagers to show appreciation of their hospitality.

Fishing: The "harvesting" of the waters around Fiji is strictly allocated to the various villages. It is one of their most important sources of food. You must remember that when you are fishing with a hand line or spear you are catching fish that villagers identify to be theirs and the use of fishing nets is strictly forbidden. If you wish to fish be quite clear in requesting permission to do so and ensure that it is sufficient only for meals, particularly at anchor. And please be moderate in your catch. Trolling for fish outside the reefs while on passage is unlikely to cause any offence.

Alcohol: The Methodist religion in particular positively discourages the consumption of alcohol. In many villages alcohol is not permitted. It is therefore discourteous to your hosts, the village, to offer alcohol to villagers even though, on occasions, some people may request it. You may consider you have made a friend in acceding to such a request, but you will almost certainly have offended and upset the turaga ni koro and your presence at anchor in the waters of the village will no longer be appreciated. Of course, having initially accepted your sevusevu and welcomed you as an honoured guest, the village will have the greatest difficulty in informing you that you are really no longer welcome. Fijians are by nature gentle, humble and above all polite.

Dress: You should dress conservatively whenever you are in close proximity to villagers, particularly if invited into the village or into a house. Swimwear and long trousers or shorts worn by women are not appropriate. For women, knee length dresses and skirts are more acceptable. For men it would be more appropriate to wear long trousers or "sulu". Whenever you are carrying such things as rucksacks, handbags, cameras, etc. they should be carried in the hand and not slung over the shoulders. Nor should you wear sunglasses or hats, specially when meeting people. Footwear is normally taken off at the doorway when entering a house.

Finally do not overstay your welcome. Consider for how long you would like to welcome a total stranger onto your yacht. Do not place any burdens upon the villagers. Remember, your permit and introductory letter asks the villagers to make your visit "pleasant and memorable". Consideration of the above will help ensure it is."

Yaqona (Kava):

The first question usually asked regarding yaqona is how much should you give. The general consensus is an amount of about half a kilo of root, worth about $7 in 1992, although I have heard of as little as one third of a kilo being acceptable.

Many yachtsmen and women to whom I have spoken find themselves at odds with the presentation of yaqona to the 'turaga ni koro', or other local dignitary, when first visiting a village.

"If I have to give something why can't I give something useful to the village - say books for the school - rather than grog for an old man!? "

Such a sentiment, though admirable in its own right, neglects two fundamentals; first, the importance of age and seniority, and second, tradition. Quite simply, it is the 'Fijian way'.

Other yachties see yaqona as a 'payment' to permit the use of an anchorage or beach, which they wrongly feel to be public property, and as such look up on it as a 'rip-off', This is of not so; it is a ceremonial presentation and a mark of respect.

In the days before the Europeans came to Fiji, visitors from one area to another would always place before the turaga a suitable gift as a symbol of recognition and honour. The recipient was bound to accept the gift or he would be guilty of the gravest misconduct, tantamount to a declaration of war. Once the gift was accepted however, obligations fell to the recipient. He became responsible for the safety and well-being of his guest, and to see that he wanted for nothing. There was a reciprocity inherent in the giving and receiving of gifts that is still effective today.

When presenting yaqona to your host there is a proper Fijian greeting:-

"Noqu sevusevu gor."

The present (sevusevu) is placed on the floor in front of the person, NOT handed to him. Presumably this allows the recipient to decline to pick up the gift, and supposedly chase you out of his territory!

When the yaqona is picked up, thus accepting the sevusevu and the responsibilities that go therewith, the turaga will formally greet you in the Fijian language, in a small ceremony in which he may bestow on you, your crew, and your relatives in your home country, his blessing, regards, protection and help.

You may well find that, as your stay in an area progresses, reciprocity manifests itself by way of an invitation to drink yaqona with the men at the end of their day's work. You may be invited to a house for a meal, or to join in a celebration feast. Possibly a young relative of the turaga may visit your yacht with a gift of fresh fruit or coconuts.

Finally, it is also polite to bid farewell to your host when you leave. The stylised farewell is:-

"Noqu yaqona ni tatau."

A formal farewell absolves your host from any further responsibility.

Departure From Fiji:

By the time that you decide to depart from Fiji you should be well conversant with the customs and immigration formalities and where the various offices are. Only two authorities are involved in departure; in order of visit they are immigration and then customs. If you have 'imported' or recruited additional crew for your ocean passage, you will have to complete form 'B' to sign them on as crew. You will already have signed off any crew that have left.

After completing immigration formalities you will then clear customs outward. You will recover any firearms and bonded stores, and you must depart within 24 hours of obtaining your clearance.

You must then proceed directly from your port of departure to your next destination. Calls at outlying Fijian islands MUST NOT be made, and permission to do so will not be granted.

Further Reading:

For a better understanding of the culture and ways of the Fijian people, and to make your stay even more enjoyable, I would recommend reading the short but concise book:

The Fijian Way of Life, by Asesela Ravuvu, published by the Institute of Pacific Studies of the University of the South Pacific in 1983.

For a concise history of the country:

FIJI - A Short History, by Deryck Scarr, published by George Allen & Unwin, 1984.

A short introduction to the language can be found in a little book:

Say It In Fijian, by A.J.Schutz, Pacific Publications, 1984.

3

Navigation in Fijian Waters

The following section deals with those aspects of navigating a yacht in Fiji that are common to all areas. It does not cover the subject in the detail to be found in the Admiralty Sailing Directions, Pacific Islands Pilot Vol II., or the United States Sailing Directions for the Pacific Islands - Volume 2.

Tides and Tidal Streams:

The range of tide within Fijian waters is between about 1.4 and 2.5 metres. It is semi-diurnal (two highs and two lows per day) with little diurnal inequality.

Tidal streams are generally moderate in strength in open waters but can become very strong in the reef entrances and in areas where islands tend to create choke points.

Charts:

The range of navigational charts available for Fiji is most satisfactory for the major ports and for passage making through the group with the notable exception of the Yasawa Group. Unfortunately for the yachtsman, many anchorages sought by the cruising yacht are not adequately covered. Also, particularly in the outer islands, many charts are based on old surveys and the amount of reliance that can be placed upon inshore areas is often difficult to assess.

The major chart series covering Fijian waters is that produced by the British Admiralty (BA), and numbers some 28 charts. There are three Fiji Hydrographic Unit charts that are only available locally. The coverage provided by the United States Defence Mapping Agency has now been reduced to five medium to small scale charts

In this book I have quoted and provided a catalogue of the BA charts. However, the most recent chart catalogues, available at all chart agents, should be consulted to ensure that new charts have not been published or old ones withdrawn. Official chart catalogues are reprinted regularly (usually yearly) and should be kept in date from Notices to Mariners.

GPS Positions:

Those yachts that intend to use GPS for inshore navigation should pay particular attention to the notes occurring on BA charts regarding "SATELLITE DERIVED POSITIONS" and corrections to be applied to allow direct plotting on the chart. Corrections vary from chart to chart, and in some cases they are not stated. This does not necessarily mean that there are none. It may mean that they vary in different areas on the same chart.

Buoys and Beacons:

Fiji has adopted the IALA System A for buoys and beacons, but there is an additional local system of pile beacons used throughout the group to indicate passages, channels, and isolated dangers among the coral reefs. The beacons are of steel or concrete, with distinctive topmarks indicating on which side the craft should pass. They are as follows:

White triangular topmark point up.
Pass to seaward of the beacon.

White diamond topmark. Isolated danger.
Pass either side of the beacon.

Black or red triangular topmark point down.
Pass to shoreward of the beacon.

Pennant topmark painted orange Day-Glo.
Points to the clear channel.

Topmarks may be equipped with red or white reflectors.

It is inevitable that when navigating among islands some confusion will arise as to which is the shoreward side, and therefore these beacons should be used in conjunction with the largest scale chart available, and should always be used with caution. Beacons may be some metres in from the edge of the danger and, at times, colours may be indistinct. Non-standard private beacons may occasionally be met. It is an offence to moor to pile beacons.

As Fiji is subject to occasional hurricanes, buoys and beacons cannot be relied upon to be found as charted. Topmarks are often lost, making identification of the purpose of the mark extremely difficult. This was found to be particularly so in 1992. The worst occurrence that can befall a beacon is that the pennant type can have the metal 'finger' bent by the wind so that it indicates the wrong side to be passed.

I have also been informed that young Fijian boys think that it is great fun to twist the pointer and then watch the ensuing mayhem!

Lights:

An extract from the 1993 Admiralty List of Lights appears at the end of the index. All lights in the Fiji Islands are UNWATCHED.

Fiji is far too beautiful a country to be steaming or sailing around at night, but should this be necessary for the longer passages the lights will be found to be reasonably well maintained and far more trustworthy than in many other island nations. Nevertheless, at times very heavy rain squalls can completely obliterate a light as most have ranges of less than 15 miles.

Radio:

The coast radio station 'SUVA RADIO' 3 Delta Papa, provides 24-hour coverage on calling frequencies 2182 and 6215 kHz. and VHF ch 16. Working frequencies are international RT(HF) Channels 406 and 810, with Radphone channels 602, 1202 and VHF ch 26. WT(MF) service is also available.

Medical advice, address RADIOMEDICAL SUVA, in English can be obtained through 3DP.

A maritime surveillance safety service involving ship reporting is established for all vessels, including small craft, within 200 n. miles of Fiji. Reports should be sent to 3DP daily in the following form:-

        (a) Vessel's name.

        (b) Position.

        (c) Date and time of reporting.

        (d) Port of destination.

        (e) ETA.

This information was correct at the time of publication but comprehensive and up-to-date details should be checked in Admiralty List of Radio Signals, Vol 1, Part 2 - Coast Radio Stations.

Amateur radio stations can be operated from a yacht after first obtaining authorisation from the Department of Posts & Telecommunications in Suva. There is no charge for this authorisation.

Weather:

Fiji lies within an area affected by hurricanes. The season is considered to extend from November to April, which coincides with the hot and humid 'wet' season. The remainder of the year, when it is cool and dry with an overall south-east trade wind pattern, is exceptionally pleasant. The weather is, however, much modified by the effects of the winter frontal systems moving across the Tasman Sea and over Australia and New Zealand.

Marine Weather bulletins and forecasts are plentiful, both on entertainment radio and 3DP. The broadcasts on 3DP are on 4372 and 8746 kHz., at 0803, 1203, 1603 and 2003 Fiji local time.

The main weather centre for Fiji is located at Nadi Airport. The forecasters suffer from a lack of reports from sea and welcome 'ship' reports from offshore yachts. These reports can be in plain language, if brief, and can contain as much or as little as you care to observe. If the observation is detailed, code should be used (Refer to ALRS Vol 3 - Radio Weather Services). The report is transmitted to 3DP and might be as follows:-

Address:	METEO NADI from Yacht....
Position:	....South.....East.
Wind:	South-east 15 knots.
Sea:	ESE 1 metre.
Swell:	Low Easterly.
Cloud:	Cumulus - little vertical development.
Barometer:	1010 rising - (make sure your barometer is OK.).

This is more than enough but it will be greatly appreciated, especially if you are more than 100 miles from the main islands.

Sea conditions experienced around Fiji are variable and modified very much by the proximity or otherwise of reefs and islands. In areas where there are strong tidal streams, such as Somosomo Strait and parts of the Koro Sea, short, steep and uncomfortably rough seas can be experienced.

Inshore Passage-Making:

The ideal time for passage-making in coral waters is, as ever, from two hours before apparent noon to two hours after. The sun should, ideally, be behind you. The positioning of a man aloft to con the boat not only ensures that reefs will be seen earlier but they will also be seen more easily. Polaroid sunglasses are essential for good reef spotting; ordinary sunglasses will not do.

When departing from an area in which a yacht has spent several days, and which should by then be reasonably well known, the light will not be so critical.

Nevertheless, LEAVE EARLY - ARRIVE EARLY, is a good policy to adopt.

On arrival at a new anchorage, check it out. If restricted in its entry and at all likely to become untenable in changed weather, make sure you know how to leave in the dark, or can change to a more comfortable position in the anchorage.

Although many of us 'eyeball' our passages in the familiar waters of home, one is quite likely to come unstuck in Fiji. Fiji lends itself well to the practice of navigation. There are many objects that can be used as marks ahead or astern, and often in transit (as a range) with other marks. Selecting a safe course with a conspicuous high hill dead ahead, even though you may have to sail an additional mile or so (10 minutes?), is always a good policy.

I can assure you that you will be far more relaxed and able to enjoy the excellent Fiji Bitter, if you know that you are on track, and that the track is a safe one.

Naturally, if the wind is contrary and you have to tack to your destination, things are a little different and you will have to select a safe area and navigate within it. Of course, 'Only racing yachtsmen and fools go to windward!' so that problem should not arise.

If fixing by GPS in inshore waters, great care must be taken to ensure that the correct datum is used or that corrections are applied.

Nautical Almanac:

The Fiji Marine Department publishes a pocket-sized Nautical Almanac annually. This handy little book provides ready reference to local navigational in formation including tides, lights, radio beacons, weather bulletins, sunrise and sunset, and a table of distances. It is well worth the few dollars that it costs.

Units Of Measurement:

All units of measurement used in this book are metric. Fiji is a metric country. Chartlets in this book are in metric units. Depths are in metres, or metres and decimetres if appropriate. Whenever the unit 'mile' occurs, it is the nautical mile.

There is one exception to this. Whenever a feature charted on a current 'fathoms' BA chart is referred to in the text, and its height is part of that description, the height shown on the chart is used .

e.g. Hill (1160) not Hill (354m.)

Bearings:

All bearings used in this book are TRUE and from seaward. The approximate magnetic variation throughout the group was 13° East (1992).

PART TWO

Suva,

The Central

and

Eastern Division

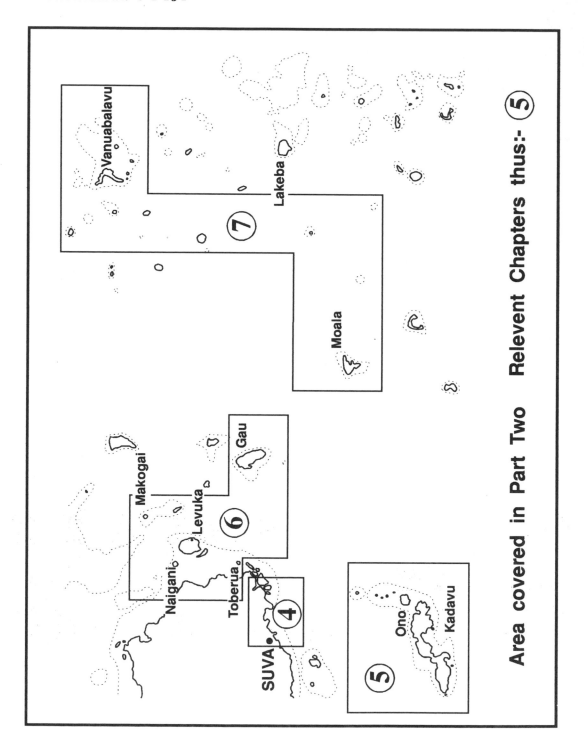

Area covered in Part Two   Relevent Chapters thus:- ⑤

Suva

    Suva and the surrounding area do not lie in the Eastern Division but, as it is the preferred Port of Entry and the logical place from which to begin a cruise through the Eastern Division, it has been included in this section together with the other few anchorages that may be used during a passage east.

As the capital of Fiji, the seat of government, the administrative centre for the Central District, and Fiji's largest port, it can be safely said:-

"If you can't get it in Suva you can't get it in Fiji."

A modern and progressive city, it is well served by all the facilities required by the international traveller. International telephone and telex facilities are available at the Post and Telecommunications Head Office adjacent to the G.P.O. and the Fiji Visitors Bureau.

Nausori Airport, about 20 km. north-east of the capital, is served by the county's domestic airlines. There are frequent connections to Nadi International Airport and daily flights to most islands.

Banks:

Banks with the greatest representation throughout Fiji are those based in Australia or New Zealand or, to a lesser degree, the United Kingdom and India. The following will be found to have substantial overseas connections:-

The Australia & New Zealand Banking Group (ANZ).
Barclays Bank International.
The Bank of Baroda.
The Bank of New Zealand (BNZ).
WESTPAC Bank.
The National Bank of Fiji.

Major offices of American Express and Diners Club can be found, and Visa and Mastercard are well represented at various banks.

Hospital:

The medical facilities found in Suva are excellent in regional terms, and should more than meet the needs of the cruising yacht. The major hospital is the Colonial War Memorial Hospital which is well equipped to carry out all but the most specialised surgical procedures.

Recompression Chamber:

There is a recompression chamber close to the yacht club in Walu Bay and two resident doctors qualified in diving medicine.

Victualling:

Victualling a yacht in Suva is a joy. The central markets, colourful and always bustling with activity, contain every sort of fresh fruit and vegetable available in Fiji and even some of the much more expensive imported produce from Australia and New Zealand, although this is often better bought at a super market or speciality shop. Unlike the 'duty free' shops in the retail area, you do not bargain at the market. The prices are adequately displayed, often written on the particular piece of fruit. Prices are fair and, with the intense competition that the market provides, the lowest you will pay for quality produce. The yachtsman should note the price paid for the more common items, as this will give him a good guide to a fair price to pay out-of-the-way villagers if he asks them to sell him local produce.

Locally produced beef in Fiji is very good. The best reputedly coming from the island of Taveuni, and Yaqara on the north coast of Viti Levu

Most other meat is imported from New Zealand and is of high quality.

For cruises away from Suva, all major outlets will package large orders in daily requirement packs and freeze if required. The co-operation of Leylands Limited, at Lami Industrial Estate, used prior to sailing to New Zealand, was excellent and they are highly recommended. The meat was vacuum packed in strong plastic bags, heat sealed, frozen, and delivered to the yacht at 0800 on the morning of departure in a freezer truck; all at a discount price.

For all other staples and packaged goods of Australian or New Zealand origin there are several supermarket chains; Morris Hedstrom (MH), Motibhai, R. B. Patel and others. Most lines are available always, or an acceptable equivalent, although on occasions all stores will run out of the same line because the shipment from overseas has been delayed. Fresh milk, in two litre cartons, is available only in Suva and Lautoka. UHT milk is generally available.

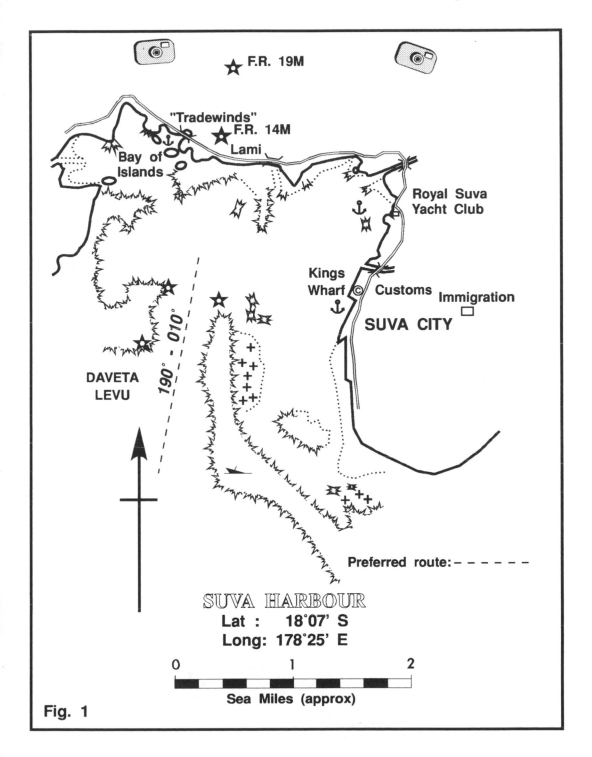

F.R. 19M

"Tradewinds"
F.R. 14M
Lami

Bay of
Islands

Royal Suva
Yacht Club

Kings
Wharf © Customs   Immigration

SUVA CITY

190° - 010°

DAVETA
LEVU

Preferred route: - - - - - -

SUVA HARBOUR
Lat :   18°07' S
Long: 178°25' E

0   1   2

Sea Miles (approx)

Fig. 1

Repair Facilities:

Repair and haul-out facilities are available in abundance. Most of the requirements of a yacht can be met from shipyards, automotive engineers, electricians and others of that ilk in the Walu Bay industrial area between the yacht club and the city. Even inflatable life rafts can be serviced by the local RFD agent at extremely competitive prices. There is still more industry, including a sail loft, at Lami. The availability of yachting chandlery is somewhat restricted and tends to be limited to that required by the smaller boats.

Fiji Visitors Bureau:

Suva has so much for the visitor and tourist and is an ideal base for visiting other areas of Fiji where a yacht is not the appropriate means of transport. To attempt to describe all tourist options in this section would fail to do them justice. Suffice it to say one can plan on spending at least two to three weeks at Suva (many yachts never seem to leave). There are many tourist publications, and the Fiji Visitors Bureau, available in the city to guide you during your stay.

Approach—(BA1660, 1673):

The waters in the approaches to Suva, outside the fringing reef, are clear and deep. Providing the approach course, from whichever direction, maintains a distance off the reef of one mile, no dangers will be encountered.

Suva Harbour can be approached from the east via Nukulau Passage. However, for a yacht that has just completed a lengthy ocean passage, such an approach is not recommended on first arrival in view of the navigational complexities. On the other hand, if the passage has been easy and the skipper and crew is well rested, the charts are reliable and with proper planning and good visibility, a safe entry can be made. In terms of distance there is little difference in the approach via Nukulau Passage and the main entrance through Daveta Levu.

Daveta Levu:

The leads into Suva Harbour consist of two square beacons, painted Day-Glo orange with a white vertical stripe. The front lead is situated slightly inshore near Lami Town at an elevation of 39.6 metres; the rear lead is situated on the first range of hills inland about 1/2 mile, at an elevation of 103 metres. They are lit by fixed red lights at night, but are sometimes difficult to see by day, particularly in the early morning, due to smoke from the nearby cement factory.

Three lit beacons mark the reefs on either side of the entrance channel. The western reef carries beacons on its south-east and north-east ends, while the eastern reef carries a beacon slightly to the north of its inner, or north, end.

A yacht should aim to place itself on the leads about 2 miles south from the outer western reef beacon, and then alter course to 010° to keep the leads in transit ahead (Fig. 1).

Once the beacon off the north end of the eastern reef is abaft the beam, the yacht should alter course for the desired anchorage, avoiding the shoal patches that are shown on the chart.

Anchorage:

On first entry a yacht is advised to contact Suva Port Control on Ch16. You will probably be told to anchor near the Quarantine Anchorage as marked on the chart. Unfortunately the depth here is about 20 metres, to anchor further northward in lesser depths will usually be acceptable as long as one keeps clear of the other yachts at the RSYC anchorage. You will then be advised as to where to berth to carry out your first arrival formalities. In 1992, the various authorities would not board a yacht while at anchor.

An alternative anchorage, when first arrival formalities are not required, may be obtained in the area south of the main wharf, near Nabukalou Creek and, about 100 metres offshore. Here the bottom is mud and sand and good holding. This position is handy to Customs and to the markets and city centre.

Having completed ALL formalities the crew is then free to go ashore for an initial visit to the city and the markets. Unfortunately this may necessitate foregoing the ritual lengthy hot shower as such facilities are only available at the yacht club or the Tradewinds Hotel.

Royal Suva Yacht Club:

The Royal Suva Yacht Club has been in existence since 1932 and was granted its Royal Charter in 1950. It is one of the most active and lively clubs in Suva with a large active membership, an excellent bar, a handy restaurant, a full social programme and all the facilities required by the yachting fraternity. The boats on its register are both power and sail and its membership is representative of Fijian society as a whole.

On arrival at the RSYC you will be supplied with an information sheet that clearly sets out the facilities available to, and the obligations expected of, the yachtsman. You will be made most welcome and after the first few days you will soon see why so many find it difficult to leave! The following summarises the facilities available:-

Honorary Membership:

Visiting yachts anchored in the waters adjacent to the RSYC are required to pay a facility fee of $F 20.00 per week (1992), at which time, honorary membership cards will be issued to all crew members.

Anchorage:

The anchorage is in mud and sand with good holding, and comfortable in all weather. There is a large landing pontoon alongside which tenders may be left in full security. Yachts are requested not to anchor too close to the race starting area.

Marina:

There are also about 20 stern to marina type berths available to visitors.at the yacht club. Rates start at $37.50 for a 9 metre yacht including power and water (1992).

During 1985 there were several instances of theft from yachts moored off the club. This was probably an inevitable growth in petty urban crime in Suva. A type of Neighbourhood Watch system was introduced amongst the yachts, which appeared to combat the problem successfully. In 1992 I did not hear any further adverse reports.

Showers:

Hot and cold with toilet facilities are available.

Laundry:

There are tubs adjacent to the ablutions block. The washing machine that was unserviceable for most, if not all, of 1985, has at last given up the ghost As its operation was not really viable financially for the club, it is doubtful if it will be replaced. With laundry ashore costing about 30 cents. per item (dry but unironed) this is not too great a financial burden to bear.

Fuel and Water:

The fuel jetty is situated at the head of the marina. It is open from 0900 to 1800, seven days a week. Water is also obtainable at the fuel jetty. Diesel, petrol, and outboard mix (1 in 50) are provided. The depth alongside the fuelling jetty and in the channel leading thereto is 0.78 metres at LAT, which is sufficient water for yachts drawing 2.0 m. at High Water Neaps.

Club Activities:

Honorary members are most welcome at any social functions advertised at the club. There are also regular yacht races and regattas and visiting boats that wish to compete are most popular.

Courtesy Flags:

Fijian flags (yacht size) are generally available at the club manager's office, together with T shirts, club shirts, sulus, and, usually, copies of "A Yachtsman's FIJI".

Transport:

The RSYC is only 2.0 km from the city centre and an easy walk for all 'fitness freaks'. For others the local buses pass the door about every 15 minutes and cost only 25 cents. Taxis, often parked outside the club, cost about $F 2.00, or whatever is showing on the meter, if used. Other taxis, which sometimes cruise into the city markets and multiple hire en route, may pick you up from the roadside (even at a bus stop). They all terminate at the markets, and your 'contribution' for this form of transport is 50 cents, or about double the bus fare. Buses do not travel to the other side of the city. All terminate at the interchange alongside the market. To travel to any of the suburbs north and east of the city from the RSYC you have to change buses at this terminus.

Tradewinds Hotel:

As an alternative to the anchorage off the RSYC, there is a limited number of anchorages in the Bay of Islands, on the shores of which is situated the recently renovated Tradewinds Hotel. The hotel is 7 km. from Suva; just past Lami Town.

In previous years, moorings in the bay, and stern-to berths on the hotel sea wall were available at the Tradewinds but the intentions of the new management are not known in this regard.

The Bay of Islands provides a quiet alternative to the bustle of the yacht club, with all the facilities of a resort hotel near by - unfortunately at resort hotel prices.

The following comments from the earlier edition are included in case the "Tradewinds Marina" should be reactivated in the future.

The costs at the Tradewinds in 1985 for a stern to berth were $F 35.00 per week or $F 5.00 per day. Water was available but the power points ashore did not work. These fees include the use of the swimming pool and associated change rooms with showers and toilets.

To provide clearance for the rudder, the yacht's stern will generally be no closer then 3 metres to the top of the wall and a long plank will be required.

There are no in-house laundry facilities. Laundry, if required, is sent out and charged for accordingly.

The nearest limited shopping is at Lami, within walking distance, but there is not nearly as extensive a range of goods as at Suva. The bus fare to Suva (half hourly service) is 45 cents. A taxi costs $F 6.00.

Bar prices are two to three times those at the RSYC and phone calls suffer the usual hotel mark up. The restaurant serves excellent food in an idyllic setting, particularly on the verandah that is cantilevered out over the water; service is unhurried to the extreme! The Tradewinds accepts most credit cards.

Hurricane Hole:

The western bay of the Bay of Islands, and the creek flowing into it, is considered to be a hurricane hole. The charted depth at the entrance to the creek is 0.5 metres that may limit its use.

Suva To Nukulau—(BA1660, 1674):

Once the yachtsman has the necessary permits to visit any offshore islands in the Eastern Division and the obligatory customs clearance the cruise can commence. The initial leg will probably only be as far as Nukulau, some 7 miles from Suva. The route inside the reef is clearly marked by beacons. The use of power is recommended, at least as far as a position south of Suva Point. The remaining short sail can be used to familiarise any new crew with the gear and blow away the cobwebs of Suva.

Nukulau is a well-maintained picnic spot and is well patronised by boats from Suva at week-ends. The islet was originally the quarantine station for the port of Suva and is now under the control of the Suva City Council. A caretaker is in residence.

Anchorage:

Although the charts show the western side of the islet as part of the 'Prohibited Anchorage' area to the eastward from Suva, it is the practice of yachts to anchor off the north-west corner of the islet near the old swimming enclosure (concrete piles) north-north-east of the concrete jetty.

The anchor should be let go about 30 metres off the beach in about 10 to 12 metres of water on a steeply shelving bottom of fine sand and some mud. The anchor must not be dropped out in the middle of the channel because of its use by coastal shipping, and the submarine cables that are laid along it. To prevent the boat swinging into the channel, with the likely result of dragging the anchor into deeper water, a stern line should be taken to one of the piles and the moor set up taut. Holding for the anchor is good. On completion of the moor, you will probably enjoy a brief stroll around the islet and your first clean salt water swim since arriving in Suva. Do not go too far off the beach because of the tidal stream.

A cold freshwater shower ashore, a barbecue and/or a sundowner, watching the sunset, will probably conclude a perfect day.

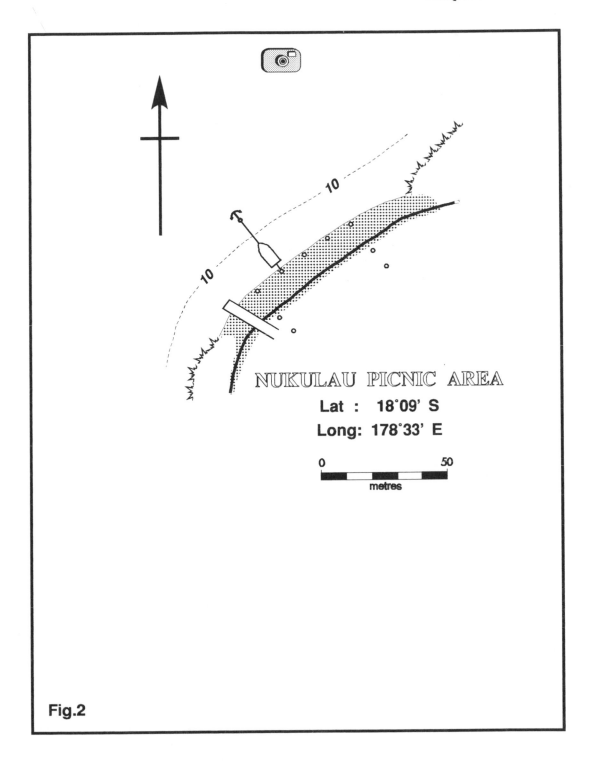

NUKULAU PICNIC AREA

Lat : 18°09' S

Long: 178°33' E

Fig.2

Nukulau Passage And Eastward—(BA1674, 488):

The track through Nukulau Passage is not difficult and is adequately marked by beacons. A yacht may proceed directly southward, leaving Makuluva to port, until about one to two miles clear of the outer edge of the reef, when course can be set to the eastward to clear Nasilai Reef. Care must be taken to give Belcher Rocks a wide berth.

An alternative track to the north of Makuluva, leading into Rewa Roads, shortens the distance to the eastward by about 3 miles. It is generally into the prevailing winds and does not lend itself to short tacking. Power is advisable in these circumstances.

Once clear of Rewa Roads course should be adjusted to remain one to two miles to seaward of Nasilai Reef. Fixing along this section is difficult as the land backing the reef is low and without prominent relief. The wreck (18°09.8'S. 178°36.9'E.) is conspicuous together with Nasilai Reef Light. The small wreck south-east of the light appears to have moved. The charted 6.4 metres should be given a wide berth - at least one mile. From abeam Nasilai Reef Light a safe north-easterly course should be held past the mouth of the Nasilai River and on until about 4 miles southward of Mabualau, when a decision can be made on entering Toberua Passage or carrying on towards Ovalau.

5

Kadavu and The Great Astrolabe Reef

The island of Kadavu, often nicknamed by Fijians 'New Zealand Lailai', lies about 50 miles south of Suva. It is about 30 miles long, 5 miles wide, and lies generally east/west. At its western end is its highest point, a most conspicuous peak named Nabukelevu, and this peak or the light on Cape Washington, close westward, is usually the first land sighted by yachts arriving in Fiji direct from either Australia or New Zealand. At its eastern end there extends to the northward, for about 19 miles, a number of islets and rocks that are fringed by the Great Astrolabe Reef.

It is unfortunate that one has to bypass Kadavu, and proceed to Suva to enter, as yachts then have to return to the southward to visit this most interesting island. Nevertheless the island has some beautiful cruising areas, particularly on the south coast. The waters surrounding it are sparkling clear and the diving is excellent.

The island is generally satisfactorily charted for the yachtsman although in areas where reefs are numerous, such as the eastern end, good light and a lookout aloft are essential. Chart BA745 covers the area. I was unable to revisit Kadavu in 1992, but reports from other yachts indicate that little has changed.

Cape Washington—(Fig. 3):

Although the light on Cape Washington is difficult to identify, a vessel will have no difficulty in navigating in the area as ample other points exist for fixing. After a particularly rough passage a yacht may feel the need to rest in the lee of Denham Island before making the final approach to Suva. The quietest water will usually be found tucked well in between Denham Island and the main island. The village on the cliffs above, which is difficult to see, is equipped with VHF radio telephone, and the earlier remarks on the correct procedures to be observed must be borne in mind.

On the other hand, if you are visiting Cape Washington after clearing into Fiji you will find it an excellent spot to dive. The villagers of Nabukelevuira are very friendly.

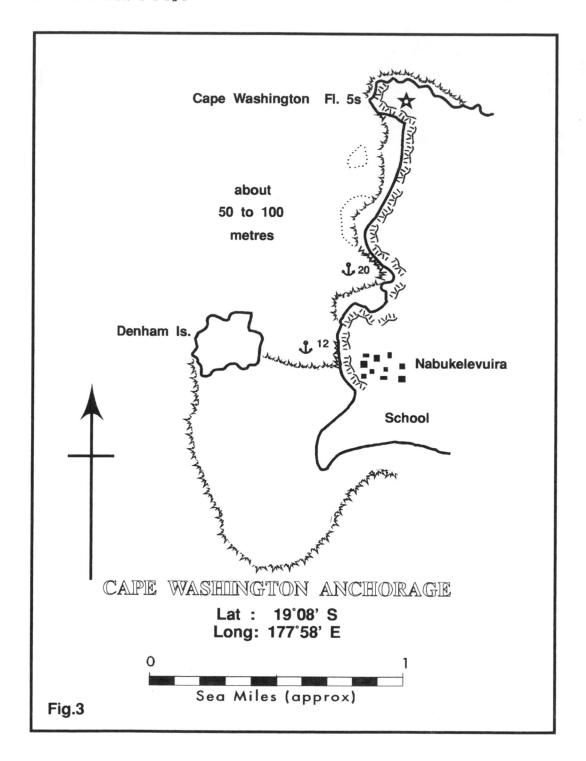

Cape Washington Fl. 5s

about
50 to 100
metres

⚓ 20

Denham Is.

⚓ 12

Nabukelevuira

School

CAPE WASHINGTON ANCHORAGE
Lat : 19˚08' S
Long: 177˚58' E

0   1
Sea Miles (approx)

Fig.3

By prior arrangement, and depending on the season, you will be able to buy tropical fruits, vegetables, fish and, with luck, some succulent freshly caught lobster (crayfish).

Anchorage:

The anchorage is over coral and rock, and the holding only good, unless the anchor snags the bottom, when it becomes too good! The general depths are about 12 to 20 metres. Due to excellent water clarity the best place to let go the anchor can be decided by inspection. Two anchorage sites are shown in the chartlet (Fig. 3).

Southern Side Of Kadavu:

Many yachtsmen seem to feel that the south side of Kadavu is exposed to bad weather and to be avoided. This is no more so than the south coast of Viti Levu, between Suva and Navula Passage. There are far more safe reef entrances, at intervals of about 10 miles, on Kadavu than on Viti Levu. Further, except for the 20 miles from Denham Island to Galoa Harbour (Sea Reef), and the 10 miles from Soso Passage to Toba ni Korolevu, the passage along the south coast can be made inside the reef.

Usually a yacht would make a landfall, after sailing from Suva, at Herald Passage or to the west of Ono and then proceed westward. This has the advantage of a more favourable morning sun. However the author traversed the south coast of Kadavu from west to east, and this is the sequence here adopted.

After departing from Denham Island, an open water passage must be made as far as the first major bay, Toba Yauravu, 11 miles to the east or on to Galoa Harbour. The bay was not visited but appeared deep and secure when viewed from the air. As Galoa Harbour is only a further 10 miles eastward and offers more for a protracted stay, it is the preferred first stop.

Galoa Harbour:

Although the old Plan BA103 has now been withdrawn, little difficulty should be encountered entering Galoa Harbour using chart BA 745. Most of the beacons shown have lost their topmarks but are otherwise visible.

The inner harbour, north-west of Galoa, provides a tranquil anchorage and access to the south end of the runway that now cuts across the isthmus where the original village of Vunisea once stood.

A closer anchorage to the present Vunisea will now be found in the north-west arm of North Bay, and it is just possible for a yacht drawing 2 metres to anchor close inside the small islet at the head of the bay. The bottom is mud and the holding excellent - But at LAT the boat may just take the bottom.

Vunisea:

The government station for the island of Kadavu is situated at Vunisea, at the head of the inlet at the north-west of North Bay. There is a District Office, an Assistant Roko Tui, an Agriculture and Fisheries office, a limited hospital, police station, post office, and telephone exchange. On the northern shore there is a substantial concrete jetty alongside which a yacht could lie. Vunisea has an airstrip, and is served daily by domestic flights from Suva.

Close westward of Vunisea is the village of Namalata. There are two stores at Vunisea, one a Co-op, the other privately owned. Both carry a similar range of dry stores, with the Co-op also stocking a limited range of frozen meat/chicken. Ice-cream is NOT available. There is a bakery where fresh bread is baked daily, including Sundays. The Co-op also sells a full range of fuels. Your own containers are required as usual. No attempt was made to obtain water but Kadavu does not appear to suffer from a shortage, and has a town water supply.

A small market operates on Saturday at the foot of the hill leading down from the government station. It commences at about 0730 and the best is sold early! When visited at about 0900 little remained except dalo and eggplant, but there was evidence that tomatoes, lettuce, pawpaw, bananas, English cabbage and even a large lobster (which changed hands for only $F 3.00) had been available earlier.

The Fisheries Department has recently installed an ice making plant and ice, in large blocks only, is available to customers other than fishermen, at a cost of 9 cents per kilogram.

One should attempt to call on either the Assistant Roko Tui or the District Officer if visiting Kadavu, although they are sometimes difficult to locate.

Toba Ni Soso—(BA745):

To the east of Galoa Harbour, and forming part of the same water enclosed by the barrier reef, is Toba Ni Soso. It is generally as charted, and there are numerous bays and indentations in its northern and eastern shores where an anchorage can be found.

There is a good anchorage in mud with some coral near Soso Village, but clearer water and a half-tide sandy beach are close at hand if a yacht anchors to the east of Vonobia, at the eastern end of the bay. The bottom is fine sand with a little mud, in about 10 metres, just out from the reef fringing the sandy beach. The area belongs to the village of Chomah.

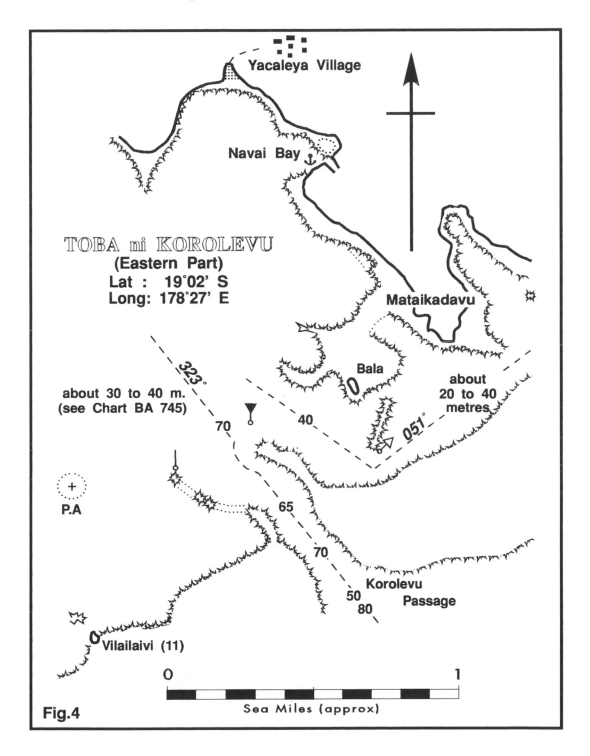

Yacaleya Village

Navai Bay

TOBA ni KOROLEVU
(Eastern Part)
Lat : 19°02' S
Long: 178°27' E

Mataikadavu

Bala

about 30 to 40 m.
(see Chart BA 745)

323°

70

40

051°

about
20 to 40
metres

+
P.A

65

70

Korolevu
Passage

50
80

Vilailaivi (11)

0   1

Sea Miles (approx)

Fig.4

49

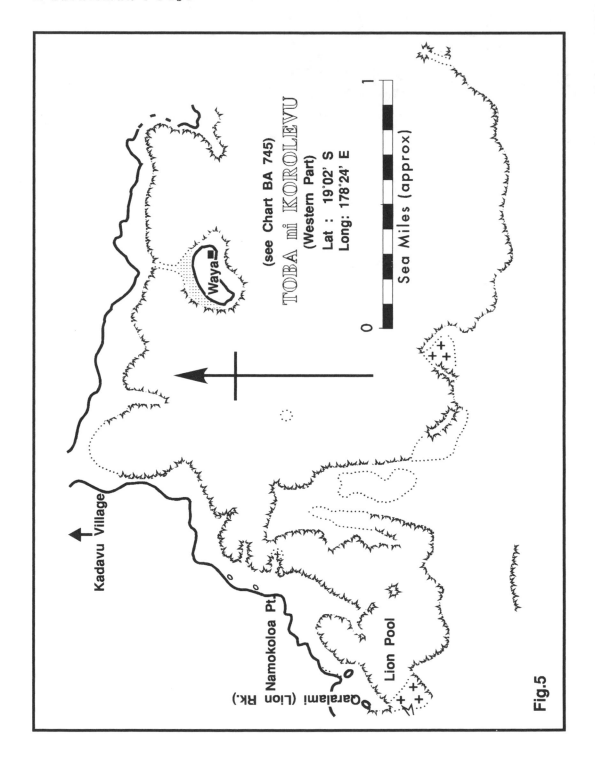

(see Chart BA 745)

TOBA ni KORDLEVU

(Western Part)

Lat : 19°02' S
Long: 178°24' E

Sea Miles (approx)

Waya

Kadavu Village

Namokoloa Pt.

Qaralami (Lion Rk.)

Lion Pool

Fig.5

If proceeding to the eastward, a vessel may leave Toba Ni Soso via Soso Passage.

The reef on the southern side is steep to and a yacht should favour this side when using the passage. A beacon without topmark marks a sunken reef on the north side but this should not be passed too close as the reef extends to both the south and east. In view of the proximity of Main Channel into Galoa Harbour, yachts should not try to enter Soso Passage unless conditions are good.

Toba Ni Korolevu—(BA745):

Although there is a small reef harbour about 4 miles east from Toba Ni Soso, the next major entrance is Korolevu Passage.

Toba Ni Korolevu (Figs. 4 and 5) is a bay with essentially two arms, each about 3 miles long. One runs away to the west, the other generally north. The entrance to the bay is through a reef passage, about 200 metres broad, which is deep with steep to sides. The inner end of the passage is marked by beacons on either side, both with topmarks missing. There is a natural transit leading through the passage, with a round hill on the skyline, unfortunately no longer indicated on the BA chart, in line with the line with the hill forming the point of land about 1/2 mile south of Korolevu village (View 1).

323°

View 1.   **View entering Toba Ni Korolevu**

The bearing of the transit is 323° The entrance is easily identified by Vileileivi (East Islet) and Bala (West Islet) which lie about 1/2 and 3/4 mile respectively on either side of its inner end.

The transit should be used as a guide to entry as, when it is exactly on, it leads over the end of a tongue of the reef on the eastern side. The round hill should be kept very slightly open to the west (port on entry) of the point hill.

Toba Ni Korolevu is as charted and movement within the bay is unrestricted within the limitations of the charted dangers. There is an orange sand beach, which does not cover at high water, at the western extremity of the bay close east of Qaralami (Lion Rock), this rock being quite remarkable for its likeness to a lion and most distinctive. There is a coral pool with good anchorage off the beach, the bottom being sand and broken coral. To reach 'Lion Beach' and 'Lion Pool' it is necessary to pass through a narrow reef passage, clearly shown on the BA chart, between a northward extension of the barrier reef and the fringing reef of the main island. The width of this opening is much narrower than charted, being no wider than about 50 metres. A tidal stream of about 2 knots will be experienced at springs. The Lion Pool area belongs to Kadavu village.

Waya, with a conspicuous white house, is privately owned by an American and a caretaker is in residence. It has a full tide beach on its northern side.

Excellent swimming and snorkelling can be had in the reef area near Vileileivi, but there is no beach.

The village of Yacalea was visited and the turaga and the other villagers were most friendly. The village gardens are not particularly fertile and fruit and other crops would be hard to obtain without disadvantage to the village. A good, quiet anchorage was found in Navai Bay about ¼ mile south of the village in about 10 metres, sand and coral.

Toba Ni Korolevu is well worth a stay of two or three days at least.

Passage Eastward—(BA745):

A safe passage to the east, toward Ono, can be made from Toba Ni Korolevu, past Ucuna Naigoro and on to Ono and the Great Astrolabe Reef. The route is marked by beacons and, with the exception of a narrows about ¼ mile south-west from Vanuatabu is generally over 20 metres deep and of ample width.

Leave Bala and the extending reef, marked by a beacon, to port and steer 051° with Vanuatabu Light in transit with the right hand edge of Tikiratu (View 2).

View 2.   **Vanuatabu Lt. Ø RHE of Tikiratu**

When close aboard Tagitu point, about 50 metres, alter course to 081°, with the 'Cat's Ears' in transit with the left hand edge of the land astern, bearing 261° (View 3).

On approaching Vesi Passage some tidal effect may be experienced. This course is held until Vanuatabu Light is positioned midway between the next two beacons that currently carry topmarks.

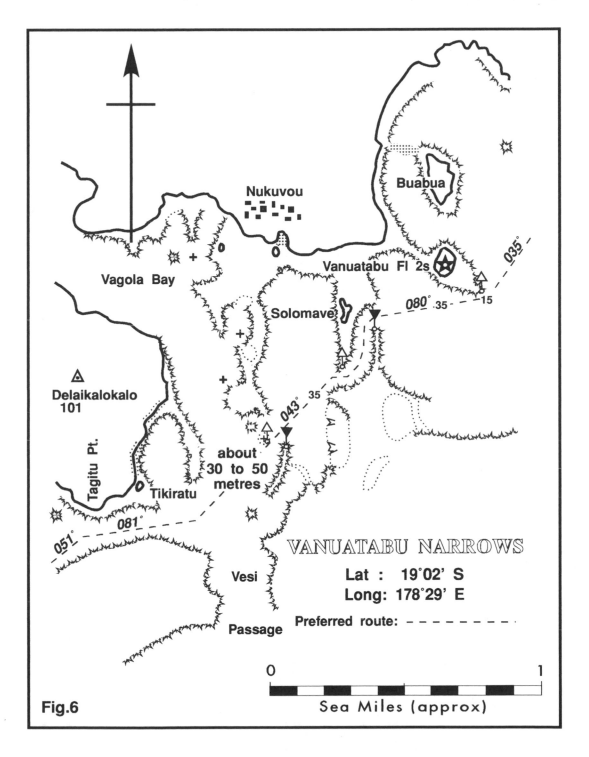

Nukuvou

Buabua

Vanuatabu Fl 2s

035°

Vagola Bay

Solomave

080° 35 - - - -15

Delaikalokalo
101

043° 35

Tagitu Pt.

about
30 to 50
metres

Tikiratu

051° 081°

Vesi

VANUATABU NARROWS

Lat :   19°02' S
Long: 178°29' E

Preferred route: - - - - - - - -

Passage

0   1

Sea Miles (approx)

Fig.6

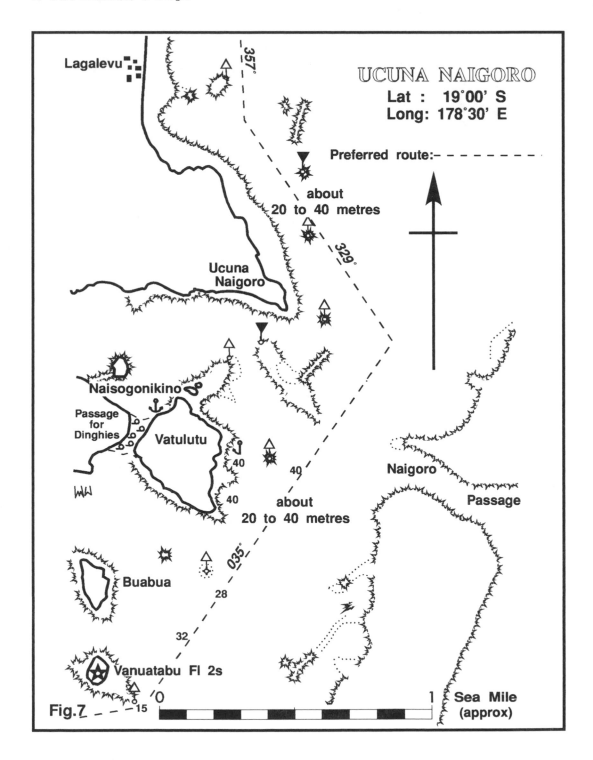

Lagalevu

357°

UCUNA NAIGORO
Lat : 19°00' S
Long: 178°30' E

Preferred route:- - - - - - -

about
20 to 40 metres

329°

Ucuna
Naigoro

Naisogonikino

Passage
for
Dinghies

Vatulutu

40

40

40

40

Naigoro

Passage

about
20 to 40 metres

035°

Buabua

28

32

Vanuatabu Fl 2s

0

1

Sea Mile
(approx)

Fig.7 - - -15

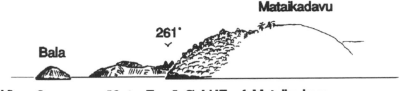

View 3. **"Cats Ears" Ø LHE of Mataikadavu**

Course is then altered onto the light bearing 043° to pass between the beacons.

On passing between the beacons, course is maintained until close up to the narrows when eyeball navigation is necessary. The narrows are marked by two beacons, one at either end, without topmarks. The first is left close to port as the yacht makes a jink to starboard; the second is left to starboard as the yacht alters course around it to 080° to pass to seaward of Vanuatabu and the beacon close south of it.

A small islet, Solomave, whose position is best seen in the chartlet (Fig. 6), will be astern bearing approximately 260° (View 4).

View 4. **Solomave from South of Vanuatabu**

The narrows are about 40 metres wide and have a least depth of 4 metres. A strong tidal stream may be experienced.

Having rounded Vanuatabu, course is then set to leave the next three beacons to port and to pass to seaward of a coral spit running south-east from Ucuna Naigoro. The spit does not carry a beacon. A course of 035° was found satisfactory.

On rounding Ucuna Naigoro, passage may be continued by staying within 1/2 mile of the coast and using the remaining beacons to identify shoals that are passed as indicated in the chartlet (Fig. 7), then as described below.

Toba Ni Korolevu to Ucuna Naigoro:

There are three bays that provide safe anchorage for yachts, the best being the one with the village of Matasawalevu at its head. A good, snug anchorage, in about 12 metres, can be found north of the southern headland, Vatulutu. Vatulutu is in fact an island, connected to Kadavu by mangroves. A dinghy passage was reported (1992) to exist through the mangroves. It is also understood that a small time-share resort is planned for the island which has two fine sandy beaches facing east towards Naigoro Passage. Unfortunately the anchorage off the beaches is in about 40 metres.

Naigoro Passage:

About 1 mile south-east from Ucuna Naigoro lies Naigoro Passage. It is deep and free of dangers, the reefs on each side being steep to. It is about 150 metres wide, but the pilot states that the sea breaks across the entrance in bad weather. Strong tidal streams set in and out through the passage but in fair weather, and with adequate power, a yacht should be able to enter safely. This passage provides the southernmost entrance into the lagoon formed by the Great Astrolabe Reef. The next entrance is about 20 miles to the northward.

Ucuna Naigoro to Ono or Kavala:

On rounding Ucuna Naigoro there are four beacons along the eastern end of Kadavu as far as Manuqiwa; only that off Manuqiwa carries a topmark. The beacons are left alternately shoreward and seaward with the boat steering 328° for the transit of the right-hand edge of Manuqiwa and Waisalima Point (View 5).

View 5.   **View from the vicinity of Ucuna Naigoro**

Leaving the shoreward beacon off Lagalevu village to port, alter course to leave the last beacon to starboard, and steer 357° for the summit of Ono (not charted on BA745) just open to starboard of the right-hand edge of the southern headland of Ono (View 6).

View 6.   **Ono from the vicinity of Lagalevu**

Pass the beacon about 200 metres off and maintain the course until the two points, Muiakoronibelo and Waisalima, north-west and east of Tiliva village, are in transit (View 7).

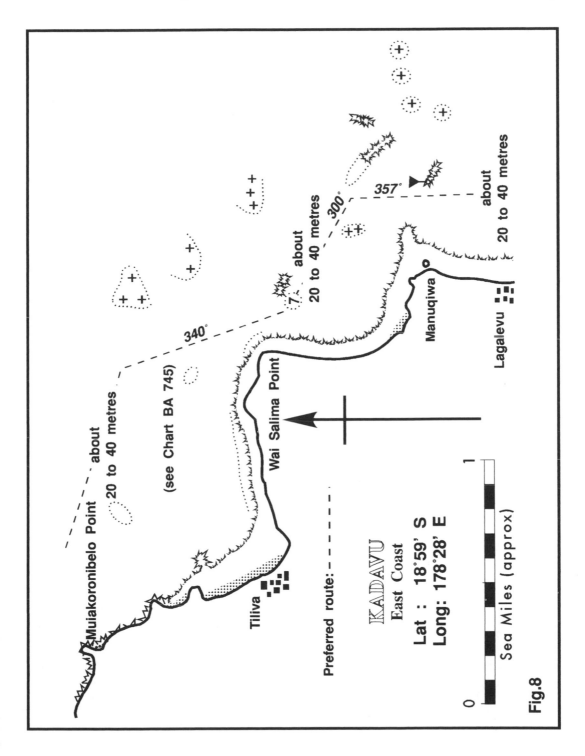

KADAVU
East Coast

Lat : 18°59' S
Long: 178°28' E

Preferred route: ------

Sea Miles (approx)

Fig.8

View 7.   **View from North-east of Manuqiwa**

Alter course to maintain this transit ahead bearing 300°.

Approaching Waisalima Point the yacht may pass over a 7 metre patch of small extent that is clearly visible. At this time the left-hand edge of the land near Ucuna Naigoro will come in transit with Manuqiwa astern, bearing 160° (View 8).

View 8.   **Ucuna Naigoro Ø Manuqiwa**

Alter course to 340° and maintain the transit. This transit will lead about 200 metres east of the isolated shoal about 0.6 miles north of Waisalima Point. Once clear of the shoal a yacht is clear to sail as necessary between Toba Ni Kavala and the island of Ono.

Toba Ni Kavala—(BA745):

This fairly substantial bay provides safe anchorage in all winds and is adequately described in the Sailing Directions. There are no beaches within the bay and the water is slightly clouded due to the mud bottom.

There are several sand beaches on the outer western side of the bay, and one particularly inviting one on the headland north west of Tiliva.

In 1992 it was reported that there was a good local store with excellent access for yachts at the south-eastern head of the bay. The shop is to the south and separate from the village of Solotavui, and is a little hard to find as it is hidden from view until you are almost upon it. A yacht can anchor within about 50 metres of the shop, in a depth of from 5 to 7 metres, sand and mud. The shop stocks a good range of local goods and sells petrol, premix, and diesel. Good water is available from a tap at the water's edge. The north coast of Kadavu contains at least three bays, all of which provide safe anchorages. Although not visited they were overflown by helicopter and appeared as charted on BA745.

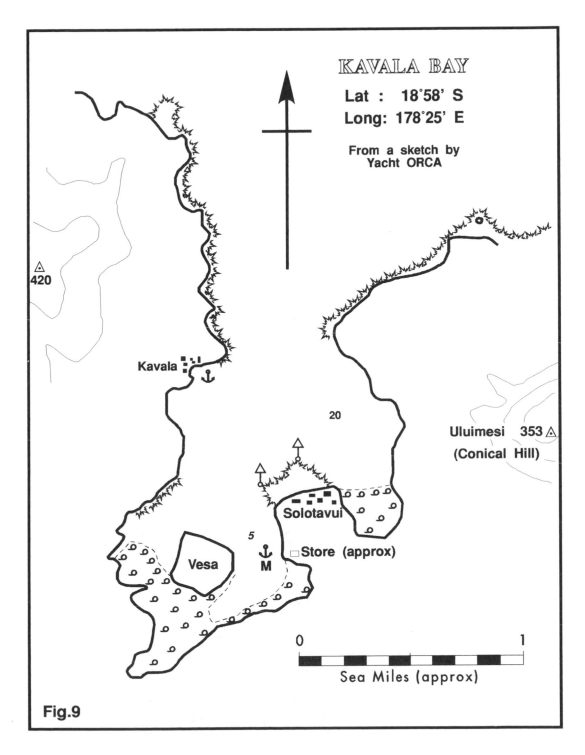

KAVALA BAY

Lat : 18°58' S
Long: 178°25' E

From a sketch by
Yacht ORCA

420

Kavala

20

Uluimesi 353
(Conical Hill)

Solotavui

Store (approx)

Vesa

5

M

0   1

Sea Miles (approx)

Fig.9

Sailing westward from Toba Ni Kavala they are, in order, Toba Ni Kasaleka, Toba Ni Daku, and Toba Ni Namalata. The latter is the main port for the island and has a concrete wharf with sufficient water for a yacht to proceed alongside.

Toba Ni Namalata is on the north side of the isthmus upon which Vunisea is situated. The bay is entered from the west, between John Wesley Bluffs and the reefs and foul ground about ½ mile to the north. The route is marked by beacons.

Ono and The Great Astrolabe Reef:

Only the western side of Ono has been visited by the author, however the islands and the reef north and east were overflown by helicopter and appear much as charted in BA745.

Nabouwalu Bay:

Situated to the north of Madre (Nabouwalu) (344), on the western side of Ono, this bay provides easy access and a safe anchorage at its head in about 8 metres, mud; inside an isolated rock that is marked by a perch. The bay provides a good base to explore Great Astrolabe Reef. There are two sandy beaches that provide other anchorages in other than westerly winds. One lies about 1.5 miles south, and the other immediately north. Both are part of the vanua of the village of Nabouwalu.

The turaga ni koro is most friendly, as are the other villagers, and will readily grant permission to use the other beaches. The village straddles a large stream that is dammed towards its head. Providing the level is high, water can be drawn from a tap in the village. Other provisions are not obtainable.

The small bay to the south provides a reasonable anchorage in about 10 metres, in sand and coral. It is backed by a beach and provides good swimming. An intermittent stream lies at the northern end of the beach. The bay is open to the west and could become a bit uncomfortable at times.

The bay to the north has a long beach of coarse sand. There is good swimming but the beach is not suitable for a picnic, being fairly steep and backed by scrub. Anchorage can be found off the centre of the beach in a clear sandy bottom in about 8 metres. Winds from the north-east tend to blow along the beach, but it is sheltered from the east to south-west. Some swell may be experienced at times.

There are several other villages on Ono, the most important being Vabia, in the south-west, which is the seat of the Tui Ono; and Naqara, at the head of the large bay in the north. Both have a postal agency, VHF radio telephone, and a store.

North from Ono, and inside the reef, are a number of islands, all possessing open anchorages of doubtful quality. One island, Dravuni, is used regularly by the cruise liners as their 'mystery island'. The villagers are not really interested in yachties!

Approaches to Ono—(BA745):

Ono may be approached from the north, having entered the reef through Usborne, Herald or Alacrity Passes. In the cases of Usborne and Alacrity, suitable leading transits may be established using the islands nearby. Herald Pass was marked by beacons, most of which were missing in 1985 as a result of the cyclones earlier in the year.

If one does not wish to enter the reef because of poor light, a safe approach may be made south of Alacrity Rocks directly into Nabouwalu Bay. At the head of Nabouwalu Bay is a two story church that has replaced a church with a bell tower, that was used as a transit mark before 1992. Providing that the new church is equally conspicuous as the old, a course of 113° with this church in transit with the left lower summit of hill (338), and a prominent black rocky outcrop on the hill close northward of the village, will lead about 70 metres south of the dangers south of Alacrity Rocks, and about 200 metres north of the isolated shoal about 0.5 miles from the mouth of the bay.(View 9)

View 9.   Nabouwalu Bay from south of Alacrity Rocks

If one wishes to give Alacrity Rocks a wider berth an initial approach may be made south of the transit, moving on to it after Alacrity Rocks is passed.

Ono to Suva—(BA745, BA1673):

Nabouwalu Bay is about 50 miles from Suva with clear water between. With an early start, a safe arrival can be made in daylight hours. The trip northward is most enjoyable in the prevailing south-easterlies.

A Yachtsman's FIJI

6

Bau Waters and Western Koro Sea

Introduction:

The major port in this area is the old capital of Levuka. Although it is possible to pass through this area, and to visit islands en route to Vanuabalavu or Savusavu, without clearing in and out of Levuka, this can only be done if you do not visit the island of Ovalau. If visiting Ovalau, you must clear at Levuka.

The island of Ovalau and the other islands in the western Koro Sea are collectively known as the Lomaviti Group. Ovalau is of obvious historical interest to the yachtsman while the island of Gau provides several pleasant anchorages and a genuine opportunity to visit traditional Fiji.

The other islands of the Lomaviti provide convenient stopping places overnight but are, in themselves, not of particular interest.

If a yacht has departed from Suva or Nukulau she will probably make her next stop at Toberua, Ovalau, or Gau. Gau is an obvious stop if headed for Vanuabalavu, while the others would be visited if en route for Savusavu or Taveuni.

Toberua—(BA488):

A yacht would be unlikely to visit Toberua unless proceeding to Bau Waters via Toberua Passage.

The islet of Toberua is entirely occupied by the Toberua Island Resort. This is an exclusive 'hideaway' resort with accommodation for about 40 guests. Yachts are welcome to anchor off and make use of the bar and restaurant by prior arrangement with the manager, Mr. Michael Dennis.

The best anchorage is in the area near the resort boats, in about 10 metres. An alternative, a little further away, is on the other side of the channel as indicated on the chartlet (Fig 10). Check with the boatmen on the suitability of your anchorage.

At Toberua all fresh water has to be shipped in and you are not welcome to use the resort showers, even after a dip in their salt-water pool. The resort cannot provide supplies to yachts.

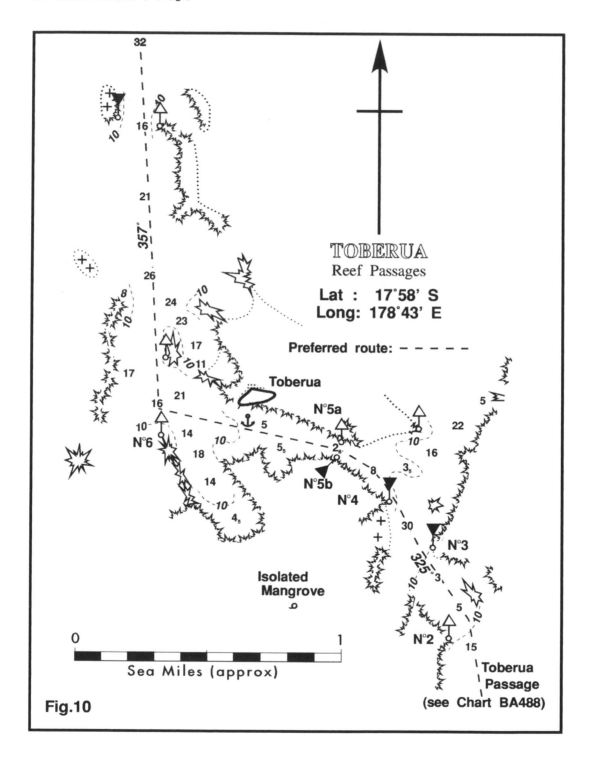

TOBERUA
Reef Passages
**Lat : 17°58' S
Long: 178°43' E**

Preferred route: – – – –

Toberua

N°5a

N°6

N°5b

N°4

N°3

N°2

Isolated
Mangrove

Toberua
Passage
(see Chart BA488)

0   1
Sea Miles (approx)

Fig.10

Because of the river outlets in the south of Bau Waters, diving close by Toberua is not good, however the outer reef is not far away. Nonetheless, the swimming is very good and, if the hip pocket can stand it, it is an excellent place to wine, dine and dance.

Toberua Passage:

From a position south of Mabualau steer for the island until the right hand edge of Togaravu Islet bears 298°, then alter course to 306° to enter Toberua Passage. During this approach an isolated mangrove will be seen nearly in line with No 1 beacon. This is not a leading transit, but it can be used to help assess any leeway or drift during the initial stages of the approach. During this leg the bottom will rise steeply from more than 100 metres to general depths of about 20 metres.

When about 0.4 miles short of the first entrance beacon, some isolated coral heads about 30 metres off the main reefs will be encountered. The first is to port and the second, about 200 metres short of the beacon, to starboard. Usually they can be identified by surface eddies. An 8 metre least depth on this leg will be found in this area. Toberua Passage suffers from patches of dirty water on the ebb, which can cause doubt as to the depths that will be encountered. It is sound advice to enter on the flood, and preferably before noon.

No 1 beacon should be given a wide berth and rounded to starboard onto a course of 350° to leave No 2 beacon about 50 metres to port. A least depth of 5 metres will be found in this area.

On passing No 2 beacon (no topmark, 1992), alter course to 325° to leave No 3 beacon to starboard. A least depth of 3 metres will be found on this leg. Continue on this course (a slight adjustment may be needed to counter a variable tidal stream) to leave No 4 beacon (missing, 1992) to port, again about 50 metres off. In 1992, there were two beacons marking each side of the "narrows" on the final approach to Toberua. On passing No 4 beacon, continue on until No 5a beacon, the northernmost of the two, is in transit with the centre of Toberua, then steer for it. This will ensure that you stay clear of the reefs on the southern side of the approach. As Nos 5a and 5b beacons are approached, adjust course slightly to port to pass between them then adjust further to port to steer for the outermost boat, moored south of the island.

Anchor nearby, but clear of the boats. Any vacant moorings will invariably be required before nightfall. Check on your position with one of the boatmen.

It should be noted that all beacons in the immediate area of Toberua carry topmarks referring to Toberua Island as the land.

Should you plan to be more than just a casual visitor to Toberua, it is understood that one of the boats will come out and pilot you in through the passage. This will have to be arranged in advance with the resort over the phone from Suva. The resort does not monitor VHF.

Bau Waters—(BA488):

Bau Waters is an area encumbered with many reefs and patches of foul ground. To navigate the area without either of the reference charts, and preferably both, is considered foolhardy. Nevertheless, if the charts are used, with proper planning safe routes can be plotted and a smooth water passage to the north can be enjoyed, as an alternative to the Koro Sea. Unfortunately, the previously indicated recommended tracks have been removed from the 1987 New Edition of BA488, and several of the beacons are damaged and difficult to see. Good visibility is essential.

Leluvia:

Eleven miles north of Toberua is the island of Leluvia, which is now a low cost backpackers' resort. It is quite small, and has nothing to recommend it except a superb beach and excellent swimming, however you are welcome to use the very basic facilities, eat at "mess hall", and patronise the simple shop that sells beer and small eats. Leluvia provides a safe anchorage, in about 4 metres, sand, to the west of its south-western shore. The island is about 15 miles from Levuka, which leaves only a short hop for the following day.

Toberua To Leluvia:

Depart from Toberua anchorage to the vicinity of No 6 beacon and then steer 357° for a point midway between the final two beacons in the Toberua area. No 6 beacon will be in transit astern with a position about one third of the way in from the right hand edge of Togaravu (View 10).

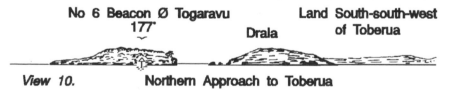

No 6 Beacon Ø Togaravu   Land South-south-west
177˚   Drala   of Toberua

View 10.   Northern Approach to Toberua

On passing between the two beacons 1.1 miles northward of Toberua, maintain course until Toberua bears 170°, then alter course to 350° with the island astern. Maintain this track until the right hand edge of Cagalai is in transit with Nadalanikoro Trig (133m.) on Moturiki, bearing 049°, then steer this transit. The anchorage to the west of Leluvia is approached on a course of 090°.

Leluvia to the Northward:

From Leluvia a yacht has the choice of a passage to Levuka via the Moturiki Channel, which is straightforward, or around the northern end of Ovalau, with more time in Bau Waters. A yacht may also proceed direct to Naigani Island Resort or on to Vanua Levu, or both may be approached via Natovi, a ferry terminal on Viti Levu.

Natovi:

The ferry terminal of Natovi is used by small ferries to and from Ovalau, and the resort ferry to Naigani. It is connected to Suva by road, and a bus may run. A taxi is generally in attendance at the end of the jetty and, if not, one can be summoned on the phone from the store.

The store at Natovi is well stocked with provisions and has a deep freeze chest and a liquor counter. Fresh bread is available. Water, petrol, diesel, and mix are all available (provide your own containers).

There is a small jetty with about 1.3 metres alongside at low water, so it can be used by a yacht for short periods. It is rough in parts, so good fendering will be needed. Tidal stream and wind could also affect its use.

The anchorage off the jetty is in 6 to 8 metres, sand, and should be well protected from any sea by the enclosing reefs.

Leluvia to Natovi:

With Leluvia astern, bearing 150°, steer 330° to leave Challis Reefs to starboard, and to pass between Doole Reefs and Mermaid Shoal. When approaching Rask Reef, leave it to starboard and alter course to 280° for the beacon on the outer end of Vuidrana Reef. When about 0.2 miles short of this beacon, adjust course to pass south and west of Ballance Reef, and anchor south of the jetty at Natovi.

Natovi to the Northward:

Proceed from the anchorage off Natovi jetty to the north of Ballance Reef to pass south of Ramsay reef and between Patricia and Joan reefs.

If wishing to complete a circumnavigation of Viti Levu, via Ellington Wharf, a yacht should proceed as detailed in Chapter 12. Ellington Wharf also provides an alternative departure point for Vanua Levu by way of Yadua.

If proceeding to Vanua Levu, alter course to the north-westward on passing Ramsay reef and pass between Cox and Elsie reefs, then on to the northward and out into Vatu-I-Ra Channel. If proceeding to Savusavu, re-entry into reef waters may be made at the entrance, which is lit, 5 miles north-east of Vatu-I-Ra (17°18.8'S. 178°28.2'E.)

If proceeding to Ovalau, choose your own route!

If proceeding to Naigani, alter course for the summit of the island bearing 010°, after passing Patricia reefs. On closing the large drying reef, close southward of the island, a decision can be made whether to proceed to an anchorage off the resort on the eastern shore, off the village on the south-western shore, or to Cagabuli Bay on the northern coast. Although the pilot recommends Sova Bay as an anchorage this should be avoided, if possible, as the bay is a sacred fishing ground.

The reef to the south of the island is marked at its eastern and western ends by beacons. As these beacons are slightly in from the ends they should not be taken too close.

Naigani—(Fig 11):

Although the island was at one time wholly owned by the Riley family, having been presented to the original Riley by the Chief of Verata for services rendered during the tempestuous days of the early 1800s, it has now reverted to the villagers except for the area of the resort on the south-eastern point.

Yacht crews are welcome to use the dining room and bar, and if available there is one resort heavy duty mooring off the south-eastern beach that will facilitate a late return on board! The best anchorage is, however, at Cagabuli Bay.

The mooring off the resort is exposed to the south-east and, although strong and safe, it can be a bit uncomfortable if the breeze is up. If making a passage around the northern end of the island the reefs should not be taken too close as there are many small off-lying heads.

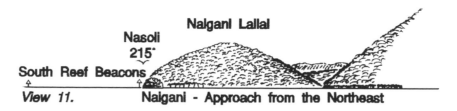

View 11. **Naigani - Approach from the Northeast**

The final approach toward the resort from the north-east should be made on a course of 215°, with the western beacon on South Reef, the south point of the island, and the right-hand edge of Naisoli, all in transit (View 11).

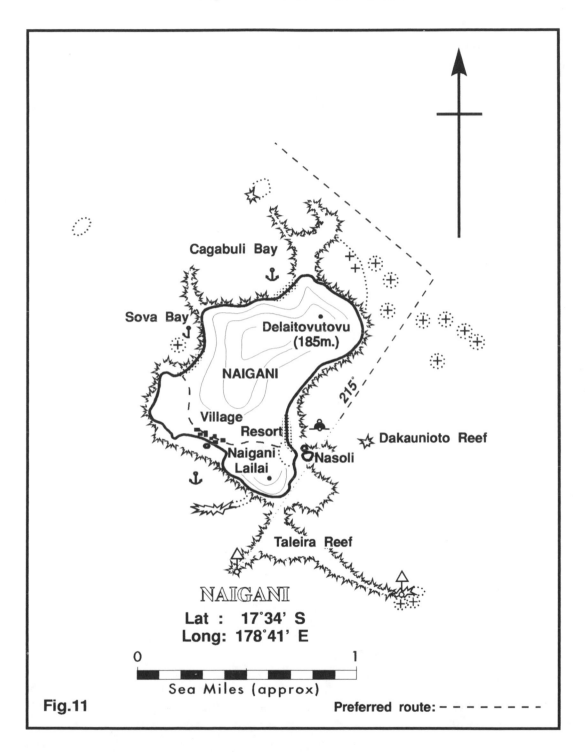

Cagabuli Bay

Sova Bay

Delaitovutovu
(185m.)

NAIGANI

215°

Village

Resort

Dakaunioto Reef

Naigani
Lailai

Nasoli

Taleira Reef

NAIGANI
Lat : 17°34' S
Long: 178°41' E

0   1

Sea Miles (approx)

Fig.11

Preferred route: — — — — — — —

It is difficult to identify Naisoli against the similar background of the main island, and binoculars are essential.

The anchorage at Cagabuli Bay is off a beautiful white sandy beach in depths of 5 to 7 metres, sand. There are several coral patches, all carrying about 3 metres at LAT, which pose no problems for yachts. There is an extensive coral reef from the northern point of the island that provides good shelter from any winds from the north-east.

A safe entry or departure to the northward from Cagabuli Bay can be made on a line of bearing of 197° on the western edge of the island.

Ovalau and Levuka:

Levuka is a port of entry and as such all yachts visiting Ovalau must clear in and out at Levuka. As a yachting anchorage Levuka is not good. It is open to all winds from north through east to south and the holding is variable, particularly reasonably close to shore. The boat landing is also exposed, although at about half tide it is possible to enter the creek spanned by a yellow bridge, and proceed to a calm landing alongside the Royal Hotel.

The wharf at Levuka is controlled by the Ports Authority of Fiji, and charges are levied for its use. Charges are the same as at Suva or Lautoka, as are those for water. However, water can be collected in containers from a tap in the public toilets near the boat landing.

The wharf is next to the new fish factory, opened in 1992, and it is frequently used by trawlers which run their auxiliaries constantly. There used to be an all-pervading stink of fish, and anchoring off was pleasant by comparison. With the new factory things may have changed.

The town of Levuka is steeped in history and to step ashore is to go back in time some 50 years.

The town contains two reasonably large supermarkets, MH, and Ranchrods, with good stocks of frozen and canned goods. Fresh vegetables are available in a haphazard fashion at the supermarkets and other stores. The only 'market' is held on Saturday. It is reported to be poorly stocked. The following fresh provisions were found on a Tuesday after visiting numerous stores - potatoes, carrots, beans, buck choy, English cabbage, pumpkin, onions, tomatoes, pawpaw, bananas, and dalo. Ice is available at the fish factory, the block, is very large, but can be cut. One quarter block costs $2.00.

There are branches of Westpac and ANZ Banks.

The Royal Hotel and two clubs, the Ovalau Club and the Levuka Club (members only, but visitors welcome) provide the local watering holes. Meals may be had at the Royal (by prior arrangement) and at several restaurants.

Diesel super, and mix are all available a short distance from the wharf.

An effort is being made to boost Levuka as a tourist attraction with its history as the main theme. A good couple of days could be spent at Levuka to absorb some of Fiji's colonial past.

Buses to other parts of Ovalau are rare and are mainly geared to transporting workers to and from Levuka in the morning and afternoon. Taxis, at a price, are plentiful.

There is a resort at Rukuruku, on the north-west coast, not shown on the chart but sited on the northern side of the bay north-east of Vunisinu Point, off which a yacht can anchor. It was not visited.

Levuka—(BA488, 1244):

The directions given in the Admiralty Pilot provide all that is needed by the yachtsman. The approach from the north, inside the reef, is uncomplicated. The main entrance from the eastward, Na Tubari, is well marked by leads (a green strip and a green cross on the church), and has a light and beacon on the reefs either side.

Nalulu Entrance, to the south, can be used but eyeballing is essential in the area around Balolo Point.

The most convenient anchorage for a yacht is in front of the church in about 10 metres. An alternative anchorage can be found in the area north-east of Nasova Point.

Hurricane Hole:

The pilot describes the area between the south-western side of Ovalau and the north-eastern side of Moturiki as a good hurricane refuge. A yacht can tuck well into Wainaloka Bay and anchor in 5 metres, mud.

Directions:

Once in the area east of Moturiki steer 112° with the left tangent of Ladoyalewa, in transit with the left tangent of Yanuca Lailai. When Ladotagane bears 237°, put it astern and steer 057° for the anchorage.

There is a dinghy landing in the northern curve of the bay that gives access to the main road to Levuka. A bus runs twice daily. Wainaloka Mission, run by the Church of England is close by.

Islands North-East of Ovalau—(BA905):

Two islands lie close north-east of Ovalau: Makogai and Wakaya. The former was the site of the Leper Hospital but this was transferred to Suva in 1979. The site is now used for a government aquaculture operation and an experimental sheep station. Makogai can be visited en route to Savusavu via Makogai Channel, and being three hours from Levuka makes a handy overnight anchorage after viewing the old hospital, particularly the graveyard, and the research station.

The island of Wakaya is a privately owned island and is currently being developed and sold in lots as individual holiday/retirement homes. Only 9 miles from Levuka, it is in easy reach and one can find a safe anchorage in the open bay on the north-western end of the island. The island's caretaker will not allow visitors to proceed above the high-water line. The anchorage is in 10 metres, sand, and the holding is reasonable. In view of the 'closed' nature of the island it does not appear to offer much to the yachtsman, but it can be used as an alternative to Makogai for a night anchorage.

Makogai—(BA905):

Makogai is adequately charted and well described in the Admiralty Pilot. Although the weather was foul, little difficulty was found in identifying the leading beacons shown on the chart, once in the vicinity of Daveta Yawa-Levu, even though the rear beacon was not readily apparent as one approached from further northward.

The beacon mentioned as standing on the southern side of the entrance has been destroyed (1992), but a "local" mark of PVC pipe had been erected in its place. The off-lying reef, Vatu Vula, was easily seen breaking. The reefs on the northern side of the entrance were not as distinct as those on the south.

The passage into Dalice Bay was made without difficulty and anchorage in about 10 metres found off the old Leper Hospital. The staff of the research station welcomes visitors.

There are two moorings for the station's vessels immediately seaward of the jetty and some other buoys marking agricultural sites on the southern shore of the bay. One should keep well clear of the latter. A reef north-east of the jetty was marked by a pole.

My visit to Makogai was made at the time of a 30 knot easterly and did not allow an examination of the north-eastern entrance, Daveta Loboni, although the custodian of the research station advised that, in good visibility, EUREKA would have no trouble in negotiating this alternative passage. Exit through this passage would save 4 miles on the passage to Savusavu.

Wakaya—(BA905):

Daveta Ni Kavu is the entrance to be used by yachts. Although the beacon on the south side of the entrance was missing, the reefs are clearly visible and entry was made as described in the Admiralty Pilot, page 288.

If proceeding northward a yacht can depart from Wakaya by Daveta Na Kaile, or the unnamed entrance on the 249° transit of the two northern points of the island.

The latter entrance is narrow, but the reefs can be easily seen. The beacons are wooden poles with a very limited life.

Daveta Na Kaile is wide and deep, and a natural transit of 'north point house' and a hill provides adequate guide to the entrance from the anchorage, on a course of 007°.

Good visibility is necessary at any time when sailing in this area.

Gau—(BA1251):

Gau, some 45 miles east from Nukulau, is an easy day sail although probably hard on the wind.

The island is fringed with a large reef containing, on the western side a large deep lagoon. The BA chart is adequate and would appear correct in most aspects. There are four entrances to the lagoon; three on the north-western side of the island and one to the south-west. All are clearly shown on the chart. All are possible for yachts, although the south-western one is not for the faint-hearted as it is narrow and the shallows over the lip of the reef are clearly visible. Least depths of 5 metres were encountered in 1985. The leading line as described on the chart is difficult to identify without prior know ledge as 'grassy hill' is now wooded!

Of the three north-western entrances the one preferred is the centre unnamed one with Lion Pk. transit Leading Point, bearing 115° (View 12).

Shoulder Pk.   Lion Pk. Ø Leading Point

115°

View 12.   **Approach to Gau through "Centre" Passage**

This entrance is wide and I believe has been deepened in recent years. The transit is not critical, and one may be off to the southward without danger. The least depth obtained in 1985 was 7.5 metres.

The northernmost entrance was also used and would appear as charted.

There are many anchorages within the lagoon, but two have characteristics that lend immediate appeal. The first and most obvious is,

Herald Bay. This bay is backed by an excellent sandy beach, which is often used by the locals for picnics, and it is also close to the village of Sawayake, upon whose Turaga ni Koro one should pay a visit as he is also the turaga for the island. It is also the nearest anchorage to Qarani, where there is the post office for the island, the co-op store and the assistant Roko-Tui. Qarani is situated on the eastern fork of the Siguma reef harbour but such an anchorage has little to recommend it.

The second recommended anchorage is in Somosomo Bay, the next bay south from Herald Bay. This bay is well protected from the weather. Somosomo is connected to the island's road 'network' but it was noted that children invariably went to school at Sawayake by punt. So much for the road!

The other large bay, with the village of Waikama on its eastern shore, is excellent for larger vessels. A jetty with depths of about 5 metres alongside is situated on its north-eastern shore about ½ mile north-west of Waikama.

Unfortunately most of the anchorages are in about 15 metres. To try to anchor in less water generally puts one too close to the reef. Both Herald Bay and Somosomo Bay have dead coral/sand bottoms and a trip line on the anchor is recommended. Waikama Bay is charted as mud and reported as being so. It is believed to be a popular hurricane hole for the Fijian Navy.

The island is connected to Suva by air, the airfield being at the south-eastern end of the island.

The Lau Group

Introduction:

The easternmost of the island groups that go to make up Fiji is known collectively as the Lau Group. The islands are generally small and widely dispersed. The provincial capital is the island of Lakeba, about 150 miles east of Suva. This island is the home of Ratu Sir Kamisese Mara, the immediate past Prime Minister of Fiji, current First Vice President, and Tui Lau.

Tourism is not encouraged in the area because the people of many of the smaller islands are relatively unsophisticated and there is a desire to preserve their current lifestyle. It is possible to fly to Lakeba, and to the best of my knowledge a permit is not required. Similarly, if you are hardy enough, the trip can be made on the inter-island cargo vessels.

As with the other outer islands a yacht will require a permit to visit this group, presumably through the Ministry of Fijian Affairs. The situation was not clear in 1992 as permits to visiting yachts had been "temporarily suspended since the last Provincial Council Meeting". In the past, approval for a visit to islands in the group was not automatic. A valid reason, other than tourism, was essential. Even with an acceptable reason, the time to obtain approval could run into weeks. As this situation is likely to prevail for some time, any request should be made early and the visit planned as a separate excursion to your main tour of Fiji.

I was unable to revisit any of this group in 1992.

Vanuabalavu (The Exploring Isles)—(BA416):

At the northern end of the Lau Group is a collection of six islands, named on British charts The Exploring Isles. They are surrounded by a large barrier reef and, outside the Yasawas, provide some of the best beaches and cruising in Fiji.

The largest of the islands is Vanuabalavu. At its northern end is a large freehold plantation that is currently being redeveloped as a privately owned, exclusive, marine-oriented tourist resort.

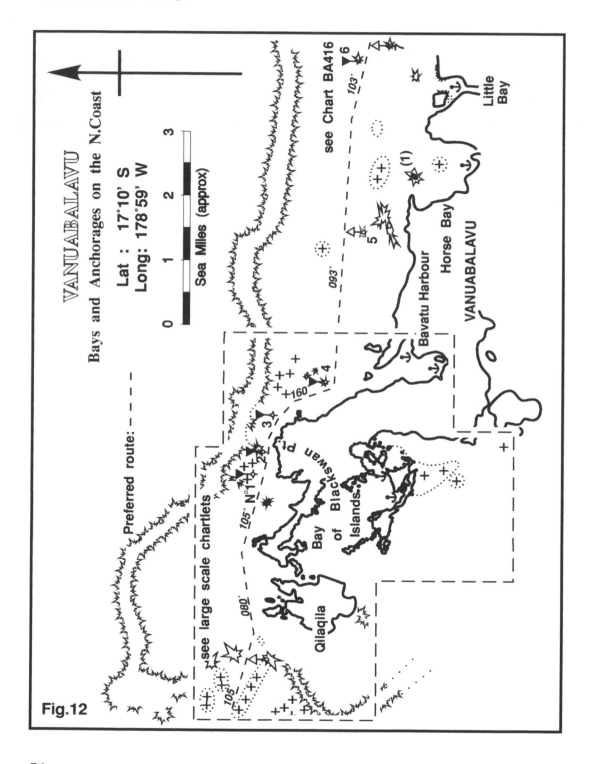

Fig.12

VANUABALAVU
Bays and Anchorages on the N.Coast

Lat : 17°10' S
Long: 178°59' W

Sea Miles (approx)

0 1 2 3

Preferred route: — — —

see large scale chartlets

see Chart BA416

Little Bay

Horse Bay

Bavatu Harbour

VANUABALAVU

Bay of Blackswan Pt

Islands

Qilaqila

103°

093°

160

105° N°1

080°

105

At the present time, in line with the Provincial Council decision mentioned above, permits to visit Vanuabalavu are not being issued but should this policy change the general area of Vanuabalavu and its magnificent lagoon and surrounding reef will become more accessible to the cruising yacht.

The island contains literally scores of bays, indentations and safe anchorages. Because of its shape it is possible to find a calm, windless and serene anchorage, somewhere in the island, no matter what is the direction of the wind.

Two anchorages, Bavatu Harbour (Turquoise Harbour) and the Bay of Islands, are part of the "resort". They are totally land-locked and provide a safe haven in all weather.

Approach—(BA416):

There are three major passages through the barrier reef associated with Vanuabalavu. These, together with other lesser passages are well described in the Pilot.

Tongan Passage is the closest entrance to Lomaloma, where yachts are required to call on arrival for the customary visit to the assistant Roko Tui. However, as the passage from Suva or Levuka will be dictated by the wind direction, one is most likely to fetch up at the northern entrance, Qilaqila Passage. This passage is highly recommended for yachts as it is down sun in the afternoon. The two white leading beacons, 3metres high, provide an excellent lead even in restricted visibility. For those arriving late, a satisfactory overnight anchorage can be found a short distance inside the entrance, allowing passage to Lomaloma to be completed next day.

Qilaqila Passage to Lomaloma—(BA416):

A yacht should place herself on the leads at least 2 miles offshore to ensure she is settled down well clear of the reef that extends to the north and southward of the leading line. The leads are clearly visible at a distance of about 5miles on a bearing of 105° (View 13).

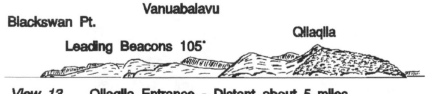

View 13.   Qilaqila Entrance - Distant about 5 miles

The leads should be rigorously maintained as there are off lying dangers on either side (Fig.12).

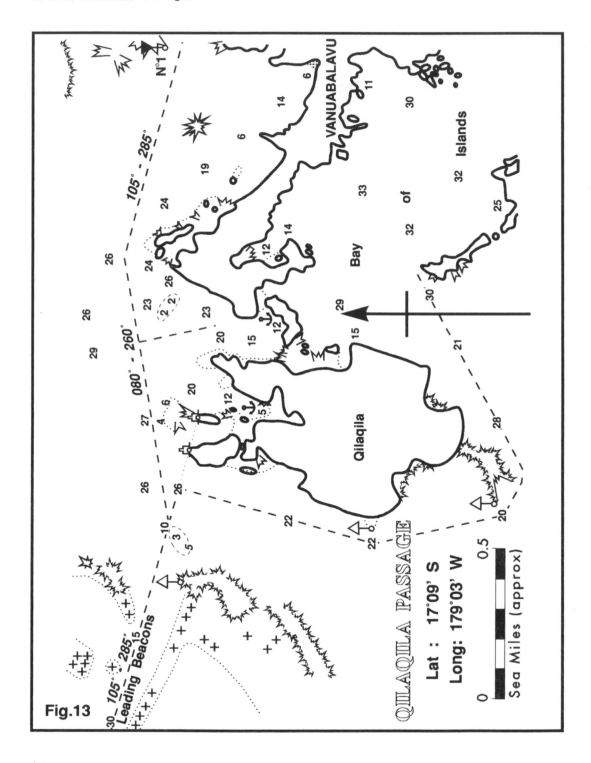

Fig.13

QILAQILA PASSAGE

Lat : 17°09' S
Long: 179°03' W

Sea Miles (approx)
0   0.5

Just inside the entrance, the south side of which carries a beacon, is a visible 3-metre patch. When abeam of this patch course should be altered to port to 080° to clear the shoal patches to the north and east of Qilaqila. An overnight anchorage can be found to the southward of this track in a bay as shown in Fig. 13, in a depth of about 15 metres. A course of 080° should be held until Blackswan Point comes in transit with the right hand summit of Avea bearing 105° (View 14).

105°

View 14.   Blackswan Point Ø RH Summit of Avea

Continue to steer 105° until close aboard Blackswan Point, keeping the beacons to port.

When abeam No 2 beacon, about 100 metres short of Blackswan Point, alter course for Sovu, bearing 091° (Fig. 14). When No 3 beacon is in transit with the main summit of Avea (600), bearing 105°, alter course to this lead. When close aboard No 3 beacon alter course to 130° for the middle of three sandy beaches with an uncharted high hill behind. When the islet in the middle of the entrance to Bavatu Harbour bears 160° steer this course and enter the harbour.

To continue on to Lomaloma (Fig 12.), steer 160° until No 4 beacon is abeam to port when a wide swing to port should be made to steer 095° for the left - hand edge of Avea, which will then be seen to be open to port of No 5 beacon. This course is now held for about 1.1 miles, until the summit of Avea (600) bears 103°, then steer for this mark, leaving No 5 beacon well clear to starboard. No 6 beacon will now be seen open to the north of the summit of Avea. This course is held for a further 1.9 miles.

The vessel will pass No 6 beacon to port and No 7 beacon to starboard. No 8 beacon will be seen open to the north of the summit of Avea, and other beacons open to the south of the right-hand edge of Avea.

When abeam No 8 beacon to port, No 9 to starboard, alter course to 127° for the right hand edge of Cikobia-I-Lau. The remaining beacons are passed to starboard and course progressively adjusted around the east coast of Vanuabalavu until the gap between Vanuabalavu and Namalata bears 221°, when this course is steered. This is held until hill (660), northwards from Lomaloma bears 268° with a beacon open to the north when this course is steered (See plan—BA416).

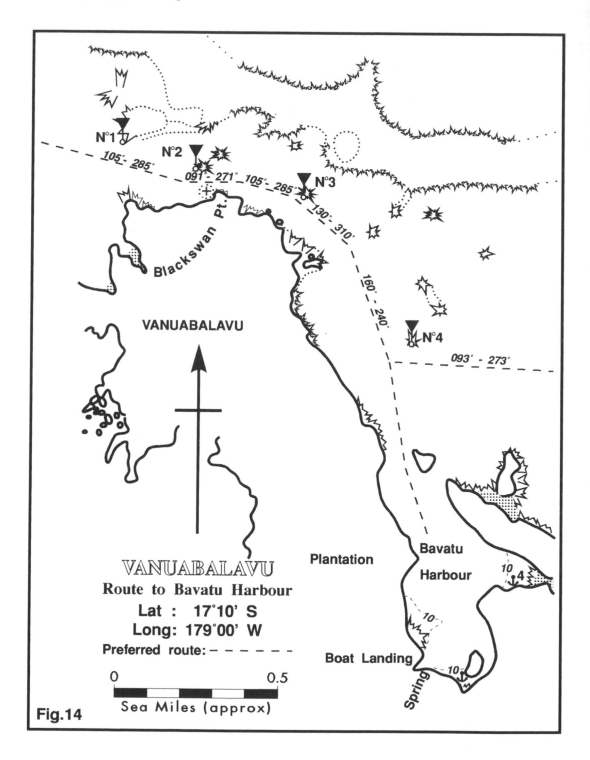

N°1

N°2

091° - 271° - 105° - 285°

N°3

105° - 285°

130° - 310°

160° - 240°

N°4

093° - 273°

Blackswan Pt.

VANUABALAVU

Plantation

Bavatu
Harbour

10

VANUABALAVU
Route to Bavatu Harbour
Lat : 17°10' S
Long: 179°00' W
Preferred route: - - - - - -

Boat Landing

Spring

10

10

10

0   0.5
Sea Miles (approx)

Fig.14

The final approach to Lomaloma is made with the radio mast in transit with the end of the wharf bearing 243°. When north of Yanu Yanu alter course as necessary to leave the beacon off Lomaloma to starboard and take up an anchorage in the area to the south-eastward of the wharf in a depth of 10 to 15 metres, sand.

A vessel can proceed alongside the wharf inside the 'T', there being about 3 metres at LAT.

Lomaloma—(BA416):

The administrative centre for Vanuabalavu and surrounding district is the village of Lomaloma. The assistant Roko Tui has his office here and he should be called upon on arrival in the area. There is a hospital, post office, telephone exchange, airfield and two stores. There is little difference in the stock the stores carry, which depends upon when a ship last called, or on what the last plane could carry.

Generally the stores carry only those requirements of the Fijian villagers in the area, with the co-op carrying diesel and 1 in 50 mix. Ice-cream is sometimes available (it depends on the plane) and beer.

Flights to Suva are on Tuesdays and Thursdays and the mail closes at 0930 on those days.

Ratu Sir Kamisese Mara owns land on Vanuabalavu and has a fine bure at Lomaloma.

Water may be obtained depending on the weather but it should not taken for granted.

The anchorage off the Lomaloma wharf is subject to the prevailing easterly and south-easterly winds, although some relief can be found by anchoring closer to Yanu Yanu.

Susui:

About 3 miles south-east from Lomaloma is the island and village of Susui, with a population of about 100.

The anchorage off the village on the eastern side of the bay, a little to east of the school, is in sand in a depth of about 5 to 8 metres. It is well protected from the prevailing weather and has a fine sandy beach.

The senior member of the village is the Tui Susui. Although the village also has a Turaga ni Koro, it is to the former that one should present the sevusevu.

The anchorage is a pleasant spot, and the villagers appear most friendly.

Tongan Passage—(BA416):

The general directions for Tongan passage are given in the Admiralty Pilot and are quite satisfactory for passage to Lomaloma. If, however, a boat wishes to proceed directly to the northern end of Vanuabalavu she may do so by steering directly for the north-eastern end of Avea, bearing 336°, after leaving the patch in the centre of Tongan passage to starboard. This course will pass clear between the shoals and reefs to the south-eastward of Avea. When about 1 mile from the north-eastern end of Avea the vessel should alter onto hill (670), close north-westward of Mavana village, on a bearing of 259°. The beacon to the east-north-eastward of the hill will be just open to the northward. This course should be maintained until south of the south-western end of Avea, when the recommended track between Qilaqila Entrance and Lomaloma will be joined.

Anchorages on the North Coast—(BA416):

There are 3 anchorages on the north coast of Vanuabalavu: Bavatu Harbour and two unnamed bays, one between hills (580) and (420), and another to the westward of hill (420). These two bays, though not as snug as Bavatu Harbour, possess fine sandy beaches along their shores. The western bay has been assigned the name Horse Bay and the eastern bay Little Bay.

Entry into Horse Bay is made with No 6 beacon astern and a sandy beach, Horse Beach (so named because of the horse that inhabits the small coconut plantation backing it), ahead on a line 230° - 050°. A coral head, small but clearly visible, lies on this approach with the drying rocks at the west of the bay bearing 300°. This may be passed on either side during the latter stage of the approach. Anchorages may be found off any of the sandy beaches in about 10 metres, sand. Although protected by the barrier reef from any major wave action, a slight movement can be felt when the reef is covered at high water.

Entry into Little Bay is made leaving No 7 beacon to the eastward (port) and navigating by eye between the reefs that fringe the two headlands. Once inside, the bay will be found to be snug and, with a bottom of sand and mud, the holding is very good. There is a good sandy beach on the eastern shore.

Both Horse and Little Bays have sizeable lagoons backing them. Although the entrances to these are shallow, access by dinghy is easy and they are worth a visit. These bays are part of the vanua of the village of Mavana.

Bavatu Harbour is part of the freehold property mentioned earlier and may well become the centre for a marine-oriented tourist facility.

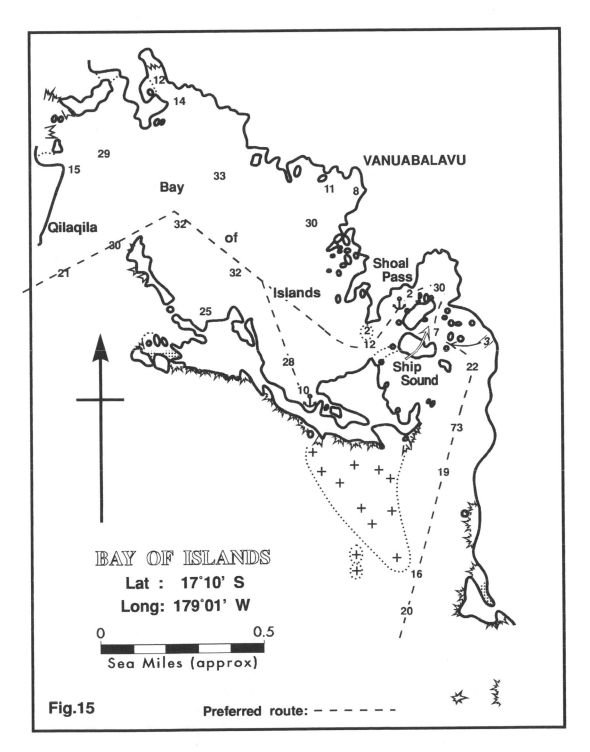

VANUABALAVU

Qilaqila

Bay

of

Islands

Shoal
Pass

Ship
Sound

BAY OF ISLANDS
Lat : 17°10' S
Long: 179°01' W

0   0.5

Sea Miles (approx)

Fig.15   Preferred route: – – – – – –

The bay is completely land locked but totally lacking in other facilities such as beaches. It is surrounded by high cliffs and is deep throughout, with the exception of two anchorages in indentations on its southern and eastern sides as shown on the chartlet (Fig. 14). Nevertheless these provide perfectly safe anchorages and good swimming. Access to the homestead on the plateau above, which has now been completely restored and is occupied, is by a track leading from a small (shaded) beach in the south-western corner of the bay. There is a caretaker in residence in the grounds of the estate.

A fresh water spring issues from a hole in the cliffs just east of this beach. The cement 'dam' is now open to the sea, and the water is only fresh at low water after all the salt water has been flushed out.

It is understood that a landing pontoon has been installed near the small beach. Visitors are only welcome by prior arrangement.

The Bay of Islands—(Fig.15):

The area to the south-east of Qilaqila is dotted with a multitude of islands varying in size from almost one mile in length to the size of a small boat. They are virtually impossible to land upon, being volcanic/coralline rock, which jut out of the water with sharp rocky shores that have been undercut by the action of the sea. They do provide some fantastic scenery and several satisfactory anchorages.

It is possible to take a yacht through the islands by a winding route as shown. The many inlets provide numerous places to explore in the dinghy. Unfortunately, the area itself is devoid of beaches.

The two best anchorages, in order of preference, are Shoal Pass and Ship Sound.

The Bay of Islands is a reserve trust park and is the vanua of the village of Daliconi.

Adavaci Passage and the Western Side of Vanuabalavu—(BA416):

Adavaci Passage provides access to the lagoon on the western side of Vanuabalavu but it requires a lengthy approach through the reefs and is not an easy route. There is a beacon on the southern side of the entrance and a course of 066° approx. on the south-eastern end of Yanucaloa provides a fair lead, but good visibility is essential. The opening over the lip is narrow and only carries about 8 metres of water.

Safe passage may be made down the western side of Vanuabalavu as far as the village at the back of Lomaloma, known appropriately as Daku ni Lomaloma.

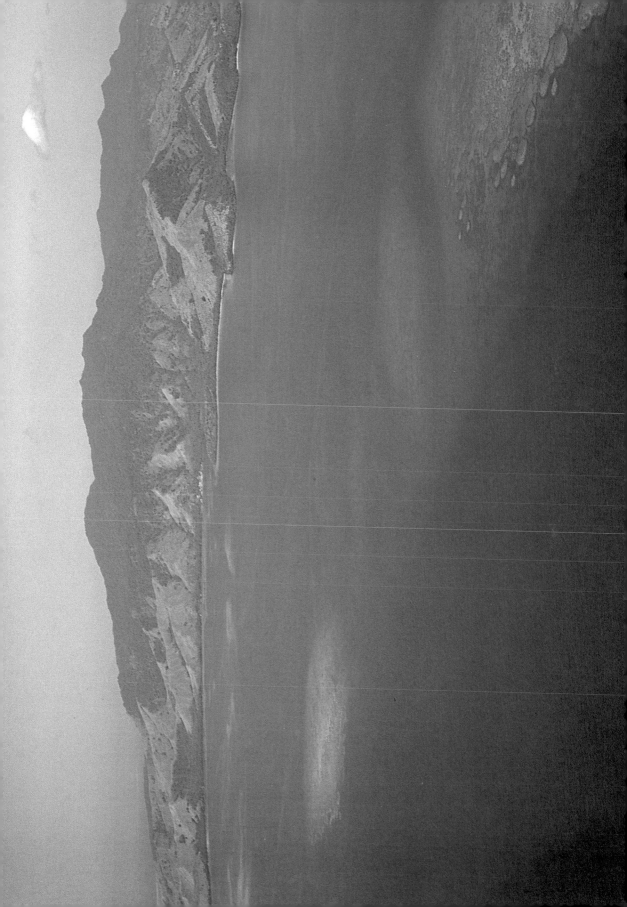

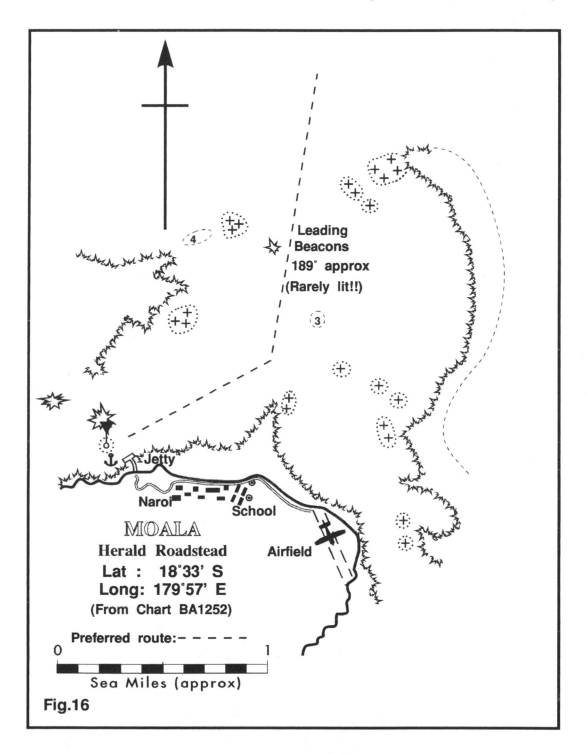

Leading Beacons 189° approx (Rarely lit!!)

Jetty

Naroi

School

MOALA

Herald Roadstead
Lat : 18°33' S
Long: 179°57' E
(From Chart BA1252)

Airfield

Preferred route:- - - - -

0   1

Sea Miles (approx)

Fig.16

From here it is about a mile by road to Lomaloma and this does provide an alternative to the passage down the east coast. The anchorage off the village is not ideal, but satisfactory for a short period. Sand flats back the reef, which extends about ¼ mile offshore.

Moala—(BA1252):

Permission is needed if a yacht wishes to visit Moala, one of the islands of the Lau group. The island is handily placed if one is taking passage from Suva to the main islands of the Lau or if sailing from Kadavu to them, as the journey can be broken into two comfortable one-day passages instead of a lengthy two-day passage.

Except in the north the island is well protected by reefs, and there are several excellent anchorages well sheltered from the prevailing south-easterlies.

The island is now connected to the mainland by air and has a new concrete jetty with about 4 metres alongside the head on the north coast near the main village of Naroi.

There are two small stores at Naroi, a post office and radio telephone link. There is also a small hospital, and a secondary school.

Directions:

The island is adequately charted by BA 1252 and described in the Admiralty Pilot, although there have been some changes to beacons as are shown in Fig.16. There are now two leading beacons, (occasionally lit by kerosene lamps) on the point south from Observatory Rocks, which lead into Herald Roadstead on a course of 189°. The leads pass 0.2 miles east of an isolated reef, marked with a beacon, 1.3 miles north of Observatory Rocks.

On a passage to Kiti-i-Ra, at the head of the deep bay on the east coast, all charted dangers were clearly visible from aloft and no others were seen.

Although the majority of yachts would be unlikely to plan a special visit to Moala, if such a stop fitted logically into an itinerary, at least three or four days could be spent exploring the bays and reefs.

PART THREE

Savusavu

and

The Northern Division

Area covered in Part Three Relevent Chapters thus:- ⑩

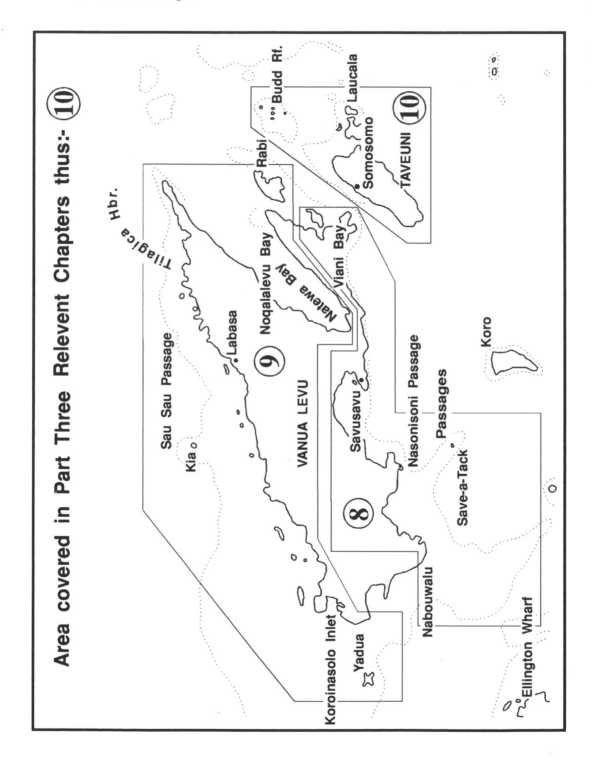

South Coast of Vanua Levu

Ovalau to Savusavu:

After departing from the north of Ovalau or from Levuka, proceed via Makogai Channel or Wakaya on into the Koro Sea. A vessel may then sail via Namenalala, where there is an exclusive resort, at which yachts are not welcome and a bird sanctuary, or pass outside the Namena Barrier Reef, sailing direct for Savusavu. The Koro Sea has a reputation for being decidedly rough at times and is also subject to tidal streams that can be quite strong. Generally, with average visibility, there are ample navigational marks in view and the effect of tidal streams can be overcome by diligent position fixing. Except in the areas close to the charted islands and reefs the water is very deep and clear of dangers.

The approach to Savusavu is through Point Passage leaving Point Reef, which is lit, to starboard. The charts and the Admiralty Pilot are more than adequate.

Namenalala and Save-a-Tack Passages—(BA382):

Should a yacht wish to break the voyage at Namenalala, she should enter the Namena Barrier Reef at South Save-a-tack Passage and depart via North Save-a-tack Passage.

Namenalala Ø Hill 150△- 059°

View 15.   **Approach to South Save-a-tack Passage**

South Save-a-Tack Passage:

Approach Namenalala on a course of 059°, with the summit of the island in transit with Hill (150) Trig (View 15). This will lead to the best entrance.

A clearly visible beacon, without a topmark, marks the southern side of the entrance.

A small submerged, detached reef, probably carrying about 4 metres, prevents direct entry along the transit.

Once the entrance has been located the beacon should be brought in line with the left-hand edge of the island, bearing 054°, and this should be held until about 50 metres from the beacon. Course is then cast to port, to maintain a distance off of 30 to 50 metres until inside the reef, when a course of 054° is again set on the left-hand edge of the island. There is then a clear passage to the north-west coast of the island.

Namenalala:

Namenalala now hosts an exclusive (20 guests) resort and, although visitors can anchor off the island and proceed ashore as far as the high water line they are generally not welcome. No facilities are available. Anchorage off the north-west coast, at the south-western end of the island away from the resort, is fair in coral and sand with a long line astern to a tree. The island is a rookery for boobies. Diving in the lagoon is excellent but fish cannot be taken as the whole area has been zoned as a reserve.

North Save-a-Tack Passage:

As with the south passage, the north passage is easily located on a line of bearing of 020° from the south-west point of Namenalala. In clear visibility, a stern transit with the dip in the summit of Makogai bearing 200°, will be seen (View 16).

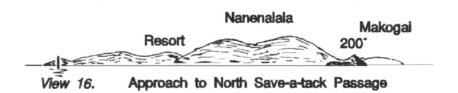

View 16.   Approach to North Save-a-tack Passage

Only one beacon exists, on the south side of the entrance. The transit does not appear to agree with the charted position of the entrance but it gives a clear channel with a depth of 20 metres. There are some submerged coral heads inside the entrance carrying about 6 metres.

On leaving North Save-a-tack Passage course can be set direct for Point Passage.

Vatu-I-Ra Channel to Savusavu—(BA379, 382, 378):

Enter the reef at the opening, which is lit, 5 miles north-east of Vatu-I-Ra (17°18.8'S. 178°28.2'E.), and steer 039° for the Rocks (3 ft. high), 11 miles distant. Adjust course after sighting the rocks to pass about 0.7 miles to the west, and then steer towards Nabouwalu, if an early anchorage is desired, or to the north-east if proceeding directly to Nasonisoni Passage. Depending on the strength and direction of the wind, anchorages can be had in Solevu or Nadi bays.

Nabouwalu—(BA379, 382):

The anchorage at Nabouwalu is an open roadstead, but is generally well protected by reefs from all but the south-west. There is a government station and a substantial village with at least one store. There is a concrete jetty with 4 metres at its head alongside which a yacht can lie. Further investigation may reveal a more sheltered mooring inside the head of the jetty but this area is generally occupied by several small craft. Care is required when navigating the reefs south of Nabouwalu.

Solevu Bay—(BA382):

Although not visited by the author, Solevu Bay is reported as being a snug anchorage for a yacht, well up into the bay where the reefs give good shelter. Winds from the south-east would still, however, be experienced.

Nadi Bay—(BA382):

Nadi Bay is approached more along the southern shore than directly for the middle as there are several shoal patches at its entrance. The anchorage is in mud and sand and would appear to offer good holding. As with Solevu Bay, Nadi Bay is open to south-easterly winds. The village was not visited.

Nasonisoni Passage—(BA382, 378):

The route across Wainunu Bay is clear except for Nole, which is easily avoided. Wainunu Bay is fringed with mangroves and holds little for the yachtsman.

Nasonisoni Passage is about 300 metres wide at its narrowest, and is deep and steep to alongside the reefs on either side. It is well described in the Pilot.

Once clear of the passage, a yacht can find a snug anchorage in the small craft harbour immediately east of Nasonisoni in the area south-east of the small islet, Navatu, as described in the Pilot. The depth is about 10 metres and the anchorage is well protected from all winds. The villages in the area were not visited.

Nasonisoni to Savusavu—(BA378):

If the visibility is good a yacht can proceed to Savusavu inside the reefs, but the area is full of coral heads, the scenery is uninspiring and it is 6 miles further. Extreme caution is needed as the water clarity is poor, particularly in the area between Kubulau and Nyavu Passages. It is not recommended. Nevertheless, a snug anchorage amongst mangroves does exist in Nadivakarua Bay, about three miles west from Kubulau Passage, in 3 metres, mud, if required.

The normal route is outside the reef to Point Passage.

Savusavu Bay has not been checked out but a yacht will obtain the best information on the area from the Savusavu Yacht Club.

Savusavu—(BA378):

The town of Savusavu is situated on the southern shore of Nakama creek at the eastern end of Savusavu Bay. It is a pretty spot and the town has grown considerably over the past few years. Of signal importance to cruising yachts is the Copra Shed Marina, and Savusavu Yacht Club, which is situated in the recently restored and renovated "Copra Shed", the town's oldest and most historic building. Although not on a par with Suva or Lautoka, the shopping is quite adequate and Savusavu makes an excellent base for sailing in the eastern waters of Fiji. It is the base for the crewed yacht charter operation, Emerald Yacht Charters.

Copra Shed Marina:

The Copra Shed Marina complex includes many services required by yachts, all housed under the one roof. These include the following:

Sea Fiji Travel.
Fiji Air Travel Office.
Dive Shop.
Captains Cafe (Pizza Restaurant).
Hot Bread Shop.
Boutique.
One double and one single serviced apartment.
The Savusavu Yacht Club.
Public Telephone (ISD).

The marina contains seven stern to berths, holding off buoys are provided, with 240 volt AC power and water available. There are also seven swing moorings owned by the yacht club. The fees from the latter are used to promote junior sailing in the club's fleet of Optimist dinghies.

There are two "hurricane" moorings at which yachts may be left long term under the supervision of the marina. Hot showers and toilet facilities are available dockside. During the hours that the offices and shops in the complex are not attended (approximately 2100 to 0700) a security guard is in attendance.

The 1992 marina rates were as follows:-

Stern to Berths and Moorings....$10 pd, $40 pw.

Hurricane Moorings.............$150 per month.

Use of facilities (anchored off)$15 pw.

All visiting yachts crews are invited to the Savusavu Yacht Club (bar available) however after two weeks a Visitors Membership of $10 per year will be charged.

Additional services which can be obtained are: Fax, Phone, Word Processing, Mail Service.

Fuel. By small tanker at main wharf.

Washing (Machine) sent out ...$5 per bag.

To give your cook a break, Emerald Yacht Charters will also cook and freeze entrees, and provide cakes, cookies and the like to order. Two to three days notice may be required for large orders. They can be contacted on VHF Ch.08.

In 1992 the rates for the serviced apartments were $80 per day (two bedrooms) and $60 per day (one bedroom). However these are negotiable depending on season and occupancy rate.

The Copra Shed Marina and Savusavu Yacht Club may be contacted on VHF Ch.84, Phone 850457 or 850561 and Fax (679) 850344.

There are several supermarkets, including MH and Gulabdas. All have a similar range of goods. There is another bakery besides the Hot Bread Shop, and an excellent butcher. The market is open from about 0700 daily and has a good range, particularly on Saturday. Banks are ANZ, Westpac, National of Fiji, and Bank of Baroda. The first two provide cash advances using Visa and Mastercard respectively.

There is a small hospital.

The Hot Springs Hotel welcomes non residents. The normal dress rules for Fiji apply. There are several restaurants, including the hotel dining room and two clubs, Savusavu and Planters, members only but visitors are welcome.

The bus station is adjacent to the market. Newspapers are sold at the Prakash barber shop, opposite the market, from 1200 daily.

The post office is about one kilometre out of town, near the government jetty.

Savusavu is connected to the capital by sea and daily air services.

At the head of the creek are the government buildings, including the post office. There is a launch jetty where a dinghy can secure if you do not wish to walk the kilometre from the marina.

Directions—(BA378):

Savusavu Bay will usually be entered from the Koro Sea via Point Passage, although it is possible to make a passage inside the reefs from the vicinity of Nasonisoni Passage.

Having raised Point Reef Light, proceed along the south-eastern shore of Savusavu Bay about ½ mile offshore until the mouth of Nakama creek is reached. Enter the creek and maintain a track along the middle. Adequate beacons or poles mark dangers on the shore of Nawi, which forms the north bank of the creek.

If a yacht wishes to anchor the best anchorages will be found upstream of the marina moorings. There is adequate water throughout the creek and, except for fringing coral, the bottom is mud and the holding excellent.

Savusavu to Taveuni—(BA378, 440, 416, 382,F50,F51):

This trip can be done quite easily in one day as it is only about 50 miles. Having already entered Point Passage, which is lit, an early start can be made before dawn if required. However, should it be desired to do short hops, the following bays and reef entrances provide varying degrees of shelter en route: Naidi Bay, Bakabaka Inlet (Salt Lake), Fawn Harbour and Viani Bay.

The water outside the barrier reef to the east of Savusavu Bay is clear and deep and the passage presents no problems. However, if one wishes to use the four anchorages just named, close attention to navigation will be required to ensure accurate fixing as the coastal features and inshore hills are at times difficult to identify.

In the following descriptions it is assumed which the yacht has closed the coast and identified the appropriate entrance.

Naidi Bay:

The Namale Plantation Resort is situated on the eastern headland of Naidi Bay, only about 5 miles by road from Savusavu, along the Hibiscus Highway. The bay is about 15 miles by sea. The entrance to the bay is directly north from the sea for the centre of the gap between two headlands. The anchorage is sand and mud, in 3 to 5 metres with excellent holding. A yacht owned by the resort will often be seen at anchor in the bay.

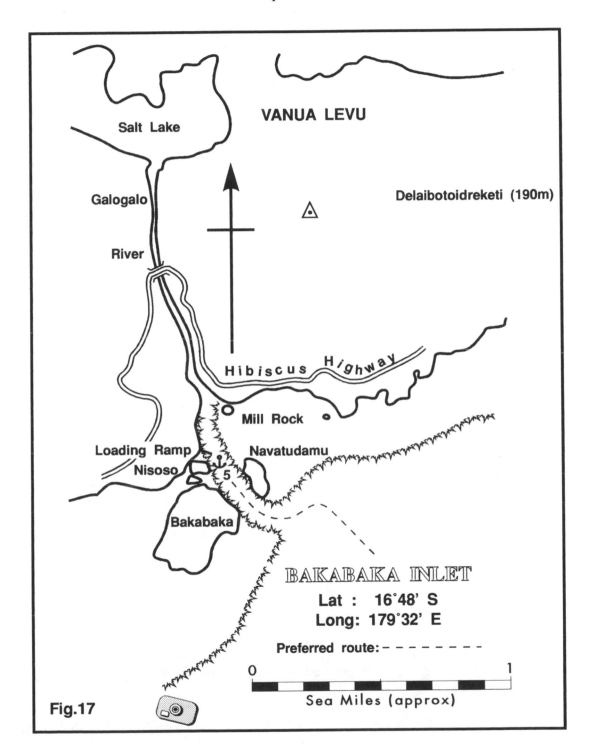

Salt Lake

VANUA LEVU

Galogalo

Delaibotoidreketi (190m)

River

Hibiscus Highway

Mill Rock

Loading Ramp

Navatudamu

Nisoso

5

Bakabaka

BAKABAKA INLET
Lat : 16°48' S
Long: 179°32' E

Preferred route: – – – – – – –

0   1

Sea Miles (approx)

Fig.17

Unfortunately the bay is often subject to residual swell from the south-easterly. The fringing coral reefs on each side of the bay are virtually parallel (not as charted) and are the same width as the entrance, thus it is not possible to tuck in to the south-east corner to minimise the swell effect. There is little to recommend the use of the bay and it could equally well be visited by bus from Savusavu.

Bakabaka Inlet (Salt Lake)—(BA382):

This is a fair weather reef entrance, being somewhat narrow and entered from an east and south-easterly direction. Once inside, and positioned between Bakabaka and Navatudamu, reasonable shelter is obtained, although swinging room is limited. Holding is sand and mud, in 5 metres and very good. (Fig.17)

The main reason for visiting this anchorage is to take a dinghy trip up the Galogalo River to the Salt Lake, some 2.5 miles, which provides an interesting passage through semi-jungle/mangrove/palm tree scenery. The lake is tidal and at springs a 2 horsepower outboard will have difficulty working against the tidal stream in the restriction where a bridge carrying the Hibiscus Highway spans the river. If you have no motor, check the tides.

There are several planters' houses in the area.

Water turbidity on the ebb tide can effect visibility of the reefs. An entry on the flood has the advantage of clear water and a rising tide.

The Buca Bay bus runs along the highway to Savusavu.

Fawn Harbour—(F50,BA440):

Fawn Harbour is a large anchorage protected to seaward by extensive coral reefs, and generally fringed on the shoreline by mangroves. There are several small islets on the inner sides of the reefs that are accessible by dinghy, and from which one can swim or walk the reefs on the appropriate tide.

Because of the extensive mangrove areas the bay is troubled to some degree by turbidity on the ebb, but on a rising tide the water is passably clear. As the general area of the bay is clear of dangers, this is not of great importance.

The entrance, Naikasa Pass, is wide and deep, although one should keep in mid channel to avoid the 20-metre deep extensions from the horns at the seaward side of the reef.

The pass is about one mile long, with a dogleg about one third of the way in. Nevertheless, entry is possible in most weather and light conditions, as there are adequate beacons and natural leads.

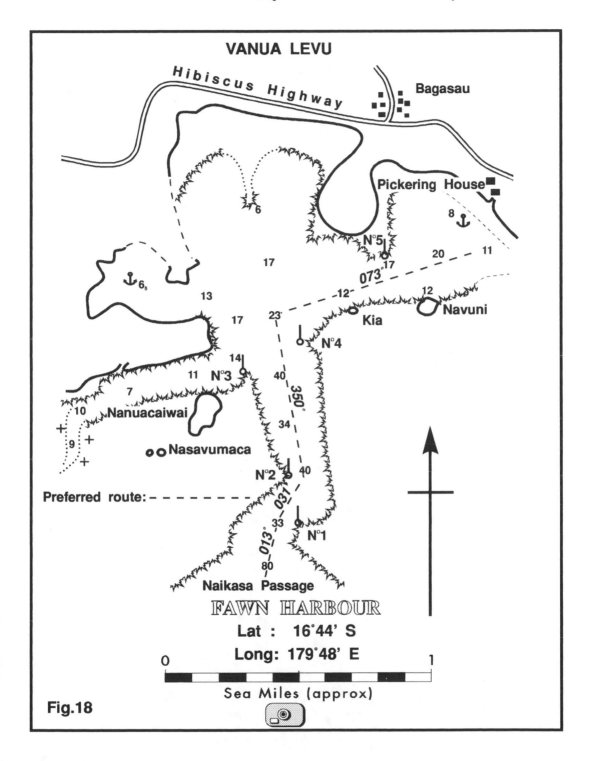

VANUA LEVU

Hibiscus Highway

Bagasau

Pickering House

8

N°5 17

20 11

073°

17

13

12

073°

Kia

12

Navuni

23°

17

N°4

14

40

350°

11 N°3

7

34

10 Nanuacaiwai

9

Nasavumaca

N°2 40

Preferred route: - - - - - - -

031°

33

013°

N°1

80

Naikasa Passage

FAWN HARBOUR

Lat : 16°44' S

Long: 179°48' E

0 1

Sea Miles (approx)

Fig.18

Holding ground is excellent, being sand and mud. The north-western arm is reported to provide a good hurricane anchorage, free from coral, and with a good mud and sand bottom.

A good anchorage can be found in the northern curve of the eastern arm of the bay, north-eastward of Navuni. Roy and Lena Pickering own one of the planters' houses on the high ground behind the mangroves. At half tide there is a boat passage through the mangroves to the Pickering's' boatshed. Visitors are welcome to call. Roy and the other men in the area generally share a bowl of kava at the end of the day, and a donation of yaqona will be well accepted. You will invariably be asked to join in.

The Pickering plantation also gives access to the village of Bagasau where, with a day's notice, some fruit and Fijian vegetables may be bought. You can also get close to Bagasau through a hole in the mangroves at half tide - if you can find the hole! Bagasau is the last access to the Savusavu/Buca Bay bus before Buca Bay. The bus leaves Bagasau for Savusavu about one hour after it leaves from Buca Bay.

Directions—(Fig. 18):

The initial approach into Naikasa Pass is made on a course of 013°, with No 2 beacon just open to starboard of the valley north of Bagasau that carries the Hibiscus Highway (View 17).

No 2 Pile 013°

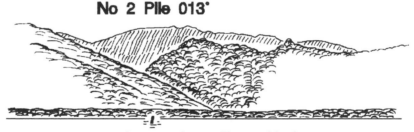

View 17.   **Approach to Fawn Harbour**

When the vessel passes over the lip of the reef, and when the two planters' houses are just open to port of Navuni, bearing 031° (View 18), steer 031°.

Planters' Houses open of Navuni - 031°

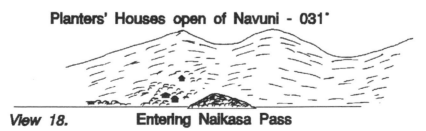

View 18.   **Entering Naikasa Pass**

Maintain this transit until No 2 beacon is abeam to port, when it is rounded onto a course of 350°, midway between No 3 and No 4 beacons. Hold this course until Kia is in transit with Navuni, then alter course to 073° midway between Navuni and No 5 beacon. When No 5 beacon is abeam to port, steer toward the planter's house and anchor in about 8 metres. The bottom shelves steeply from about 6 metres at the edge of the fringing coral and mud.

Fawn Harbour to Viani Bay—(BA440,F50,F51):

Continuing to the eastward from Fawn Harbour a vessel could enter the reef again at Dakuniba Pass, about 5 miles west of Viani Bay. Due to the complexity of the inner route this is not recommended on a first visit, unless the sun and weather are most favourable.

Viani Bay—(F51,BA416):

Viani Bay is a large bay situated at the south-eastern end of Vanua Levu, on the western side of Somosomo Strait. It has several excellent beaches and provides a very good anchorage at its head. The shores of Viani Bay are generally owned by descendants of the Fisher family. Ned Fisher owns the plantation homestead at the head of the bay, off which you may choose to anchor on first arriving. Yachts are welcome.

About 5 miles westward from Viani Bay is Dakuniba Boat Pass. Although the chart does not indicate it, it is possible to navigate within the reef between the two and gain access to the bays to the west of Viani Bay. There is a narrows adjacent to Benauiwai, but the water between the reefs is deep and the passage is marked by poles.

Directions:

Entry into Viani Bay is reasonably easy under all conditions.

Although the Pilot indicates which a vessel may pass either side of the 4-metre patch in the middle of Viani Pass, it is easier to leave the patch to port as a natural transit exists to guide a vessel, and the drying reef to starboard can usually be sighted either as breaking water or as dry rocks.

320°
Yalewalagimevu Pt.   Nacagina Pt.
Nakawa Pt.

View 19. **RHE Nakotoga Pt. Ø Navukana - 320° - 2 miles**

The pass should be entered on a course of 320°, with the right hand edge of Nakatoga Point (not named on the charts - 0.4 miles NNW of Vatudamu Point) in transit with Navukana (328m.) ahead. (View 19)

This should be maintained until a small islet with one of the longest of names, Nayalewadravudravua, bears 274°, when course should be steered for it. The islet will be seen to be in line with the head of a gully full of trees. (View 20)

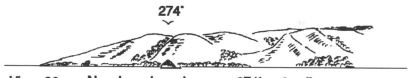

View 20.   Nayalewadravudravua - 274° - 2 miles

Maintain this course until Ned's house, the left of two buildings at the head of Vatolutolu Bay, is in transit with Naqaiqai Hill (1060) bearing 329°, when this is placed ahead (View 21).

Naqaiqai Ø Planter's House - 329°

View 21.   Approaching Vatolutolu Bay

When Tri is abeam to port alter course to bring the first high hill to the right of Ned's house ahead on a bearing of 353°. This course is held until inside the finger of reef running south-east from Vatudeni Point, then steer approximately 290° to an anchorage in Vatolutolu Bay, in 18 metres, sand and coral, with Ned's house bearing 323°, and Naviavia (920) transit Vatudeni Point, 237°.

There is a tighter anchorage a little higher up the bay in about 8 metres, but in view of the limited swinging room it is only suitable in calm conditions.

There are numerous other anchorages and beaches fronting Viani Bay, which can be visited by dinghy or by the yacht herself. The choice of anchorage will be influenced by the direction and strength of the wind. During strong south-easterly winds the best shelter from the wind will be found close westward or north-westward of Yanuyanuwiri

Ned Fisher, the owner of the plantation, enjoys the company of yachties. He has spent some time at sea as a deck hand on a US research vessel, the JOSEPH CONRAD, and enjoys a beer or a whisky. He will make you most welcome.

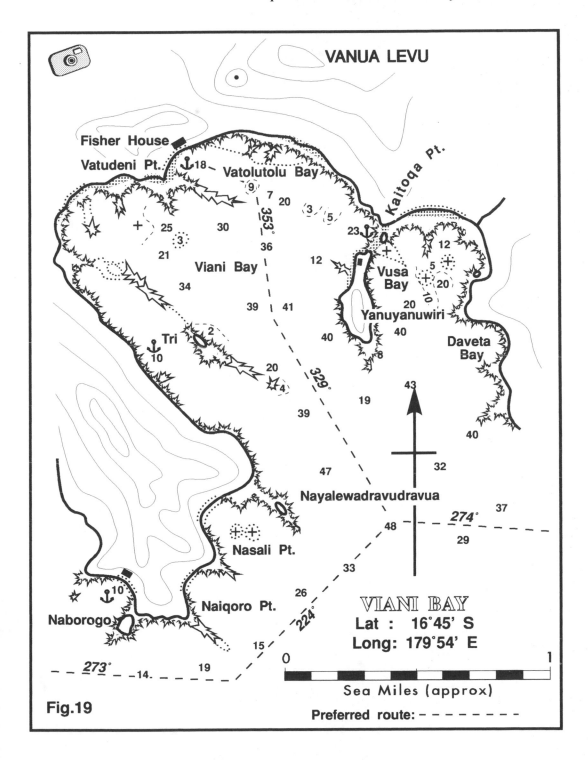

VANUA LEVU

Fisher House
Vatudeni Pt.
18
Vatolutolu Bay
Kaitoqa Pt.
9
7   20
3   5
353°   23
25   30   12
36   12   Vusa
3   Bay   5
21   20
Viani Bay   10
34   Yanuyanuwiri
39   41   20
Tri   40   40   Daveta
2   8   Bay
10
20
4   43   40
329°
39   19
32
47
Nayalewadravudravua
37
274°
48   29
33
26
Nasali Pt.   224°
10   VIANI BAY
Naborogo   Naiqoro Pt.   **Lat : 16°45' S**
Long: 179°54' E
273°   0   1
14   19
Fig.19   Sea Miles (approx)
Preferred route: - - - - - - - -

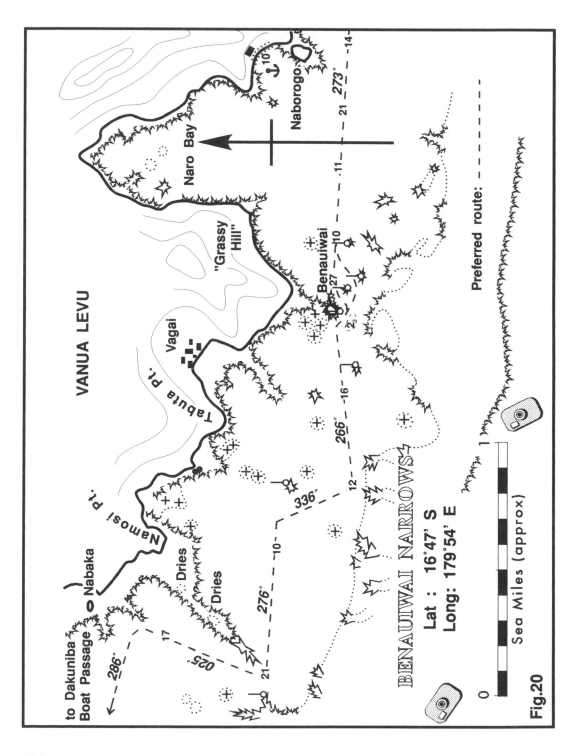

VANUA LEVU

Naro Bay

Naborogo

"Grassy Hill"

Vagai

Tabuta Pt.

Namosi Pt.

Benauiwai

to Dakuniba
Boat Passage   Nabaka

Dries

Dries

BENAUIWAI NARROWS

Lat : 16°47' S
Long: 179°54' E

Preferred route: – – –

Sea Miles (approx)

0   1

Fig.20

Viani Bay to Dakuniba Boat Pass—(Fig. 19,F51):

From a position on the approach transit, 329° on Ned Fisher's house, with hill (530) east of Daveta Bay bearing 044°, steer 224° to a position 0.3 miles south-east of Naiqoro Point, where Benauiwai bears 273°, and bring the islet ahead, steering 273° (View 22).

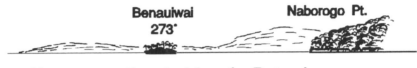

View 22. **Benauiwai from the Eastward**

On approaching Benauiwai numerous poles will be seen which mark isolated reefs. There are two routes through Benauiwai Narrows, indicated on the chartlet (Fig 22). The preferred route is which closest to Benauiwai, as eyeball navigation is more positive. The reef surrounding the islet is steep to and depths of about 10 metres will be held throughout. Two patches close by each other, the shallowest of which carries 2.2 metres, lie close south-west of Benauiwai. Keeping close to Benauiwai's fringing reef will leave them to port but they can be passed on either side. Having cleared Benauiwai Narrows, bring Benauiwai astern in transit with the right-hand edge of Naborogo bearing 086° and steer 266° (View 23).

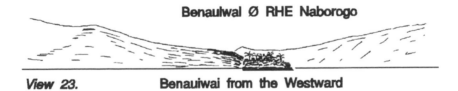

View 23. **Benauiwai from the Westward**

This course is maintained until approaching the inner edge of the barrier reef when it is altered to 336° onto Nabaka ahead. Hold this course until the point north of Benauiwai is just open of the right-hand edge of Naborogo bearing 096° (View 24).

View 24. Naborogo open of "Benauiwai Pt." - 096°

Then place this astern, steering 276° for the remains of a pole on the inner side of the barrier reef, just opposite the end of the long finger of reef running to the south-westward from Namosi Point.

Round this reef about 15 metres off, and bring Nabaka ahead 025° and in transit with a house on the beach behind (View 25).

View 25.   **House Ø Nabaka - 025°**

A pole will be seen, near the shore, fine on the starboard bow. Maintain course 025° until close by the pole and then alter to 286°, with Namosi Point in transit astern with the grassy hill 0.75 miles northward of Benauiwai (View 26).

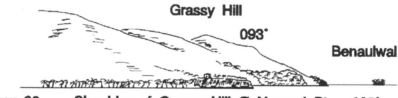

View 26.   **Shoulder of Grassy Hill Ø Namosi Pt. - 093°**

This track is maintained until the inner end of Dakuniba Boat Pass, which is marked by beacons. Thence steer to seaward, maintaining a track midway between the reefs.

The bays lying to the north of this route have not been investigated, but there is one delightful beach tucked in behind Naborogo, just after you leave Viani Bay. The beach is steep to with fine white sand and off-lying coral heads. An anchorage in fine sand can be found just outside the coral in 10 metres. The swimming is excellent.

Viani Bay to Savusavu:

Should a yacht arrive at Viani Bay without having first called at Savusavu she will find the passage from there to Savusavu an easy downwind sail. It is made offshore of the barrier reef at whatever distance one feels comfortable; the water is deep and there are no off-lying dangers. Departure will normally be made via Viani Pass reversing the directions given for entry. There are several possible anchorages inside the reef en route to Savusavu, the only notable one being Fawn Harbour. All are described earlier in this chapter.

Buca Bay—(F51, BA416):

The next major bay east, or rather north, from Viani Bay is Buca Bay. As it is most likely which a yacht will have sailed to Buca Bay by way of Taveuni rather than from Viani Bay, the route later described assumes which Viani Bay is the destination.

On its own, Buca Bay has little to offer the cruising yacht. Its main advantage is which it is connected to Savusavu by bus and can be used as a point of embarkation or disembarkation if needed. It is also a calm anchorage, with a good mud bottom that provides excellent holding in all weather.

The bay is free of dangers except for the fringing reef, and the chart is quite adequate, although the scale is a little small. The directions for entering the bay, given in the Pilot, are straightforward and can be followed without difficulty.

A small ferry operates between Buca Bay and Waiyevo on Taveuni. It lands and picks up its passengers over the beach at Natuvu Plantation. Just inshore from the beach is a general store run by the plantation. The store carries the usual staples and stocks diesel, petrol, 50 mix and kerosene. Water is available. All must be carried in containers. One of the surprises—ICE CREAM is sold! The store is a post office agency and a phone is available. The bus to Savusavu operates from here three times daily, at about 0830, 1230 and 1430, give or take a bit of 'Fiji time'. The trip takes 2 hours each way. The last bus from Savusavu departs from the market at 1430.

Often a taxi will be found at the store but, if not, one can be phoned if needed. The bus fare is about $F 3.00 each way. The taxi about $F15.00 each way.

A better anchorage than which off Natuvu Plantation is to be found about one mile further into the bay, also on the southern shore, off a small dilapidated jetty at Vatuvono School, which is run by the Seventh Day Adventist Church. The bus to Savusavu also passes here (catch it on the way out to Natuvu or you might not get a seat on the way back), and you can also obtain water. The staff are most friendly and helpful.

Just to the east of Buca Bay is the island of Kioa. This is now the home of the Ellis Islanders. The eastern side of the island is a little exposed to the prevailing weather, but the north-western shore contains some pretty sandy beaches, which are suitable for a day visit. Unfortunately they are generally fringed by reefs (which provide good diving and snorkelling) and the depths close by are about 20 metres.

Buca Bay to Viani Bay—(F51, BA416):

Passage from Buca Bay to Viani Bay can be made inside the reef with normal care and reasonable light. The dangers that exist are very much as charted and, although one of the two beacons charted is missing and the other hard to see, there are ample natural marks for fixing and use as leads.

Departure from Buca Bay is the reverse of entry as far as the beacon marking the reef at the southern end of Kioa. When this beacon bears 333°, course is altered to 153° with the beacon astern. This course is held to pass between the reefs to the east-north-eastward of Nawai village. When clear of these reefs a course of 140°, just open of the small islet about one mile north-east of Navukana, and with Wairiki mission on Taveuni ahead, can be held as far as Nacagina Point.

Overfalls may be experienced in rough weather in the vicinity of the point.

When Vatudamu Point bears 213°, alter course toward it to pass either side of the isolated rock about 0.4 miles to the east of the point, then proceed into Viani Bay and join the recommended track.

Naqaiqai and Nasau Bays:

When proceeding from Buca Bay to Viani Bay two small bays will be passed. The first is Naqaiqai Bay, a long narrow bay, which shoals to about 3 metres about half-way in. It has a mud bottom and is a good hurricane hole, being used as such by the Dive Taveuni boats. It is not particularly pretty, but is a snug, safe anchorage.

Nasau Bay, the second bay, is particularly pretty, with a beautiful golden sand beach just inside the eastern headland. The isolated rock shown on the chart is a large coral head, which should provide excellent snorkelling. The bay is fringed with coral reef, which is steep to, with depths of about 20 metres. A tight anchorage, amongst coral, exists at the head of the bay. The planter who lives on the western shore is a relative of Ned Fisher (see Viani Bay).

Navalval Ø Western Headland
206°

View 27.   Naiqaiqai Bay

A safe approach to both bays can be made using Naviavia (282m) as a rear transit mark. For Naqaiqai Bay it is used in transit with the western headland, bearing 206° (View 27).

For Nasau Bay it is in transit with a conspicuous shed bearing 223° (View 28).

Naviavia 223°

View 28.　　　　　　　**Nasau Bay**

Unfortunately Naviavia disappears behind an intervening hill soon after commencing the latter approach.

9

North Coast of Vanua Levu

Ellington Wharf to Yadua:

If proceeding to the north coast of Vanua Levu from Viti Levu, the shortest open water passage is from Nananu passage, north of Ellington Wharf and the nearby islands of Nananu-I-Ra and Nananu-I-Cake, to the island of Yadua, some 27 miles northward. In normal visibility, the summit of Yadua can be seen as one departs from Nananu passage.

Nananu passage, about 0.25 miles wide, is well charted on BA387, however BA379 or BA381 are also sufficient as there are two leading beacons, bearing approximately 169°, which mark the course to be taken. The passage is described in Chapter 12. Once clear of the passage, course may be set for either the eastern or western side of Yadua.

While the approach to the east coast of Yadua was surveyed in 1975 and is well charted on BA386, the south-western approaches are from older surveys and good visibility is necessary in the vicinity of Pascoe Reefs. The cay shown on the reef about 1.8 miles west-south-west of Yadua Tabu was not visible in 1992 and the isolated shoal 1.3 miles south-south-west of the same island was not sighted.

Yadua—(BA386, BA379):

The island of Yadua is famous as the sanctuary for the green crested iguana. This rare protected species is found only on Yadua Taba, the small island at the south-west corner of the main island. There is a small village, Denimanu, at the north-eastern end of the main island. One of the families in the village provides the "warden" responsible for the protection of the iguana. There are numerous bays and coves around the coast of Yadua, however, the two offering the best protection from most winds are Cukuvou Harbour on the west coast and Navi Laca Bay on the east coast.

Although the BA charts show both bays as being "shallow" there is, in both cases, ample water between the scattered reefs as indicated in Fig. 20 and Fig. 21.

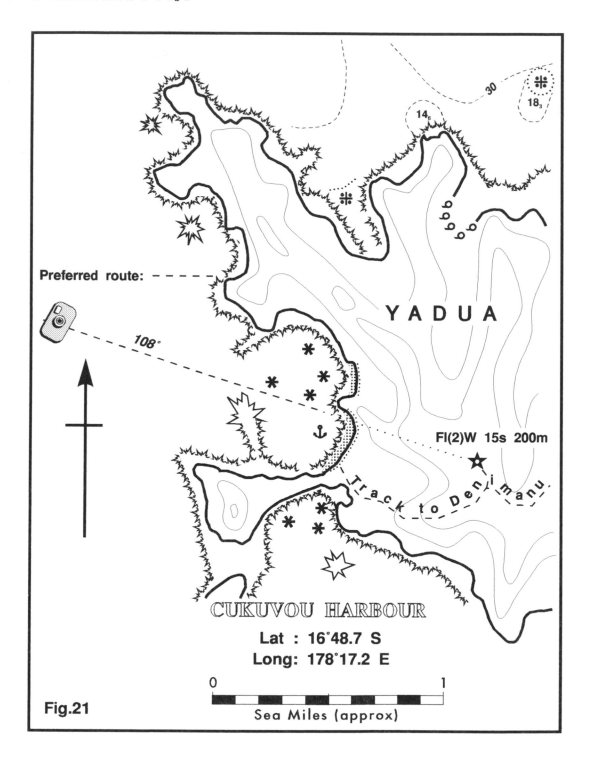

Preferred route: – – – –

108°

Y A D U A

Fl(2)W 15s 200m

Track to Denimanu

CUKUVOU HARBOUR

Lat : 16°48.7 S
Long: 178°17.2 E

0   1

Sea Miles (approx)

Fig.21

The shoals are generally clearly visible in good light and avoiding them is not difficult. Cukuvou Harbour is obviously the most protected from east and south-east winds. It will probably be the first choice of most yachts. It also possesses two magnificent yellow sand beaches and the isolated coral reefs in the harbour provide some wonderful snorkelling. It has one further advantage of being remote from the village if you are tired of socialising.

Unfortunately, you are expected to call on the Tui Yadua at the village to present your sevusevu and it may be more convenient to visit Navi Laca Bay first. Surprisingly, Navi Laca Bay provides adequate protection from the south-east, either tucked up into the head of the bay or behind Motubua Islet. The holding appears good in mud, with water depths of about 10 to 13 metres.

If weather dictates, or should you prefer to base yourself at Cukuvou Harbour, you can walk to Denimanu. There is a track that winds its way along the ridges of the hills from the southern end of the "big" beach, up past the navigation light and down to the village. It is about 3 miles walk but it could be worth it just for the views. If you have anchored at Cukuvou without making your sevusevu you will probably be visited by Pita (Peter) who has being doing the job of warden for the last few years. He will ask to see your papers and take particulars back to the village to enter in his log book.

Cukuvou Harbour—(Fig. 21):

Approach the west coast of Yadua from the south on a course about 009° with the north-western Point of the island ahead. A good lookout should be maintained on crossing the 200-metre line.

From a position west of the bay, a yacht should steer a course of 108° for Yadua Light, a red metal-framework tower on the summit of the island. (View 29.)

Yadua Light Ø Righthand Rock
108°

View 29.   Approaching Cukuvou Harbour from the West

On closing the reef, two prominent black rocks will be seen at the northern end of the "big", or southern, of two sandy beaches that lie either side of a wooded headland on the eastern shore of the bay. Course should be adjusted onto the transit of the light and the larger southern, or right hand, of the two rocks. While this track will pass close to the reef on the starboard hand, the reef is steep to and easily seen. This track will lead south of a very small isolated coral head, which is particularly hard to see. This small coral head lies right on the "natural" track one would take through the centre of the gap in the reefs. It probably carries less than 2 metres at LAT. The danger is not visible in the colour plate of Cukuvou.

Anchor as convenient off either of the beaches.

Navi Laca Bay—(Fig.22):

The approach to the narrow entrance to Navi Laca Bay is unencumbered and not difficult, however, good light is essential to feel your way past the several small coral heads which lie on the centre line of the passage once you are inside the narrowest part of the entrance.

Once inside the bay little difficulty was experienced in making a tour around the reefs shown in the chartlet, and checking out various anchorages. Due to the clearer water for swimming, the chosen spot was to the west of Motubua in about 10 metres.

The island does not get many visiting yachts and you will be made most welcome at the village. Some crews have even lived ashore for several days. It is a poor comunity with little income except for fishing, the land on the island being difficult to cultivate.

From Yadua it is but 9 miles to the western coast of Vanua Levu, where a yacht can choose to proceed either to the south coast via Nabouwalu and Savusavu, or to the north coast via the route inside the Great Sea Reef and Labasa.

Bua Bay—(BA379)

Landfall on the west coast of Vanua Levu will be made in the general area of Naicobocobo Point (16°49.5'S. 178°30.5'E.). To the south and east of this point lies Bua Bay. Large and well protected, it provides numerous anchorages around its shores. It appears to hold little to interest a yacht and is adequately charted and described in the Admiralty Pilot. The south coast route around Vanua Levu is described in chapter 8.

Vanua Levu—North Coast—Inshore Route—Charts.

The 70-mile length of the inshore route from Yadua to Labasa is well charted by the BA 1:50,000 series, BA386, BA385 and BA384. The general state of the beacons was quite good in 1992. East of Labasa, chart BA495, on a scale of 1:100,000 (with BA382 to bridge the 4-mile gap from BA384), will have to be used.

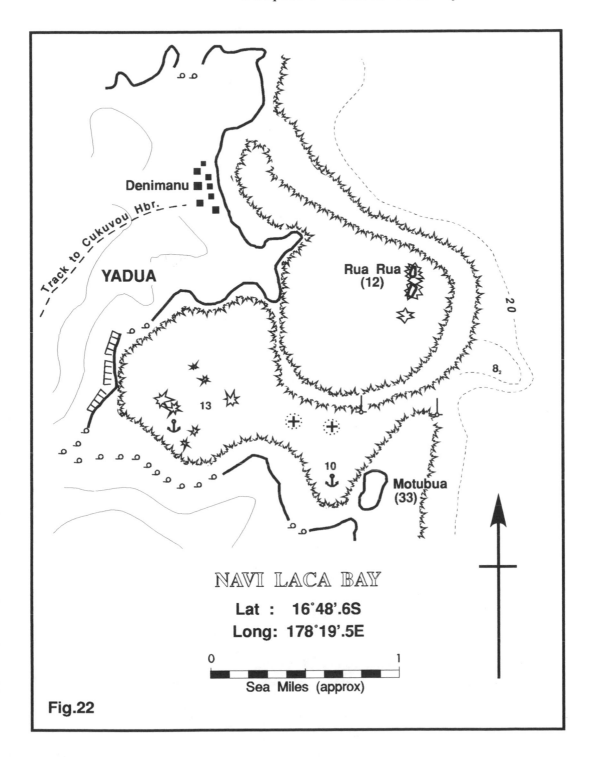

NAVI LACA BAY

Lat : 16˚48'.6S

Long: 178˚19'.5E

0   1

Sea Miles (approx)

Fig.22

In this area, where the Great Sea Reef closes and eventually becomes contiguous with the coast, passage planning is more critical and good weather and visibility essential.

The following describes anchorages along the way of the northern inshore route and supplements information available in the Admiralty Pilot.

Having closed the coast in the area of Naicobocobo Point, a yacht will steer generally to the north-east along the recommended tracks, as shown on chart BA386. A number of small bays, all of which appear to offer shelter from all but the north-west, will be passed before reaching Rukuruku Bay. Although described as a hurricane anchorage in the Pilot, a yacht will more likely choose to anchor in Koroinasolo Inlet on the southern side of Rukuruku Bay.

Koroinasolo Inlet—(BA386):

Although visited only briefly, Koroinasolo Inlet is a snug, safe, almost totally landlocked anchorage with a mud bottom that shelves gently to about 2 metres at the head of the bay. The holding is excellent. There is a small traditional village on the high ground at the end of the inlet. Although there appears to be a dirt road entering the village, the villagers said they did not have a truck and their lifestyle appeared unaffected by modern ways. They were extremely friendly and most anxious that I should remain at anchor overnight and pay them a visit. Unfortunately I was unable to do so.

Yaqaga and Eastward—(BA385):

Continuing northward from Rukuruku Bay, a yacht passes through Monkey Face pass, so named because of a remarkable basalt bluff on the western face of Uluinasiva, the highest point of Naivaka promontory. The "monkey face" is unmistakable when viewed from the western end of the passage.If you have your camera, don't wait to get a better angle!

North of Uluinasiva is the island of Yaqaga. About 3 miles long, the island is rugged and sparsely wooded; similar to Yadua but without satisfactory anchorages. Although a visit had originally been intended, the island appeared to offer little. The approaches appeared steep to and, with anchoring depths expected to be at least 12 metres, passage eastward was continued. An overnight anchorage, in calm conditions, was made close eastward of the southern point of Galoa, a small island about 5 miles east-south-eastward of Yaqaga. Naurore Bay, to the east of Naivaka promontory, was not visited but appeared to offer good protection had the weather been from the south-east.

In view of the relatively straightforward nature of the route and the adequate natural marks available should beacons have been destroyed, passage eastward was recommenced shortly after sunrise the following day. Unfortunately, the early start precluded a visit to the "cascade" mentioned in the Pilot and shown on the charts, about a mile or so east of Tavea. The passage continued without incident, as all beacons were found to be as charted and in reasonable repair.

Basa and Vunisinu Bays—(BA385, BA384):

Basa and Vunisinu Bays, lying west and east respectively of Ravi Ravi Point, were briefly visited and found to provide convenient anchorages in moderate to shallow depths and a mud bottom. Both appeared to be reasonably deserted and unlikely to require the presentation of sevusevu, at least for a short stopover.

Nukubati Resort—(BA384):

Four miles east of Ravi Ravi Point is a small bay containing the Nukubati Islands. Two of these islands appear as one on the chart as they are connected by dense mangroves.

A new lowkey resort is being opened on the western shore of the "large" island near a prominent sand spit. The resort is owned by an Australian and managed by a Fijian couple, Keith and Mary Zoing. The owner of the resort, Peter Bourke, is a yachtsman himself and yachts are welcome to anchor in the waters nearby. To quote from the resort brochure, Nukubati Resort is "a low to no activity destination where the emphasis is on fine food, friendly service and complete relaxation". Arrangements can be made to dine ashore, but the fresh water ashore has to be supplemented by desalination and is not available to yachts. During our brief stay at the island we found Keith and Mary delightful company and a wonderful source of local information. Although we anchored directly in front of the resort, it was clear that a quieter anchorage, more protected from the prevailing south-easterlies, could be found tucked into the south-east of the main island. Nukubati was an excellent spot to make an early start for Kia Island, 15 miles to the North.

Kia—(BA384):

A small island, less than a mile square, Kia is situated in a partial lagoon formed by a bow in the Great Sea Reef. The island is ruggedly picturesque and provides good clear water for swimming and immediate access to the outer reef for more adventurous diving or snorkelling.

The islanders were obviously overjoyed to have visitors. We were told we were the first yacht ever to visit the island, and were only the second "foreign" visitors in three years, Although they are purely subsistence fishermen and totally unsophisticated, a number spoke English well, and they made us most welcome.

On arrival we had made our first contact with the islanders at the village of Ligau, the southernmost of the villages on the west coast of the island. They had offered EUREKA the use of a mooring and I felt honour bound to accept the offer. I do, however, consider that the anchorage off the village of Dakau, immediately northward, is more protected from the south-easterlies. It should be noted that the BA chart has the northernmost village incorrectly named as "Ligau".

The information indicated on chart BA384 is brief in the extreme, showing little more than the land detail of the island with areas of "shoal" water tinted blue. There are few soundings either in the immediate vicinity of the island or in the south-eastern approaches thereto.

The passage was planned from Nukubati, between the reefs to the northward, and then directly for the summit of the island, sailing along the one line of soundings that do appear on the chart. The passage was made during the forenoon, not a good time to be heading generally north and east, but there were ample natural leads or transits to ensure a safe route through the reefs. For the last 7 miles through the "open" water, we steered directly for the island. The sunlight was somewhat filtered by high and some scattered low cloud, but the water was reasonably clear and reefs could be clearly seen when they were abeam, which confirmed the safe nature of the track. The echo sounder was run continuously, which confirmed the general depths were as charted.

In the open water south of the island, the skies cleared and visibility was very good. Great Sea Reef could be clearly seen, as could a slight lightening of the water colour within about half a mile of the island where the depths shoaled to about 22 metres. No dangers were seen near the track taken.

Directions.

From a position 0.5 miles north of hill (43) on Nukubati, steer 060° with No.1 beacon ahead in transit with Uluinavava (184), the south-western summit of Macuata-i-Wai. When No.2 beacon is abeam to port, adjust course progressively to port to round the eastern end of the reef marked by it, until a position is reached about 0.4 miles north of the beacon. The beacon (No.2) will then be in transit with the eastern edge of Nukubati, and a saddle on the skyline behind, on a bearing of 176° astern. (View 30.) Steer 356° for a further 2 miles, until Koronitana (234), the high hill backing Ravi Ravi Point, bears 230°.

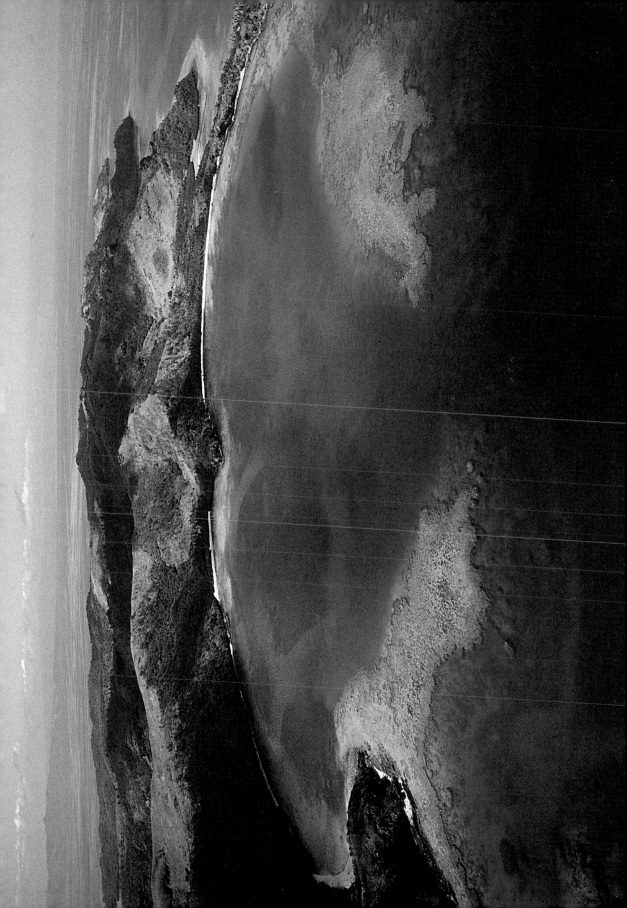

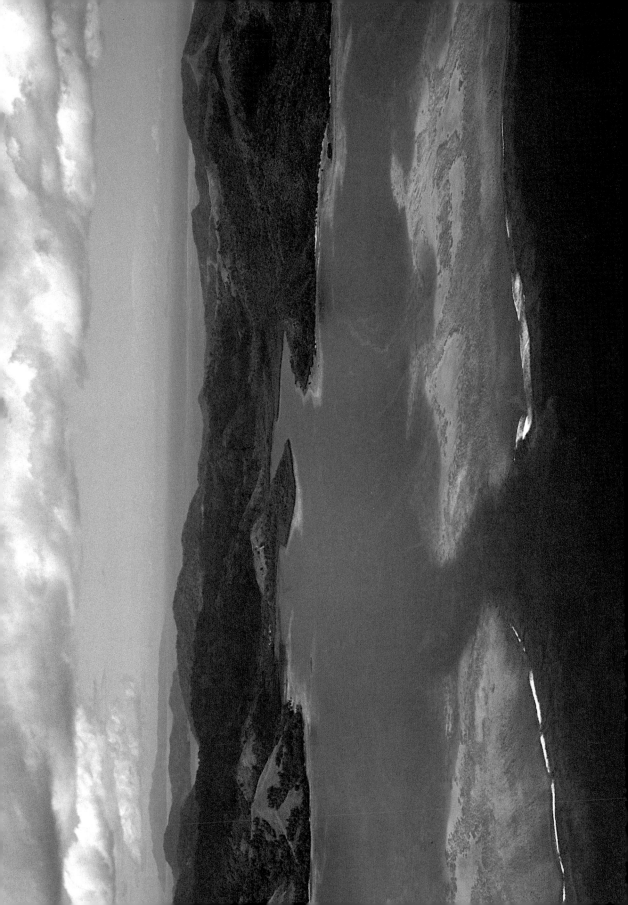

No.2 beacon Ø Eastern Edge Nukubati
176°

View 30.   **Nukubati 180° - 3 miles**

Alter course to 050° with Koronitana astern. This lead is a little difficult to maintain due to the distance to Koronitana (about 7 miles), but providing the point of land 1.5 miles south-west of Muaitana, the small island 0.5 miles north-west of Ravi Ravi Point, remains closed behind that island, a yacht will remain 0.25 miles clear of the reefs to port.

The course of 050° is maintained for about 2.6 miles until Uluinavava (184) and Bulebulewa (630) on Vanua Levu are in transit bearing 175°. Alter course slowly to port onto a course of 358° with Uluinavava astern open to port of Bulebulewa. In 1992 there was an obvious gap in the trees on the western slope of Bulebulewa in transit with Uluinavava. The gap was about one third of the way from the summit to the first saddle westward. (View 31.)

Uluinavava Ø Bulebulewa
178°

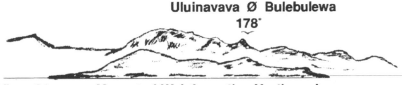

View 31.   **Macuata-i-Wai from the Northward**

This ad hoc transit was maintained for a further 1.6 miles until the summit of Kia (245) bore 015°, when course was altered to bring the island ahead on this bearing. (View 32.)

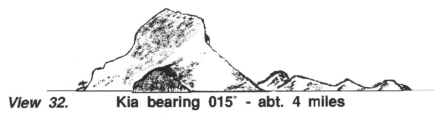

View 32.   **Kia bearing 015° - abt. 4 miles**

It was later noted that the summit of the bluff headland forming the south-west Point of Kia was in transit with the summit of the island on this bearing. This transit was maintained, and depths of 40 to 30 metres carried, until about 0.5 miles south-westward of the island when depths slowly decreased to about 22 metres.

Eyeball navigation was then used to circumnavigate the island, and examine other anchorages before returning to a mooring off Ligau, the southernmost of two villages on the west coast of Kia.

Kia to Malau (Labasa)—(BA384):

The passage from Kia to Malau, the deep water port on the north-eastern side of the mouth of the Labasa River, was again made in conditions that were other than ideal. The weather was cloudy with occasional rain, interspersed with sunshine.

Nevertheless, as all but the first 5 miles of the passage was through well charted waters and what sun there was was at the correct elevation and direction, a cautious start was made with the echo sounder running continuously to give indications of broken ground and any possibility of shoaling. The general light conditions were considered sufficient to give at least half a mile warning of any dangerous shoals. Should the weather have deteriorated, the options of heaving to or returning to Kia were available.

The depths remained at more than 20 metres until the northern edge of Cakau Nalolo (16°20' N. 179°06' E.) and the shoal water 0.8 miles northward was sighted. As showers were of only short duration and passed quickly, ample land fixing was available.

Directions:

From an anchorage off the west coast of Kia, steer as necessary to assume a course of 171° with the summit of Kia (245) astern on a bearing of 351°. Maintain this course until Ulusori (348) bears 140°, open to port of Talailau. (View 33)

The Lion's Head   **Rock (294)**

Tailailau

View 33. **Ulusori bearing 140˚ - abt. 4 Miles**

Alter course to bring Ulusori ahead on this bearing. A sharp lookout must be kept during this phase until the reefs and shoal waters have been identified and a good fix obtained. Once abeam Cakau Nalolo, the reefs to starboard and port, and the sandbank, Malavi (dries 1.5 metres), fine on the port bow, will be clearly visible. The course of 140° can be easily maintained until the recommended track of the inner route is rejoined and course altered for Labasa.

Although the inner route between Nukubati and the position north-west of Ulusori was not traversed, there are numerous small islands, which are generally steep to, on either side of the track and maintaining safe water would not be difficult.

During the latter stages of the approach to Malau, it is not necessary for a yacht to take the dogleg between Jubilee and Waterwitch Shoals providing she remains north of Jubilee Shoal beacon and steers for the right hand edge of Mali.

Anchor as convenient in the area between the timber mill and the sugar terminal.

Labasa River—(BA377):

The admiralty pilot advises that vessels drawing 2.3 metres can navigate the Labasa River at high water springs and this was loosely confirmed in discussions with local tug skippers. There are no dockside fuel or water facilities at Labasa and a yacht would probably have to anchor in mid stream if remaining overnight. In view of the times of high water (0600 - 0700) and the marginal underkeel clearance expected when crossing the bar, EUREKA did not attempt the passage.

Malau—(BA377):

In 1992, the mid channel buoy and the buoy off the timber mill jetty were not in place. There was no evidence of the post shown between the two jetties. The timber mill is owned by Fiji Forest Industries and the management is quite amenable to yachts seeking assistance for any urgent problems. Although there is no town water to the mill, this may be available in the next year and yachts will be able to top up alongside the end of the mill jetty. The head of the mill jetty consists of a sunken barge filled with earth and concrete. It carries the pumproom for the salt water used by the mill, but is also accessible to vehicular traffic.

There is a Mobil fuel depot near the sugar jetty and fuel may be available from a tanker. Otherwise it will have to be brought by carrier from Labasa in 200-litre drums. Fiji Gas also has a depot near the mill, but I was unable to ascertain if bottles could be filled there. There is a small village, Malau, next to the main gate to the mill. It contains a small store carrying most staples including bread, long lifemilk, eggs, and soft drinks. A bus runs between Labasa and Malau at roughly 90-minute intervals. The first bus from Malau was at 0700 and the last from Labasa at 1600, the trip taking about 40 minutes and a fare of 70 cents. Taxis are available at a fare of $7.00 each way, although this is negotiable.

Labasa:

Labasa is the largest town in Vanua Levu and contains all that is required by a yacht, although the selection of food and range of services is not as great as Suva or Lautoka. The range of meats available at the supermarkets is almost wholly lamb chops and shanks, but there is a butcher towards the far end of the main street about 100 metres past MH's. (There is only one shopping street in Labasa!) The butcher stocks good beef. Do not be put off by the display in the window. Ask for what you want and it is probably in the cold room.

The market carries a good range of fruit and vegetables, also yaqona if you are running short of sevusevu.

Labasa is connected by daily flights to both Suva and Nadi and to other airports by occasional direct flights. Buses run north-east along the coast as far as Visoqo and to Savusavu.

The post office has facilities for international calls and Poste Restante. There are branches of the main banks, including ANZ and Westpac.

There is a hospital and two residential hotels.

Malau to Sau Sau Passage—(BA382, BA495):

Generally the coast between Malau and Sau Sau passage is picturesque but, for a large part, bordered by mangroves.The water is inclined to be murky and the anchorages are not particularly inviting. It does, however, provide a smooth water passage that is not too difficult as far as Sau Sau passage (known by the locals as Wainikoro passage after the nearby river), which provides a convenient exit or entry through Great Sea Reef.

There are several safe anchorages along the coast providing the water clarity and visibility are not too bad: One to the west of Tivi, several arms of Vunivutu Bay, east of Tivi, and one small bay on the western side of Vatudamu Point, which I have chosen to call Blackjack Bay after the yacht which alerted me to its potential.

Blackjack Bay:

The small bay, which is backed by a sandy beach, is situated 0.3 miles south of Vatudamu Point on its western side and provides a convenient anchorage for Sau Sau passage. BA495 shows the reef as being continuous in this area, but it does in fact follow the line of the coast and an anchorage can be found in from 12 to 6 metres on a sand bottom. The occasional inquisitive "punt" may call alongside en route to or from the Wainikoro River, but you are unlikely to be asked for sevusevu.

Sau Sau Passage—(BA495):

Although Sau Sau passage is described as "dangerous" by the Admiralty Pilot, it would appear that the survey of 1891 is more than adequate for a yacht. It is necessary, however, to maintain position in the centre of the channel as there are numerous shallows extending from the edges of the reefs on either side.

Although still plagued by low scudding cloud and questionable water visibility, I was able to see the shoal water of Pasco Bank. At the same time the bottom was also visible in about 10 metres. An afternoon entry should present few problems and, with care, a morning departure is equally possible.

Directions:

Having ascertained one's position to seaward of the passage, enter on a course of 167° with the double peaked hill defined by an unlabelled 750-feet contour in position 16°18.1'S. 179°31.6'E. in transit ahead with a rounded hill backing Nasanini Point. (View 34)

Double Peaked Hill Ø Rounded Hill 167°

View 34. **Nasanini Pt. 167° - 5 miles**

When using this transit it may be necessary to cast slightly to starboard (the western side of the track) during the early stages of the approach, and later, to cast to port (the eastern side of the track) when past the southern point of the eastern reef and approaching the outermost beacon on the western reef.

This course can be maintained until the inner beacon can be rounded to starboard and the recommended track for Labasa joined. Alternatively, a yacht may choose to anchor in Blackjack Bay. To do so, proceed as follows when about one mile north of the inner beacon.

When the right-hand edge of Vatunibusa (40 ft.), the prominent conical islet 0.4 miles north-westward of Vatudamu Point, is in transit with the left-hand edge of a similarly shaped islet, barely visible on the chart, 0.5 miles south-east of the same point, bearing 134°, alter course for and maintain the transit. (View 35)

This track will just clip the tail of Pasco Bank with a depth of 10 metres, but passes northward of the two shoal patches between the passage and Vatudamu Point.

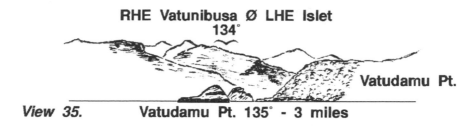

RHE Vatunibusa Ø LHE Islet
134°

Vatudamu Pt.

View 35.   **Vatudamu Pt. 135° - 3 miles**

When about 0.3 miles from Vatunibusa, alter course to the southward and skirt the reef joining the last named to Vatudamu Point.

Do not cut the corner entering Blackjack Bay, but do so on an easterly heading.

Sau Sau Passage to Tilagica Harbour:

Once more the coast is fringed by mangroves, and with several rivers discharging into the adjacent waters, the water is not particularly clear. There are several good anchorages, all in depths of less than 10 metres with good mud holding, none of which are particularly attractive. Visoqo Bay, with the large village at its head (most is hidden behind the mangroves and trees) is probably the most useful, as it is connected to Labasa by a twice daily bus service. The village was not visited but there is a store.

The boat passage to Tilagica Harbour mentioned in the Pilot is well marked and as far as Silivakatani Point can be executed using natural transits, as described later. The final mile into the clear water of Tilagica Harbour is the narrowest part and contains the shallowest depths, approximately 5 metres. Beacons also mark this final stage of the route and, although the bottom was not visible in 5 metres, good visibility is essential for seeing the reefs bordering the route, thus enabling the vessel to sail safely in the centre of the passage.

A fairly open anchorage in 10 metres, mud, can be obtained about half a mile west of the island of Tilagica.

Sau Sau Passage to Tilagica Harbour (Inner Route)—(BA495, Fig.23):

This final stage of the inner route along the north coast of Vanua Levu is convenient for those yachts that have anchored overnight in Tilagica Harbour or those who wish to avail themselves of the maximum amount of smooth water on their passage eastward. Those who are travelling westward from their overnight anchorage will find the passage easier, as the sun will be in the favoured position for forenoon transit. Nevertheless,

122

the following directions assume that a yacht is travelling from west to east.

Directions:

If continuing eastward from Blackjack Bay, rejoin the recommended track shown on chart BA495 north of Vatunibusa. It is not necessary to adhere rigidly to the track providing the beacons shown are identified. All were in place in 1992.

Having arrived at a position east of Drua Drua, set a course to leave the beacon about 0.5 miles north of Korovou about 100 metres to starboard and then adjust course to bring this beacon in line astern on a bearing of 257° and in transit with the centre of the northernmost of two small beaches on the east coast of Drua Drua. Steer 077° for 1.8 miles until in the area north of Visoqo Bay. Three additional beacons to those charted will be seen. The reefs which they mark are charted.

If wishing to anchor in Visoqo Bay, leave the track after 1.3 miles and enter the bay on a southerly heading. Beacons mark the route, but once into the bay care is needed to keep to the centre and eyeballing is essential to keep clear of the fringing reef which has occasional fingers extending into the fairway.

To continue eastward, maintain the earlier track until Silivakatani Point bears 101° in transit with a saddle in the hills north-east of Tabualago (1555). Steer this transit for a further 2.0 miles until reaching the area north-east of the village of Lakeba, when again beacons mark the route.

Tend to hold a course favouring the shoreside beacons until the right-hand edge of the mangroves surrounding Tilagica bears 089°. In good visibility, the shiny tin roof in the village of Nukusa will provide a transit. (View 36).

RHE Tilagica Ø Tin Roof

089°

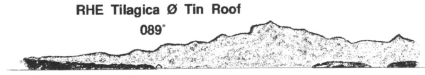

View 36. **Approaching Tilagica from the West**

Steer this transit until south of No.5 beacon, 0.6 miles north-east of Silivakatani Point.

Here will be found the shallowest water of the passage, about 5 metres. It is also the most difficult part of the passage as there are no natural transits, water visibility is often less than perfect, and eyeballing is essential. Proceed with extra caution in the area south and east of No. 5 beacon.

Round No.5 beacon on the port hand and steer generally north-east with Korokalau (1118) astern.

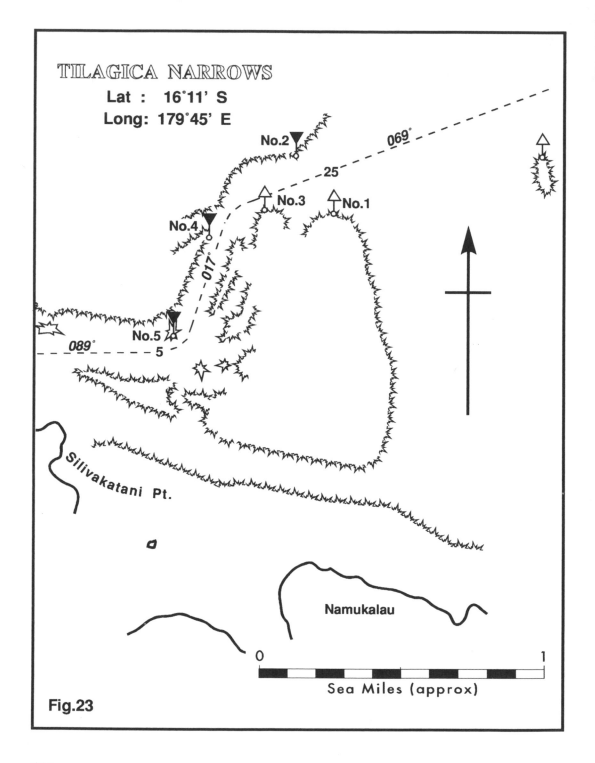

TILAGICA NARROWS

Lat : 16°11' S
Long: 179°45' E

No.2

069°

25

No.3   No.1

No.4

017°

No.5

089°   5

Silivakatani Pt.

Namukalau

0   1

Sea Miles (approx)

Fig.23

After a short time course can be adjusted to 017°, steering between Nos.4 and 3 beacons as shown on the chartlet. (Fig.23)

Round No.3 beacon to starboard about 70 metres off and steer about midway between Nos.1 and 2 beacons on a course of 069° with Borowaqa (617), near the village of Visoqo, astern. This course will lead to the deeper water of Tilagica Harbour.

A yacht may then choose an anchorage, with some lee from the prevailing wind, in a depth of less than 10 metres, about 0.5 miles west of Tilagica, or proceed directly to seaward.

If proceeding to sea, steer 352° with Saweniniu (847) astern just open to the east of the beacon about 1.0 miles north-west of Tilagica. The edges of the reefs are clearly visible and Tilagica Pass is deep and straightforward.

Bekana and Dalice Harbours—(Fig.24):

Approximately 3.5 and 6 miles eastward of Tilagica Harbour are two further harbours: Bekana, entered through Nukudamu Pass, and Dalice, entered through Nukusa Pass.

These harbours are connected by a good passage, marked by beacons, running west and south of the island of Bekana. Access to Lagi Bay, 2 miles south from Bekana, can be obtained through a channel, marked by beacons, running south from this passage.

Unfortunately, there does not appear to be a satisfactory passage for yachts to the westward to connect with Tilagica Harbour, although there is a route marked by beacons which is used by village boats.

Dalice Harbour is the easternmost harbour and safe anchorage on the north coast of Vanua Levu. There is an alternative anchorage to Lagi Bay in a small inlet about one mile east of Bekana, as shown on Fig.24. Nukusa Pass has a beacon marking the western reef, and, providing a reconnaissance has been done in good light, an early morning departure can be made with confidence.

If a yacht is continuing on to the Taveuni/Budd Reef area, the next anchorage will probably be found on the shores of Natewa Bay.

The nearest anchorage is Yasawa Harbour, some 26 miles distant.

Most yachts would probably wish to make for Naqalalevu Bay, a 45-mile passage. The direct approach to the latter is clear of dangers and an arrival shortly before sunset should be acceptable.

One further alternative is to visit the island of Rabi, the home of the Barnaban people, resettled from Ocean Island. The administrative centre for the island is located at Nuka, and an anchorage may be had at Virginia Cove.

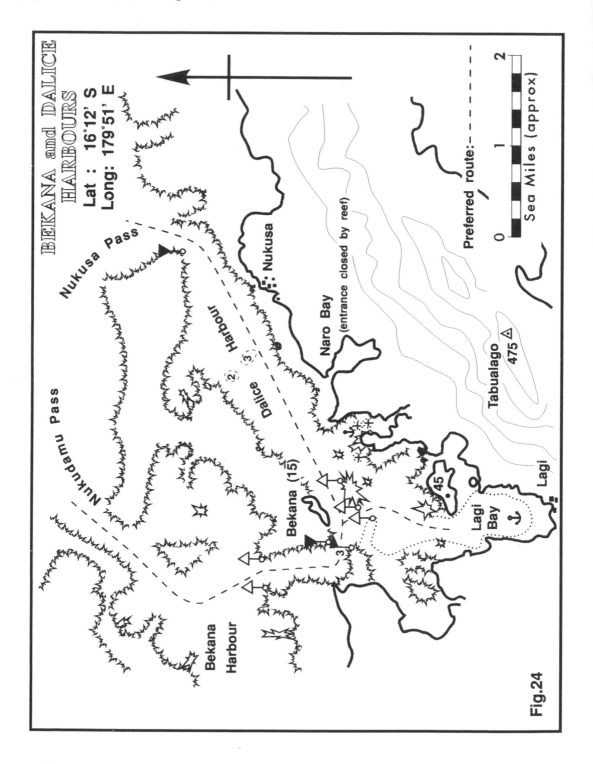

BEKANA and DALICE
HARBOURS

Lat : 16°12' S
Long: 179°51' E

Nukusa Pass

Nukudamu Pass

Dalice Harbour

Nukusa

Naro Bay
(entrance closed by reef)

Tabualago
475

Bekana (15)

Bekana Harbour

Lagi Bay

Lagi

Preferred route: ---

Sea Miles (approx)

0   1   2

Fig.24

Natewa Bay—(F50, F51, BA495, BA440):

With the exception of the anchorages at the north-eastern end of the southern shore of Natewa Bay, and possibly Yasawa Harbour on the northern shore, it would appear that a yacht has never made a landfall along the shores of Natewa Bay. As until now the only chart showing the head of the bay was BA440, this is not surprising. No doubt, the closed nature of the bay requiring a double passage in and out would also influence any decision to cruise the area.

Two other factors bear on any decision to cruise this area. Most of the attractive anchorages are to be found in the lagoons of the northern shore and these are all open to the prevailing winds. Also, as one proceeds into the head of the bay the water becomes murky, but no more so than that experienced in the inner route of the north coast.

Nevertheless, I found the four days spent in the area provided wonderful beam reach sailing, and EUREKA was the centre of attraction wherever we anchored. We were invariably invited ashore to the village, often with offers of accommodation, and never was sevusevu even mentioned, although it would have been proffered had the invitations been accepted.

When we wished to visit Savusavu for shopping we were happily escorted to the junction of the main road and, as no buses were available, assisted in obtaining a ride in a truck. On our return we were sought out by the village truck driver and given the place of honour on the upholstered seats in the front.

In all, the people we met were kind and courteous. We were visited by children poling their bamboo raft, maramas returning from an evening's fishing, and men in canoes and "punts". None overstayed their welcome or requested gifts, and we found pleasure in offering sweets, biscuits, cordial, and magazines.

One interesting incident occurred after we had anchored for the first night, offshore on the inner side of the reef at Malake Bay on the north shore. We were visited by two villagers from Tawake, the nearest village. One was a member of the Fiji Military Forces (not in uniform) and they had been asked by the police at Savusavu to check us out.

The coastwatch system definitely works!

Anchorages—(F50, BA495):

Without the availability of the Fijian chart, F50, I would not have attempted the cruise of Natewa Bay in the weather we experienced throughout the period. Except on the day we went ashore, it was generally overcast and not good for reef spotting. The chart, however, proved accurate and almost all beacons were found as expected. In spite of the weather we were able to see all reefs within about 0.25 miles of the track without having to go aloft.

The following list of anchorages runs around the bay in an anti-clockwise direction.

Yasawa Harbour—(BA495):

Having cleared Nukusa Pass on the north coast at 0800, we were able to sail close to the reef and passed Yasawa Harbour at about 1130. From aloft it looked very much as charted and the entrance wide and unencumbered. It was not entered.

Nawari Bay—(BA495):

Nawari Bay was entered through Boi Pass which, though narrow, was not difficult. There was considerable disturbed water at the entrance, caused by the outgoing tidal stream against the prevailing wind, that dictated a cautious approach, but the least depth in the entrance was found as charted with a lip of about 18 metres.

Using an aerial photograph to identify the reefs, we were able to reach the mouth of the indentation at the south-western end of the bay. We did not find the "hurricane hole" we had anticipated as the reef appeared to close off this "inner harbour". The water was also murky and bottom not visible at 5 metres.

The charted 4 fathoms 2 feet were in fact reef patches. The 3 fathoms in the southern bight of the reef may have offered a satisfactory reef anchorage. Malake Bay seemed more inviting.

Malake Bay—(BA495):

Malake Bay was entered through the northern pass. At this time the light was good, with one of the few occasions of sunshine. All reefs evident on the aerial photograph were visible and elsewhere there appeared no hazards.

A zig-zag track was run to confirm the chart. The shoreward side of the bay was not investigated as the water appeared to be murky and an anchorage was selected, in clear reef water, on the narrow sand shelf in depths of 8 feet towards the southern end of Cakaulekaleka.

The note made in the Pilot that "shelter from the south-easterly swell and sea is not complete unless Cakaulekaleka is uncovered" was borne out when the anchorage became slightly animated at a high water neap tide.

Departure next day was made at 0830 and again no difficulties were experienced in firstly closing the coast and then exiting through Levuka Pass.

It is worth noting that the road connecting Labasa and Savusavu joins the coast about one mile south-west of the pass, then continues to Savusavu along the north shore of Natewa Bay.

From Malake Bay to Nasinu Bay:

The next 11 miles of the coast, as far as Saqani village, is devoid of any suitable anchorages.

South-west from Saqani there is an intermittent barrier reef about one and a half to 2 miles offshore which provides dubious shelter from the prevailing weather to a number of rather large open bays whose position can best be seen on chart F 50.

From the conditions experienced during the passage inside this reef from Saqani to Vuinadi Pass, some 10 miles south-westward, in standard 15 knot south-east breeze, I doubt whether these bays would provide a comfortable anchorage in other than calm conditions.

Saqani Wharf—(BA495):

Not shown on chart BA495, there is a solid concrete wharf, in good condition but apparently little used, with ample water at the head for a yacht to lie alongside, at the village of Saqani.

The Labasa-Savusavu road runs close by.

In the prevailing winds described above it was too rough to place EUREKA alongside, as the head lies south-west to north-east. Further details on the village and facilities were not obtained.

Nasinu Bay—(F50):

At the head of Natewa Bay lies the village of Nasinu. Nasinu Primary School is in another village close by, Lovoniqai, which appears to be a "suburb" of Nasinu.

From Nasinu a road runs for about half a mile to a junction with the Labasa-Savusavu road. Buses run to Savusavu at least twice daily with the last one back to the junction at 1600. The fare was $1.50 each way. An alternative is to ride in a truck (carrier), usually with bench seats in the back, for a fare of $1.00. If you feel generous, offer the bus fare. If you seek out the Nasinu truck for the return journey you will save yourself the walk back to the beach from the junction. The truck is quicker than the bus.

The villagers here had never had a yacht anchored off before and we were invited to the village almost as we set foot on land. We explained that our primary mission was to travel to Savusavu for shopping and to go to a bank and were immediately assisted in our task. On our return we were invited to visit the village and drink grog. As it was then one hour before sunset, we graciously declined, citing our need to move on rapidly next day for Taveuni and then Suva.

Directions:

The approach to Nasinu Bay was made along the southern shore of Natewa Bay. Although our passage was made inside the reefs from Tagikoronadi Point about 10 miles east-north-east, an initial approach along the recommended track through Nukudrau Pass should be quite straightforward. Such an approach is accepted here.

Continue along the recommended track of 201° on the summit of Delaibotoidreketi (190) until Cololevu (245) bears 238° and the northern end of Nukudrau bears 083°, alter course to 248°, leaving the nearest beacon visible to port.

Maintain this course all the way into the bay, leaving beacons to port and starboard as shown. Anchor as convenient in depths of less than 10 metres in a mud bottom, excellent holding.

Naibalebale Bay—(F50):

During the passage to and from Nasinu, it was noted that local boats were anchored in the bay at the eastern end of the head of Natewa Bay, off the village of Naibalebale. Also, we were passed by one boat, obviously carrying people headed "into town", which entered the anchorage. It would appear that the village of Naibalebale is equally convenient to transport to Savusavu as it lies about 0.75 miles from the Hibiscus Highway.

The bay was not entered, but charted depths indicate that the anchorage may be deeper than that at Nasinu. It appears to provide a good "hurricane hole" at its head.

Drakeniwai—(F50):

From the chart, Drakeniwai would appear to be the only reasonable anchorage on the southern shore of Natewa Bay, other than those immediately next to its north-easternmost point.

An anchorage was found in about 10 metres, mud, off the reef to the north of the river mouth, but it was restricted in swinging room and the shelf fell away rapidly into deeper water. The bottom could not be seen but the holding was good.

There is a bus to Savusavu once a day, in at 0630, returning at 1800. The small store stocks very little, but there is a phone in the village. Village water could be obtained by jerry can.

The main claim to fame of this village is as the original home of Major General Sitiveni Rabuka.

About one mile north-east from Drakeniwai there is another anchorage, marked by beacons, off the houses of a freehold plantation. From the chart it would appear to offer better depths than those found at Drakeniwai and was reported as being so by the villagers that I met.

Apart from a possible anchorage off Natewa village which did not appear particularly satisfactory when viewed from seaward, there are no anchorages for the remaining 15 miles of the southern shore until Naqalalevu Bay is reached.

Naqalalevu and Naketekete Bays—(F51):

Naqalalevu Bay and a small bay close westward of Manukasi Point, which lies a further 1.8 miles north-east, provide good anchorages for yachts wishing to break their voyage between the north coast of Vanua Levu and the Taveuni area.

Naqalalevu Bay is clear of hazards in the approach and a yacht should approach from the north-west and head directly for the house at the head of the bay. The water is clear and the fringing reef can be clearly seen. There is a sand and coral shelf of reasonable extent at the head of the bay on which EUREKA found general depths of 8 metres but did not anchor. The yacht Blackjack reported the anchorage as quite satisfactory.

The approach to Naketekete Bay is again made from the north-west, but care and good visibility are needed as the approach is between fringing reefs. There is a small house at the head of the bay, to the north of the fringing mangroves. A good anchorage was found in about 10 metres, mud and some coral.

A visiting villager advised that both anchorages are part of the vanua of the village of Nailou, which lies between them, but sevusevu was not sought nor was it offered. A few magazines were gratefully accepted.

Of the two anchorages, Naqalalevu is undoubtedly the most attractive and probably offers good snorkelling.

Kubalau Point to Rabi or Buca Bay—(F51, BA416):

Although the next major destination for a yacht rounding Kubalau Point from the north would be Taveuni, this island lies generally upwind and it is assumed that a yacht would either visit Rabi en route, and possibly Budd Reef, or would enter Buca Bay and round the south-western end of Kioa before continuing on to Taveuni.

As the latter passage only totals some 30 miles, even if passing outside the reefs to seaward of Kubalau Point it can be made in one day.

Rabi possesses one of the most beautiful safe anchorages in Fiji. Albert Cove in the north could best be described as "the way the Yasawas used to be". It would be a pity not to pay a visit to the Banabans, if the opportunity presents. It is only necessary to report your presence to the Fijian police (and possibly also the local police) at Nuka, and the island welcomes visitors. By the end of July 1992 they had had only had four yachts that year.

Kubulau Inner Reef Passage—(F51, BA495, BA416):

Although appearing tortuous on the BA charts, the reef passage north of Kubulau Point is well marked by beacons (1992) and the water is beautifully clear; the bottom being visible in 15 metres even before the sun was high and in cloudy conditions.

The Fijian chart F51 is a much better scale for navigating this area. The beacons were found as plotted and the passage was obvious.

Except when crossing the sunken reef on the western side, charted as 6.4 metres, the least depth encountered on the route shown in Fig.25 was 15 metres.

A precise sounding record was not kept as the overcast conditions prevailing at the time of the passage, with the sun in the wrong position, made a vigilant lookout essential. A safe passage was aided by low water springs exposing many of the reefs. Time did not permit a re-run of the route taken.

Exit from the reef was made as shown on the chartlet and this was re-entered to check the route and marks used.

Olau Point to Buca Bay—(F51, BA416):

The inner route further southward to Olau Point and into Buca Bay was not traversed but from aloft, now with good light, it appeared straightforward and adequately marked by beacons.

The reverse passage northward into Georgia Channel is well described and illustrated in the Pilot. Having made the passage southward and arrived at a position westward of the southern end of Kioa, a yacht should proceed as described at the end of chapter 8.

Rabi (Nuka)—(F51, 495, BA416):

The administrative centre for Rabi is the village of Nuka.

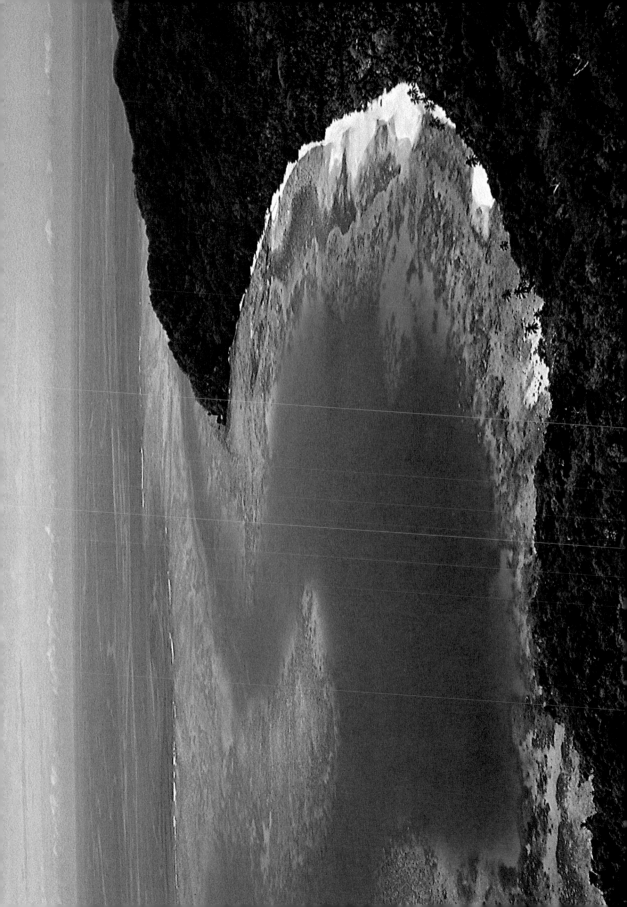

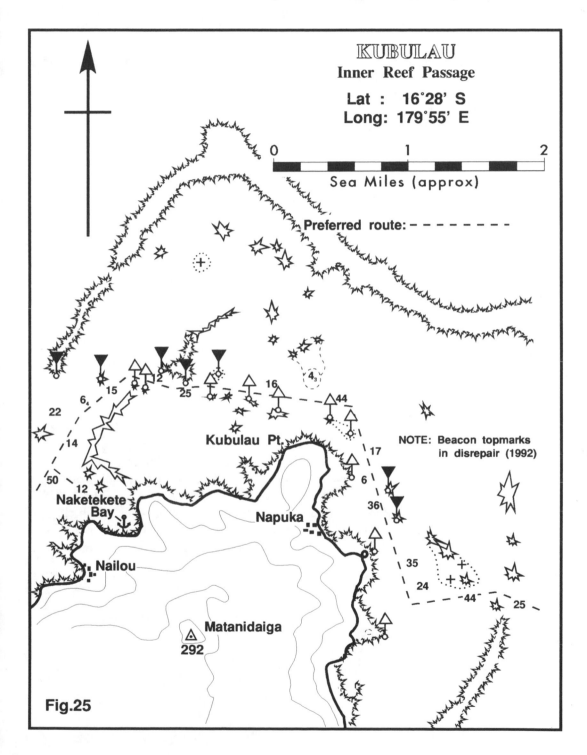

KUBULAU
Inner Reef Passage
Lat : 16°28' S
Long: 179°55' E

0   1   2

Sea Miles (approx)

Preferred route: – – – – – – –

4₃

22   6   15   25   16   44

14

50   12

Naketekete
Bay

Nailou

Kubulau Pt.

17

6

36

NOTE: Beacon topmarks
in disrepair (1992)

Napuka

35

24

44   25

Matanidaiga
292

Fig.25

The village lies in the western shore of the island near a bight in the fringing reef that forms Virginia Cove.

The southern side of the entrance is marked by a pole. The northern beacon was missing in 1992.

There is a concrete jetty at the head of the cove with approximately 2.0 metres of water at its head at LAT. A yacht can lay alongside or anchor off in about 5.0 metres over a sand and coral bottom. The holding does not appear good, but as any visit is likely to be one of short duration to check in, it is satisfactory.

There is a small store, diesel may be obtained from drums, there is a water tap about 200 metres from the wharf and there is a telephone at the Post Office that operates from 0700-2200 daily (0900-1300 Sundays). Fiji calls are coin operated. International calls must be made collect.

A bus runs about every 2 hours from the village of Eritabeta, about one and a half miles north-east, along the west coast, to Katherine Bay. A yacht must check in to the police at Nuka if visiting Rabi.

Anchorages:

The Pilot describes a number of anchorages on the coast of Rabi. However, in view of the direction of the prevailing winds, the two of most interest to yachts are Albert Cove and Katherine Bay.

Albert Cove—(F51, BA495, BA416):

Possibly one of the best kept secrets in Fiji is the beautiful soft golden sand beach, crystal-clear water, and secure anchorage of Albert Cove on the north coast of Rabi, only 3.5 miles from Nuka. Unfortunately, or possibly fortunately, it is not connected by road.

It is host to two poor but apparently contented Barnaban families, who subsist on fish, their small gardens, and occasional copra production. We made an initial visit to say hello and were warmly welcomed. At the same time we received the impression that they were happy to be left alone and had no desire to visit EUREKA.

While the rest of Fiji was subject to strong wind warnings, we remained safely at anchor with only the occasional "bullet" of wind over the high ground behind the beach.

Directions:

The approach from Nuka was made inside the reefs to seaward of Elizabeth Cove. Chart BA416 indicated a possible passage not evident on F51 or BA459. Isolated coral heads were visible in the "narrows", but the least depth found during the passage was about 12 metres. Later examination of aerial photography confirmed the passage to be quite wide, but it should not be attempted unless visibility is good.

The entrance between the horns of the inner reef to the anchorage off the beach was readily visible and of adequate width. A shallow anchorage, amongst coral and sand can be had as indicated, or deeper anchorages in about 10 metres are plentiful.

Katherine Bay—(F51, BA416):

Katherine Bay, situated on the south coast of Rabi, provides good protection from all winds except a direct south-westerly. Even then, tucked up into the head of the bay the holding is very good in mud in a depth of about 9 metres.

There is a small copra shed on a stone jetty on the outer end of the south-eastern shore. The village of Buakonikai is also situated on this shore. There are two shops with very limited stocks.

An apparently magnificent church stands conspicuously on the high ground above the village but, like most of Rabi, on closer inspection it is found to be falling into disrepair.

There is a bus service to Nuka and it is possible to visit Nuka and return the same day. In theory the trip takes about an hour, but the road is rough and can become difficult after heavy rain. While I was there the bus did not adhere to the timetable I had been given. It had been raining heavily for several days.

Directions:

From anywhere on the north-west coast of Rabi, a yacht should make her way down Georgia Channel and around Cape Georgia. I chose to pass to the west of the 3m6 shoal (a 2fm bank on chart BA416) that lies to the west of Cape Georgia. There were overfalls in the area.

The beacon shown on chart F51 about 1.5 miles south of Katherine Bay is situated on the reef close eastward. This beacon was used to provide a clearing bearing for the reef that extends about 0.5 miles south from Cape Georgia. Care must be taken not to cut the corner too closely.

Once well clear of the shoal patches extending south of Cape Georgia, a course of 040° was set directly for Katherine Bay. The beacon shown on both charts on the shore near Buakonikai does not exist.

There is a detached drying reef, missing on F51, but close to the 3m6 (2fms on BA416) 0.3 miles south of the charted beacon that carries a beacon. The reef is barely discernible on BA416 using a magnifying glass.

Katherine Bay to Taveuni—(F51, BA416):

Passage to Taveuni was made passing around the south-western extremity of Florida Reefs about 4.3 miles southward of Katherine Bay. The reef, carrying a beacon, 1.5 miles south of the bay was passed on its western side and then course set directly to clear the southern extremity of Florida Reefs. Depths found en route were generally as charted.

10

Taveuni

Taveuni, the Garden Island, is one of the four major islands of Fiji for which a permit to visit is not required. Nevertheless, it is most unlikely that one would come to Taveuni and not embrace some of the offshore islands in the itinerary for the trip, and in the name of continuity it is just as well to list it in any schedule.

The administration of Taveuni is divided between Waiyevo and Somosomo, which are within three miles of each other in the centre of the north-west coast.

The district office, post office, hospital, police and the resort hotel, Garden Island Resort, are all at Waiyevo. The assistant Roko Tui, the provincial centre and major village, and the traditional 'capital' are at Somosomo. There is a major store, Lesuma Holdings, at Waiyevo; together with the Shell depot. Somosomo has the Morris Hedstrom store with petrol and diesel pumps. Between the two, but closer to Somosomo, is the village of Naqara which contains no less than seven stores, mainly owned by Fijians of Indian descent. These stores tend to remain open late into the day, and even into the evening, and on Sundays.

Matei airport, situated close by Naselesele Point, the north-eastern end of Taveuni, is serviced by daily flights from Suva

Although most villages on Taveuni have their own stores, these are most limited in stock. A bus service connects all but the rugged south-east coast to Waiyevo/Somosomo, and taxis are also generally available. A return shopping trip from any anchorage can be done in a day. The bus runs three times a day, and the maximum fare that you are likely to incur is $1.80 each way. A taxi would cost $15.00 return for the same trip. Taxis between Waiyevo and Somosomo are plentiful and cost $1.50 for the trip. The bus, less frequent, costs 26 cents (1985 prices).

Provisioning in the Somosomo/Waiyevo area is 'quite good' or 'limited' depending on your last port of call. All staples are available: frozen meats, chickens, a few frozen vegetables, and ice-cream. Some cheese and chilled fruits (apples and pears) and vegetables (carrots, onions and potatoes) can be obtained. 'Greens' are very limited and irregular, but one sort or another can always be ordered a day before requirement, and if available, will be good and fresh. These include Chinese cabbage, English cabbage, bele (Fijian spinach), beans occasionally, cucumbers and tomatoes. Bananas and papaw are sometimes available but are generally of better quality if ordered.

Bread is also baked if the wood is not too wet to fire the ovens!

Anchorages:

The general directions for the waters surrounding Taveuni, and particularly those for Tasman Strait, are to be found in the Admiralty Pilot. The directions that follow amplify those, in particular regard to anchorages.

Generally the anchorages around Taveuni are poor. With very little in the way of a barrier reef, most are subject to swell of some kind, although it is less pronounced on the western side. Only those anchorages which have been tried personally and are considered to be of particular use for some special purpose are described in this section.

Waiyevo—(Fig.26):

The anchorage here is off the hotel/shopping area, which is below the government station (recognisable by the red and white latticed radio masts).The bottom is a flat coral shelf, mainly dead, and the holding is poor. It is advisable to set the anchor by diving if you wish to stay for any time or to leave the boat.

Although the anchorage is not often 'rough' it is totally open and the combination of wind and tide can make it most uncomfortable (and can even spill the beer!). Local advice is that it is usually so. Boat access to the shore at all states of the tide can be difficult, particularly if there is any north-west in the wind. However, if the above points are noted and due care is taken, the anchorage is tenable and has obvious advantages for doing business in Waiyevo.

Directions:

This anchorage is usually approached from the southern entrance to Somosomo Strait. The coast below the government station is closed on a course of 103°. On this course several 20-metre shoals will be passed over, with the depths ranging between 20 and 80 metres.

When about 100 metres offshore the bottom levels off at about 10 to 15 metres and it is clearly visible. A yacht should then select a convenient anchorage by eye in the area off the Taveuni Castaway Hotel.

The previous remarks should be born in mind concerning setting the anchor by diving.

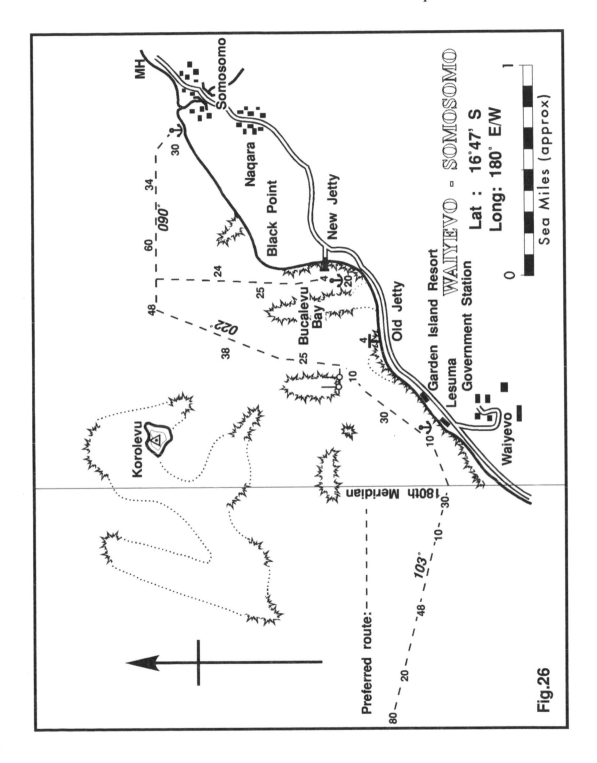

WAIYEVO - SOMOSOMO

Lat : 16°47' S
Long: 180° E/W

Sea Miles (approx)

0   1

Fig.26

Somosomo—(Fig.26):

A far better anchorage exists close south-westward of the mouth of the Somosomo River. The beach near the anchorage is black sand and gravel, and there are usually several punts pulled up on it under a large tree. This was the old copra loading area for the immediate hinterland before the wharf in Bucalevu Bay was built, and some concrete foundations of the sheds still remain.

The bottom is black sand, some mud, and gravel, and although it is not good it is adequate. The use of two anchors is recommended. There is still some movement here but it is minimal when compared with Waiyevo.

This anchorage is mid-way between the MH store and the stores at Naqara. All stores are about 10 minutes' walk from the beach. A dinghy landing can also be made on a sandy beach, with very little coral offshore, near the MH store and close south-westward, between it and a small Catholic church. The Somosomo River provides an excellent place to do the washing, and is much used by the local villagers.

Directions:

The anchorage off the mouth of the Somosomo River can be approached from Waiyevo via a passage through the reefs extending from the coast to Korolevu. The passage carries a least depth of 10 metres and is marked by one pole that is left to seaward, about 40 metres off. The approach from Waiyevo is direct from the anchorage off the Garden Island Resort, and once past the pole a boat should alter course to 202° with the Vatucu Cross astern. This course is held until Korolevu bears 270°, when the boat can alter course to 090°. When the mouth of the Somosomo River bears about 134° alter course gradually to starboard to approach the anchorage at right angles to the coast. The bottom shelves continuously and the anchor should be let go in about 15 metres.

The anchorage can also be approached directly from Somosomo Strait with the river mouth on a bearing of 134°, casting slightly to starboard as the coast is closed and when well past Phillips Rock.

Bucalevu Bay—(Fig.26):

Here the two wharves used by the local shipping are situated. I have chosen this name for the area between Black Point (a little south-westward from the Somosomo River) and Waiyevo. It is the name given to a village nearby. One wharf, which I have called "Old Jetty", is situated on the southern shore of the bay near the mouth of the unnamed river shown on the chart.

The bay is not as foul as the chart would indicate. A yacht would need to choose her time to use this wharf as surge alongside the concrete structure is often present. There are no facilities at the wharf but drum fuel could be delivered if required.

A new wharf has been built on the eastern shore of the bay, nearer to Black Point. It would appear that this wharf is be free from surge. There is ample water alongside both wharves for a yacht at LAT.

There is a passage between Korolevu and its associated reefs and Taveuni, as described earlier. Yachts can anchor off the wharves in depths of about 20 metres.

In 1985 I wrote "... there will be two wharves at Bucalevu Bay, however it is expected that the one on the southern shore, nearest to Waiyevo, will be allowed to fall into disrepair as soon as the one on the eastern shore is completed." Such are the ways of Fiji that it was discovered, on completion of the new wharf, that the major inter-island trading vessel, the "Spirit of Free Enterprise", also known as the "SOFE", was too large to gain access. For this reason both wharves have remained in operation.

Directions:

There is a reef projecting out into the centre of Bucalevu Bay, past Black Point, which prevents access to the eastern shore directly from the Waiyevo side. To reach the New Jetty, a boat must follow the previous directions for Waiyevo to Somosomo, until Black Point bears about 135°, then steer for the point. This eastern wharf can then be approached when it is bearing 173°, but this approach must be adjusted to parallel the shore about 50 to 100 metres off. There is a least depth of 5 metres alongside the end of the wharf.

A little inshore of the end of the wharf is a 20-metre deep hole. Anchorage may be found in this area. It is expected that this anchorage will be free of the swell that affects Waiyevo and, to a lesser degree, Somosomo.

Naselesele Point—(BA416, F51, Fig.27):

It was reported that an anchorage, free from the residual swell, exists amongst the reefs north-east of Naselesele Point, as described in the Admiralty Pilot. Although poorly charted, the western harbour was visited for a few hours as it is close to Matei airport.

As directed in the Pilot, the approach to the anchorage was made on a course of 137°, with the right hand edge of the (90) islet on BA416 in transit with the summit of the conspicuous conical island, Viubani (430) (View 37). Although the immediate area of the harbour is charted on F51 this should be used with caution as the small islet 0.8 miles north-east of Naselesele Point does not exist.

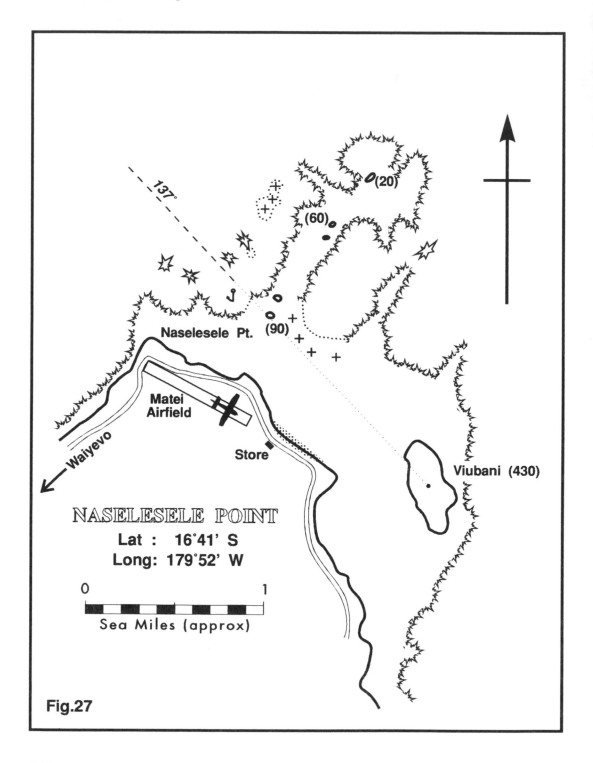

137°

(20)

(60)

(90)

Naselesele Pt.

Matei
Airfield

Waiyevo

Store

Viubani (430)

NASELESELE POINT
Lat :   16°41' S
Long: 179°52' W

0   1

Sea Miles (approx)

Fig.27

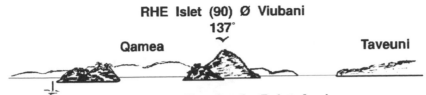

View 37.   Approach to Naselesele Point Anchorage

An anchorage was found in a depth of about 6 metres, sand. There is a store, accessible over a sandy beach, which carries limited fresh supplies including bread, ice cream. It also sells beer.

Vunivasa Estates—(Fig.28):

There is an anchorage on the east coast, between an off-lying reef and the shore, close to the homestead and plantation buildings of Vunivasa Estates. This estate is privately owned and currently for sale. It has potential for development as a tourist centre.

The anchorage is subject to moderate tidal streams and can be uncomfortable if the wind and tide are not in sympathy. The anchorage is in black sand that is quite steep to, and one must anchor close the shore to find depths of about 10 metres.

The best anchorage is a little south-eastward from the homestead, towards the cattle loading jetty. A vessel cannot berth on this rough stone construction.

This anchorage is used by the owners of the Qamea Beach Club when they visit Waiyevo/Somosomo for supplies or to collect guests.

Directions:

The approach from Tasman Strait should be made on a course of 243° with the point close north-west from the Qamea Beach Club Resort bearing 063° (View 38)

View 38.   Approaching Vunivasa Estate looking Astern

Once the reef to seaward of the anchorage has been passed to port, course should be altered towards the cattle loading jetty, leaving a pole to starboard. Here again the bottom shelves continuously and the anchor should be let go in about 15 metres.

Vurevure Bay—(Fig.29.):

This bay provides the best anchorage in Taveuni, providing the south easterly is not blowing too strongly. On its northern shore, are some fine white sand beaches that are part of Vunivasa Estates.

There are several anchorages as shown in the chartlet, but the best for an overnight stay is that off the mouth of the Wailalabi River, where anchorage can be found between reefs to the north and south, in black sand and mud in about 10 metres.

The Admiralty Pilot states that this bay is free from the prevailing south-easterly swell, as this is prevented from entering by the sunken reefs at the southern entrance to Tasman Strait.

This was confirmed by the planter, Jim Hennings, who lives on Coubrough Point.

Directions:

Proceed south through Tasman Strait until the planter's house on Coubrough Point is in transit with hill (2840) bearing 270°, when a yacht should alter course onto this transit (View 39).

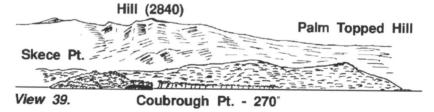

View 39.   **Coubrough Pt. - 270˚**

When about a quarter of a mile from the point, and when the '2 foot high' rock bears 323° in line with the left hand edge of a small beach, alter course for the rock. During an afternoon approach into the sun, and at high water, the transit may be hard to see. Steer this course for about 0.3 miles, until hill (2840) is in transit with the hill topped with palms that is close south-west of the mouth of the Wailalabi River, bearing 270° (View 40).

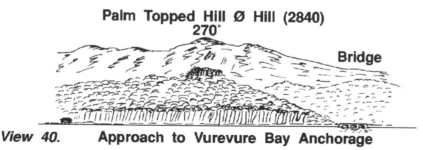

View 40.   **Approach to Vurevure Bay Anchorage**

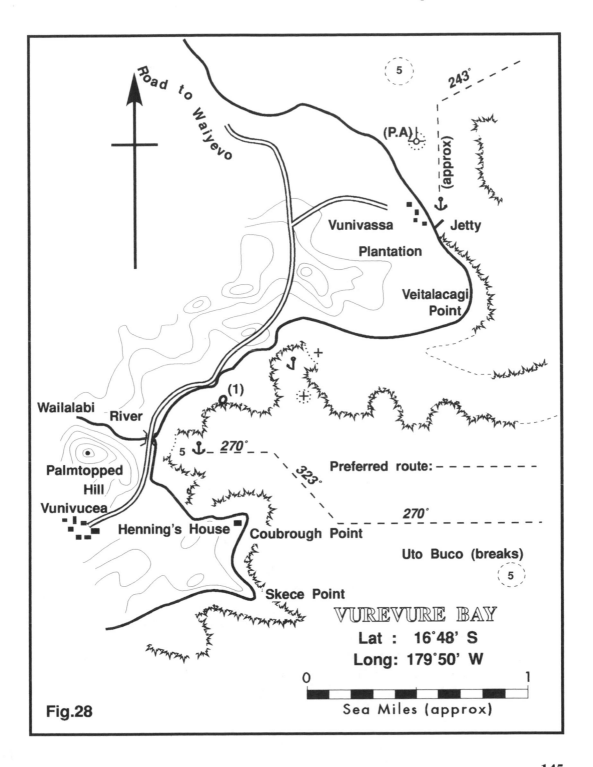

Road to Waiyevo

5

243°

(P.A)

(approx)

Jetty

Vunivassa

Plantation

Veitalacagi
Point

Wailalabi   River

(1)

5   270°

323°

Preferred route: – – – – – –

270°

Palmtopped
Hill
Vunivucea

Henning's House   Coubrough Point

Uto Buco (breaks)

5

Skece Point

VUREVURE BAY
Lat :   16°48' S
Long: 179°50' W

0   1

Sea Miles (approx)

Fig.28

Alter course onto this transit and proceed shoreward until a convenient depth in which to anchor is found. With a height of eye of 3 metres a depth of about 12 metres was found as hill (2840) dipped behind the palms on the front hill.

Laucala and Qamea:

Two islands immediately east of Taveuni are renowned as bases for some of the best game fishing and diving in Fiji. They are surrounded by deep ocean water and the tidal streams keep the water adjacent to the reefs crystal clear.

These tidal streams can be quite strong, particularly in waters confined by reefs and islands, and their effect must be taken into account. At springs, rates of up to 2 knots can be experienced in Tasman Strait between Taveuni and Qamea.

Laucala and Qamea are divided by a shallow passage that, at its northern end, is awash at low water springs. This passage is not navigable by yachts.

Approach—(BA 416.)

The islands will normally be approached either from Taveuni across Tasman Strait, or from Vanuabalavu to the eastward.

If approaching from Taveuni, passage is made along the northern coasts and south of Matagi. These coasts are fringed by reefs that are steep to, and little difficulty is experienced in sighting them in normal lighting conditions. Adequate natural leads exist to plan a perfectly safe passage.

Macomber Rock, north-west of the north-eastern tip of Qamea, has only the remains of a beacon on it and this cannot be seen at high water. As the rock itself can be difficult to see in certain conditions it should be given a wide berth on first visiting the area.

If approaching from the eastward it is advisable to make a positive landfall to the east of Laucala and then steer between the reef surrounding Laucala and Motualevu, keeping closer to the former.

This North-north-westerly course should be maintained past the north-eastern end of the reef until the northernmost point of Qamea is in transit with the northern side of Matagi. Although charted as 250°, it was found to be 246°. This transit should be steered until a vessel is off either Windseye Pass or Closeluff Pass.

The latter has a beacon on its eastern side and is entered on a transit as described later. Windseye Pass is the deeper of the two and preferred by the locals.

Windseye Pass—(View 41):

From the initial transit on the northern side of Matagi alter course onto the north-eastern point of Laucala when it bears 136°. Maintain this heading until the end of the plantation wharf is in transit with the hill 0.5 mile south-west of Palm Hill, bearing 173°.

View 41. **Entering Windseye Passage**

This transit should then be steered and an anchorage obtained in the area to the westward of the wharf.

Closeluff Pass—(View 42):

From the initial transit on the northern side of Matagi alter course onto the transit of hill (670), on the southern end of Laucala with the north-western point of Laucala, bearing 165°.

View 42. **Approach to Closeluff Passage**

Once well inside the reef course may be shaped for the anchorage.

Although the above directions are quite safe and have the benefit of being reasonably straightforward, a degree of eyeballing when close to the reefs will provide slightly deeper water. This applies particularly to Windseye Pass.

Matagi Passage—(View 43):

There is another passage through the reef close westward of Matagi. On chart BA440 this is clearly labled as Matagi Passage. However the Pilot and BA416 apply the name Matagi Pass to the northern entrance to Tasman Strait some 1.5 miles north-west.

The reef extending westward from Matagi has a number of detached submerged coral heads at the outer end which are difficult to see in bad light but with care and good visibility it provides another entry to the northen coast of Qamea. A yacht should approach on a course of 219° on the right hand edge of the northern point of Qamea in transit with hill (950) about 1.4 miles south-east. (View 43)

Qamea   **Hill (950)**
                 219°

View 43.   Approach to Matagi Passage

Anchorages:

Anchorages can be found in a number of bays, along the northern coasts of the two islands. The best of these is Namata, a large sweeping bay situated on the western side of the most northerly point of Qamea. The best anchorage is off an old copra shed in about 10 metres on a sand bottom. The shoreline is a long sandy beach and offers good swimming.

The bays on the southern side were not visited. Although protected by the reef from the sea they are open to the prevailing winds and are considered to be less than ideal.

Even though it can only be approached from outside the reef, the bay on the northern side of Matagi is reported as being 'idyllic'. There is a resort on Matagi on the south-western point of the island. There is little room to anchor off the resort as the narrow shelf is occupied by the resorts own boats.

There is a safe hurricane hole on the eastern side of Qamea, in Naiviivi Bay. The bay is surrounded by mangroves and the bottom is thick mud, providing excellent holding.

Laucala:

This island is owned by Fiji Forbes Inc., the head of which was the late Malcolm Forbes of Forbes Magazine, a prominent American investment journal. The main operation of the island is the copra plantation but there is an exclusive resort located within the plantation. One of the main attractions of the resort is game fishing. The plantation has its own airstrip. The work force is housed in a modern version of the native village. The houses are substantially built, of cement block. There is a school, village hall, church, well-stocked store, and a rugby field. Though many may not agree with the form of the Laucala village, it may be an insight into the future housing of Fiji.

Although there are no facilities for yachts they are made welcome by the manager and his wife, providing there are no untoward circumstances,

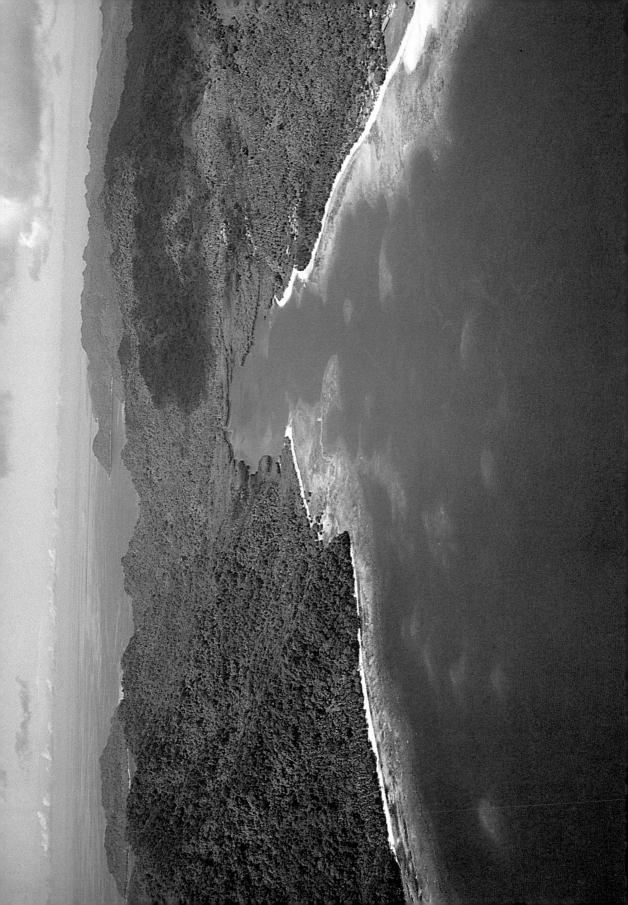

and the skipper pays the courtesy of calling to establish the convenience or otherwise of the visit before the crew proceed ashore.

There is a boat harbour, which is generally crowded with plantation boats, and a wharf alongside which coastal trading vessels (and a yacht) can berth. There are no facilities on the wharf.

If it is vacant you may be invited to secure to a boat mooring off the end of the wharf. If not, there is an adequate anchorage in about 10 metres, sand, in the light-coloured water north of the guest bure (the thatched house west of the boat harbour). However, wind gusts may be felt in this anchorage because of the dip in the hills south-west of Palm Hill. A more sheltered anchorage, which may require a stern line or anchor on to the coral reef, will be found in the next bay or indentation to the west.

The village store has a reasonable selection of tinned provisions and is available to yacht crews. It is usually open daily during the forenoon.

Passage is not possible for yachts around the eastern end of Laucala.

Qamea:

As well as Namata mentioned previously, Qamea contains Naiviivi Bay that is an excellent hurricane hole. The direct approach to this bay is guarded by a shoal that must be avoided by yachts.

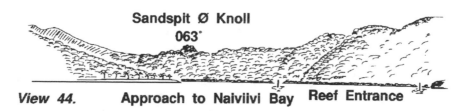

Sandspit Ø Knoll
063°

View 44.   **Approach to Naiviivi Bay**   **Reef Entrance**

The approach to the bay should be made on a course of 063° with the right hand edge of the sand-spit, on the northern side of the bay, in transit with a small knoll in the middle of a saddle in the hills backing the bay (View 44).

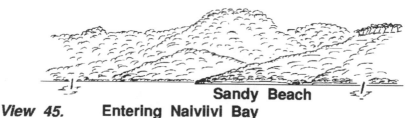

Sandy Beach

View 45.   **Entering Naiviivi Bay**

The entrance through the reef is marked by two poles. When the left hand edge of the sandy beach on the southern side of the bay is in the middle of this entrance, bearing 090°, steer this course (View 45).

Once inside the markers, and about half way to the south sandy beach, course may be shaped as convenient for the centre of the bay. A good anchorage can be found in from 5 to 10 metres, mud.

Resort:

The Qamea Beach Club resort was established in 1984 on a small steep to beach close north-westward of Naiviivi Bay.

A small resort, it has no facilities for yachts, but arrangements can be made to dine ashore if staying in the area. A dinghy trip would be involved as the anchorage off the resort is not recommended for overnight, nor is the passage to Naiviivi Bay by a yacht, particularly after a good dinner.

The resort is owned and run by Frank and Jo Kloss, who are well versed in the cruising yacht scene and who like to select their clients with care. However, if they like the cut of your jib you will be made most welcome.

Just across the Tasman Strait from Qamea is Taveuni.

Budd Reef—(BA416.):

Fifteen miles north-east of Naselesele Point lies a group of six islands known collectively on BA charts as Budd Reef. The islands comprising the group are Yavu, Yanuca, Maqewa, Beka, Raranitiqa and to the north, the breached extinct crater, Cobia. This last-named island is owned by the present Governor-General of Fiji and to visit it vice-regal permission is required.

The only island with permanent habitation is Yanuca. The village is at the south-eastern end of the island, tucked in behind a small rocky promontory. It is connected to the 'mainland' by VHF radio telephone. It is a small village engaged in subsistence farming and fishing. There is little, if any, surplus available for sale. Being a small village, the villagers would not welcome an influx of visiting yachts. This is unlikely due to the location of the group, and the occasional visitor is acceptable. As anchorages protected from the south-east are on the opposite side of the island it is easy to respect the privacy of the villagers.

In 1985, the turaga ni koro, Sairusi Raileqe, was an elderly man who did not speak English. His son-in-law, Eroni Saladromu, was most helpful and friendly.

Directions:

Passage from the north-west coast of Taveuni is made leaving the string of islets and their associated reefs to starboard, and Gangway Rocks to port. Most of the beacons in the area are missing. Constant position fixing is essential as sets of up to 10° off course can be experienced due to tidal streams. On clearing Gangway Rocks a course of about 040° can be set for Yanuca.

Entry into Budd Reef can be made according to the directions given in the Admiralty Pilot, but if the summit of Cobia is visible a better and more positive approach can be made with the summit in transit with the left saddle of Yanuca, bearing 033°. This transit can be maintained until Cobia dips below the skyline of Yanuca, when normal fixing will enable a yacht to pass either side of the reef 0.5 mile south-east of Yavu. A deep passage, which could be seen from aloft in overcast but bright conditions, exists between Yavu and Yanuca and their associated reefs.

The waters surrounding the islands appear much as charted.

Anchorages:

Although fringed with coral, the main islands all possess white sandy beaches with clean clear water. Usually the depth at the edge of the reef off the beaches is about 5 metres, with a gradual slope to 15 metres, followed by a drop to about 40 metres. These sandy areas can be recognised by the light turquoise colour of the water. As there are beaches on all sides of the islands an anchorage can be chosen as dictated by the prevailing wind.

The anchorage off the village is over sand, in about 7 metres close up to the sand-spit that connects Yanuca and Maqewa. It is uncomfortable during south-easterly winds.

An anchorage over sand, into which the anchor set well, was found in 13 metres close south of the western point of Yanuca, and north of the reef extending towards Yavu. Here good protection was found from winds from north, through east, to south. There is a fine white sand beach on the shore.

PART FOUR

The Western Division

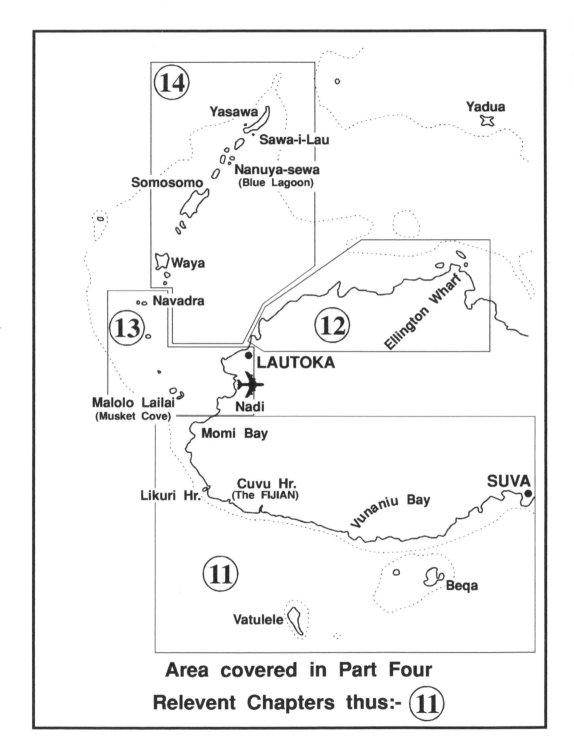

Area covered in Part Four

Relevent Chapters thus:- (11)

11

Suva to Lautoka

When taking passage from Suva to Lautoka there are several options available for the route that is selected. The overall distance is 110 miles and the voyage can be made direct with an overnight passage. Departure can be leisurely, with the only proviso being that Beqa Passage should be passed before sunset.

The route along the 'Coral Coast' is free of dangers, and the fringing reefs steep to. Although there is only one navigational light en route apart from those at Navula Passage, a yacht can stand well offshore during the dark hours, if desired. There are also the lights of the resort hotels along the coast which provide a general indication of distance offshore. Although the leading beacons for Navula Passage, at the head of Momi Bay, are difficult to see in the early morning, the light on the reef on the northern side of the entrance has been re-established, and the passage is not difficult.

A more diversified route can be planned, by way of Beqa, Vatulele and/or the Coral Coast anchorages.

A yacht could visit Kadavu, however this would make a one-day passage into a rather lengthy affair, and Kadavu and the Great Astrolabe Reef are deserving of more than a passing visit. It should be noted that a permit to visit Kadavu cannot be obtained in Lautoka although customs will clear you for Suva via Kadavu providing a permit has already been obtained in Suva.

Beqa and Yanuca (Yes! Yet another Yanuca):

Beqa, with its lagoon, and the associated islands, including Yanuca, provide an easily accessible cruising ground for those wishing to remain relatively close to the capital. They are less than 30 miles from Suva. You can even still pick up FM radio, and, horror of horrors, since 1986 - TV.

The passage is direct, and the easiest initial entry into the lagoon is through Sulphur Passage at its north-eastern end. There are ample natural fixing marks and leads, and the reef entrance is currently marked by beacons. (Missing 1992)

Once inside the reef there is a choice of several anchorages. Maluma Bay, the deep indentation at the eastern side of the island, is a breached volcano. It provides a scenic and comfortable anchorage, with good holding, in deep water. As is apparent from the topography, it is sometimes subject to violent gusts in strong south-easterly weather, and one should use ample ground tackle. There is a good swimming beach half way along the eastern shore. The area is popular with the members of the RSYC and it is important that visitors respect the villagers' privacy and property as do the locals.

The yacht club reports good trolling about 100 metres off the eastern and southern shores of Beqa and, while eyeball navigation is essential, the route to Stewart Island, south about, is not difficult. Although there is no overnight anchorage at Stewart Island it is a good place to stop for lunch and a swim. It can, at times, be overrun by day trippers from Pacific Harbour. An excellent anchorage does exist in Vaga Bay, on the south-western side of Beqa, only about 5 miles to the north-east.

Yanuca, which lies on the western side of Beqa Lagoon, has several safe, clear water anchorages on its western side. They are also popular with the Pacific Harbour people, and the large beach to the South has picnic facilities for their use and a couple of moorings for motor boats or others with a shallow draft.

The anchorage is over coral with some sand and is adequate, and comfortable, providing the wind stays in the north-east to south-east.

There is a passage through the reef north-westward from Yanuca that is not difficult.

Beqa Lagoon—(BA1673, 1682):

Although Chart BA1682 carries several warnings regarding Beqa Lagoon, the chart is a reasonable guide and quite adequate providing the usual eyeball precautions are taken. The directions given here take a yacht in through Sulphur Passage, down to Vaga Bay, to Yanuca, and out to the westward by way of the passage north-west of Yanuca.

The approach from Suva is direct and free of dangers. Sulphur Passage is entered on a course of 216° on a conspicuous saddle in the hills on the east coast of Beqa (View 46).

Two beacons (missing 1992) mark the northern side of the passage, and a detached reef inside the main reef on the southern side. Once inside the main reef course is altered to 292° with the beacon on the detached reef astern (missing 1992) bearing 112°.

This course is held until Storm Islet bears 079°, when course is altered to 259° with the islet astern.

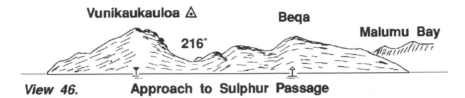

View 46. **Approach to Sulphur Passage**

The right-hand edge of Yanuca will be ahead in the distance.

The course of 259° should be maintained until close eastward of the shoal, 1.0 mile north-west of the north-west shore of Beqa, when the vessel should cast to starboard to leave the beacon (missing 1992) marking the northern edge of the shoal to the southward. The chart appears to indicate that the beacon is on the southern edge of the shoal, but such is not the case.

Once clear of the shoal, course is altered to the southward for Stewart Island. There are several reefs extending, and detached, from the west coast of Beqa. The most seaward is marked by a beacon, however the one at the entrance of Vaga Bay has been destroyed, together with several others on the inshore reefs.

The course of 192° is maintained until the left hand edge of the village at the head of the bay bears about 125° when this course is steered to enter the bay. Vaga Reef, at the entrance to the bay, is left to the northward; little difficulty is experienced in sighting this reef in all but the worst conditions.

Vaga Bay—(Fig.29):

There are two small reefs near the head of the bay, the positions of which can be best seen in Fig.29. A good anchorage can be found in about 8 metres, sand and mud, in an indentation in the reef northward of the village.

Vaga Bay appears to be a very good anchorage being protected from all but the north-west. The village on its southern shore, at the head of the bay, is known locally as Naiseuseu. It is part of the village of Naceva, which is on the other side, or south side of the hill. It does however have its own turaga ni koro. The villagers in this area, and one assumes in the rest of Beqa, are somewhat materialistic, undoubtedly as a result of their proximity to Suva. Because of this there was a degree of gift-seeking but this could be parried with fairness and firmness. I would have liked to stay longer than my one night, as I felt the villagers were otherwise most friendly. During my visit in 1992, I was asked by the son of the turaga ni koro to specifically request yachts not to offer alcohol to villagers even if was asked for.

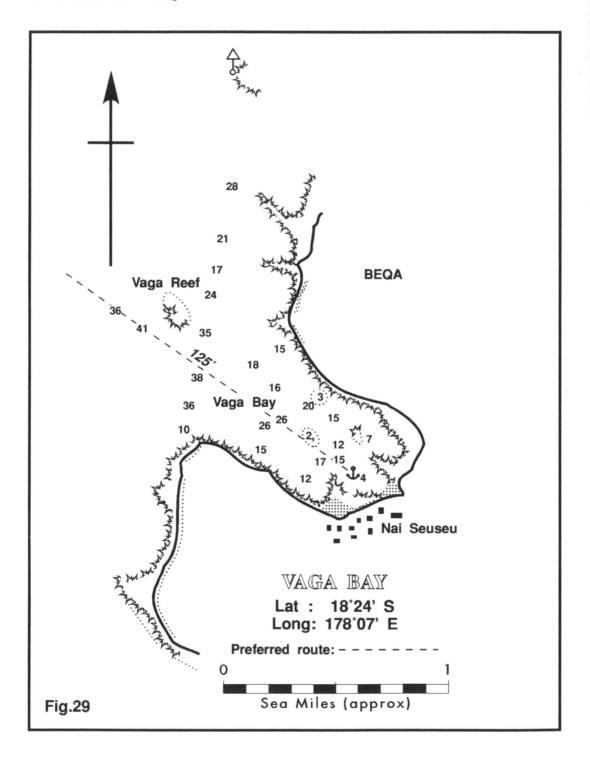

28

21

17

Vaga Reef 24

36 35

41

125°

38 18

16

Vaga Bay 36

26 26

10

15

15

17 ·15

12

BEQA

15

3

20

15

12 7

2₅

4

Nai Seuseu

VAGA BAY
Lat : 18°24' S
Long: 178°07' E

Preferred route: – – – – – – –

0   1

Sea Miles (approx)

Fig.29

I further learnt that the bay forms part of the vanua of two villages, the northern side belonging to Rukua, the next village north, the southern belonging to Naiseuseu/Naceva.

The division occurs at the small islet at the head of the bay. There are two fresh water streams that enter the head of the bay, one on either side of the small islet. The villagers obtain their water from a spring behind the village.

Yanuca:

The route from Vaga Bay to Yanuca was taken direct. Although the weather was overcast, several of the shoals close to the track were visible and the passage presented no problems.

Yanuca was rounded on its northern side which appeared clear and much as charted. The final approach to the anchorage shown on the chart was made on a course of 180° on the hill behind the beach on the south-eastern end of the island.

Departure from Yanuca through Yanuca Passage was made firstly on a course of 000°, with 'beach' hill astern, until the centre of Stewart Island was in transit with the northern end of Yanuca, bearing 132°, when this was placed astern, steering 312° (View 47).

Stewart I. **Yanuca** **"Beach Hill"**

132°

View 47.   **Yanua from Yanua Passage**

This transit leads between some large shoals to the north and some smaller ones to the south. Care should be taken not to stray off the transit as the gap in the reefs is not large, they do not appear to dry, and are sometimes difficult to see. Nevertheless, providing the north point of Yanuca is always 'in contact' with Stewart Island, safe water, least depth 15 metres, is carried.

Tidal streams appear to set diagonally across the entrance and care should be exercised. The transit is clearly visible well before the reef is reached and entry from the westward is not difficult.

Vatulele:

This island, which lies some 20 miles south-west from Beqa, was not visited by the author although it was passed close by on two occasions. Other yachts have reported the lagoon much as charted, but eyeballing is essential. The island is flat and scenically uninspiring, but it is the home of the sacred red prawn and a limestone cave complex. Although protected by the reef the eastern lagoon is generally open to the prevailing weather. A protected anchorage may be obtained off the north-west coast. A courtesy call should be made on the management of the very exclusive Vatulele Resort and yachts should be careful to anchor clear to the north of the resort's beach front.

The Coral Coast—(BA1682, 845):

Whether a yacht sails westward direct from Suva or via Beqa, she will probably make at least one stop overnight en route. Again, if sailing from the west to Suva, which is more often than not sailing into the wind, short passages have a lot to recommend them. The probable anchorages used will be the same in both cases.

Pacific Harbour:

Although carrying the name Pacific Harbour, the area off the resort is not a good anchorage. It is exposed to the south-east and the reef is some distance offshore, which allows a chop to develop when the wind is blowing. I understand that a yacht may go alongside the resort boating facility, for a short period, by prior arrangement.

Serua Harbour:

About 10 miles west from Pacific Harbour lies Serua Harbour. Although not used by the author it is described in the Admiralty Pilot and detail given in Chart BA1682 would appear adequate for the yachtsman to enter in reasonable conditions.

Vunaniu Bay—(Fig.30)

A further 5 miles west from Serua Harbour and a comfortable 35 miles from Suva, is Vunaniu Bay.

The bay is a large indentation in the reef that turns right through almost 90 degrees at its inner end. The anchorage so formed is about 5 to 15 metres deep, with excellent holding in a mud bottom. The water is usually a little discoloured and not particularly inviting for swimming.

The reefs to seaward extend for about 1 mile and provide very good protection from sea and swell and make the anchorage comfortable.

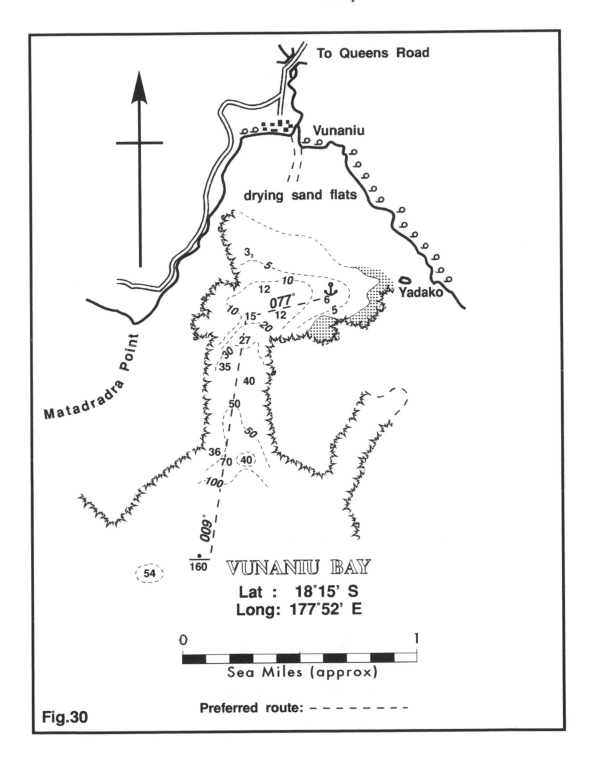

To Queens Road

Vunaniu

drying sand flats

Yadako

Matadradra Point

077°

160

009°

54

VUNANIU BAY
Lat :   18°15' S
Long: 177°52' E

0   1

Sea Miles (approx)

Preferred route: – – – – – – – –

Fig.30

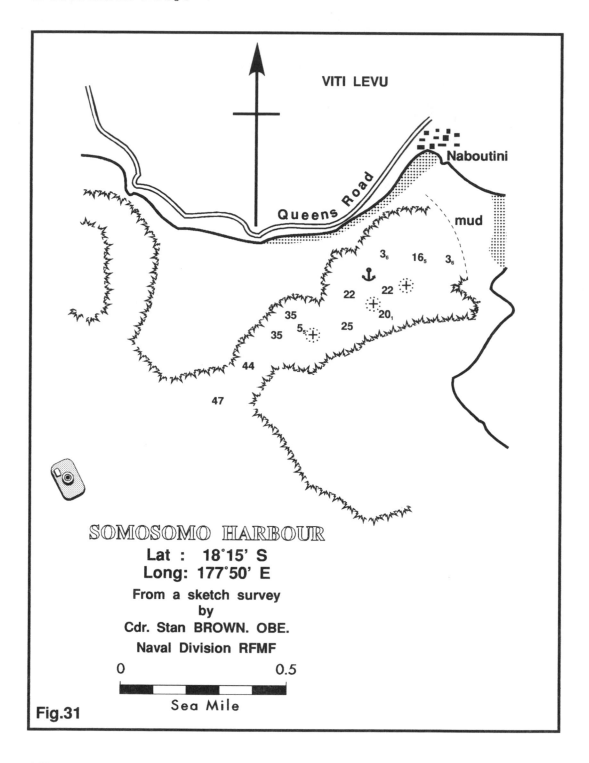

VITI LEVU

Naboutini

Queens Road

mud

3₆ 16₅ 3₆

⚓

22 22 ✛

35

5₅✛ 25

35 44

47

SOMOSOMO HARBOUR
Lat : 18°15' S
Long: 177°50' E

From a sketch survey
by
Cdr. Stan BROWN. OBE.
Naval Division RFMF

0   0.5

Sea Mile

Fig.31

Directions:

The gap in the reef is about 200 metres wide, deep, and the sides are almost parallel and steep to. It is approached and entered on a course of 009° with the centre of Vunaniu village ahead (View 48).

View 48.   **Approach to Vunaniu Bay**

About 1.5 miles in from the outer edge of the reef, when the inner end of the eastern reef is reached, course should be altered to bring the small islet, Yadako, ahead on a bearing of 077°.

The boat should then tuck itself to this eastern arm and anchor in about 5 to 7 metres. A good anchorage can be had anywhere to the south of the transit of Yadako and the radio mast on Nabouwalu (775) (View 49).

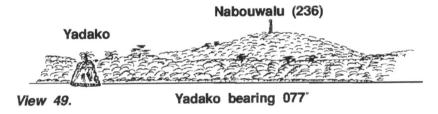

View 49.   **Yadako bearing 077°**

North of this line the sand bottom shoals rapidly and dries at low water. A safe distance in towards Yadako can be judged by keeping the left hand edge of Yanuca, in Beqa Lagoon, just open of the eastern point of land, Vatubari Point.

Care should be taken not to swing wide when rounding up onto a course of 077° on Yadako as shoal water exists on the outer, or port, side of the turn.

Somosomo Bay—(Fig.31)

Just 3 miles west from Vunaniu Bay is Somosomo Bay, not visited but reported by Stan Brown as being another good yacht anchorage. From the diagram produced by Stan, and the report of another yacht who anchored there for several weeks it offers easy access to the Queens Road, and hence Suva, if required.

Cuvu Harbour (The Fijian Resort Hotel):

Half a day's sail or 25 miles west of Vunaniu Bay is Cuvu, or Nadroga Harbour, on the eastern side of which is the Fijian Resort hotel, occupying one of the many Yanuca islands to be found in Fiji.

The harbour is well charted on the inset on Chart BA845, and detailed directions are unnecessary.

The anchorage can be subject to some residual swell at times, but a stern anchor to keep the bow into the waves is all that is needed to make life comfortable again.

On your arrival you will be handed a pamphlet detailing the facilities available, together with a form to be filled in for the hotels records as required by the Marine and Immigration Authorities. Yachts are welcome to use the resort bars, restaurants, pools, and any other of the non-chargeable facilities upon paying a fee of $25 per yacht below six persons. This includes using the shower at the Beach Office and refilling of drinking water, providing the expected standards of dress are observed. You will be issued with an official receipt which you must retain. The Fijian is one of the better resorts in Fiji and this is reflected in the prices. Providing that you do not proceed ashore, it is believed that you can avoid the charge.

Natadola Harbour—(Fig.32)

Barely 7 miles further west of Cuvu is another wide gap in the reef that forms Natadola Harbour, which has one of the best long, sandy beaches on the Coral Coast. Like Cuvu, the bay is also subject to residual swell. Nevertheless the harbour is a fair weather anchorage, with reasonable holding in depths of about 10 metres over a sand bottom. The approach is direct through the centre of the reef opening, on a course of about 048°

The islet of Navo, which is host to the navigational light, provides a pleasant alternative to the main beach for a picnic or barbecue. There are goats on the islet and it is owned by the nearby village of Sanasana.

Likuri Harbour:

Another 5 or so miles to the west, and only 10 miles from Navula Passage and the all weather anchorage of Momi Bay, is Likuri Harbour. This anchorage is also well charted on the inset on Chart BA845, and again detailed directions are unnecessary except to say that the approach through the reef was made with the centre of the island bearing 090° ahead. Eyeballing is essential. The anchorage is well protected and safe.

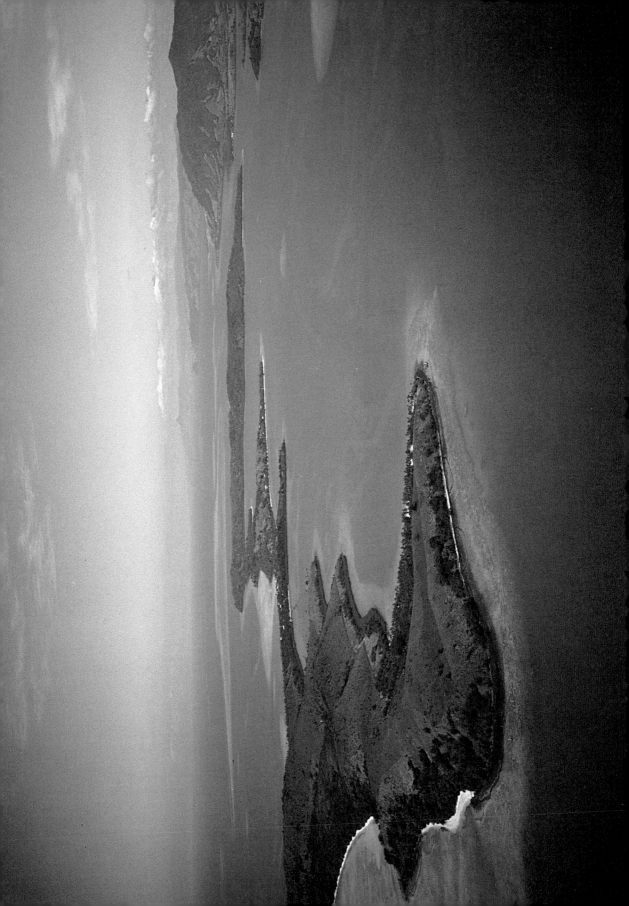

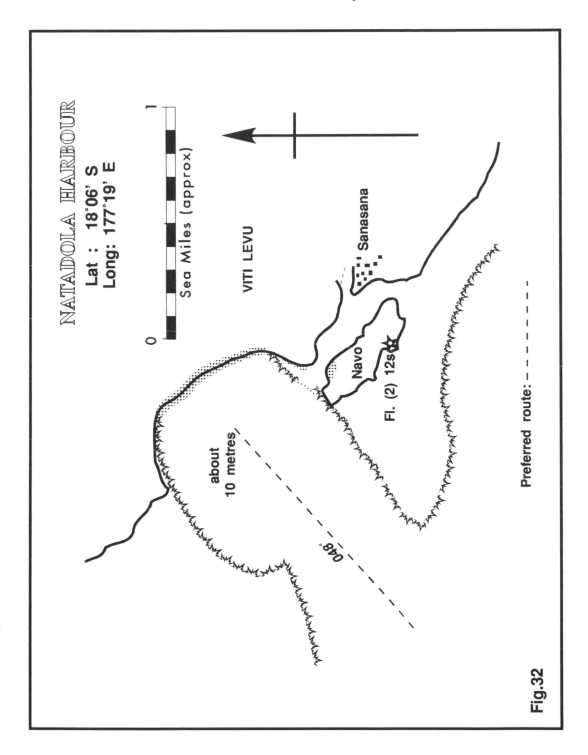

NATADOLA HARBOUR

Lat : 18°06' S
Long: 177°19' E

Sea Miles (approx)

VITI LEVU

Sanasana

Navo

Fl. (2) 12s

about
10 metres

048°

Preferred route: – – – –

Fig.32

165

The curve in the entrance traps the swell, and Likuri Island provides shelter from the south-easterlies. A small resort appeared to be under construction (1992) by villagers from near by and sevusevu was requested.

Momi Bay—(BA1670, 845):

At the head of Momi Bay are the leading beacons for Navula Passage (View 40), the main entrance from the south into Nadi Waters and thence Lautoka and the resorts and islands to the west. Directions for Navula Passage are given in Chapter 13. Momi Bay is well protected from all but the west, and the anchorage has excellent holding in a mud bottom in depths down to about 5 metres. The bay provides an overnight or anytime anchorage for those not wishing to press on to Lautoka or other anchorage en-route; and is also a good spot to wait for favourable weather or from which to make an early start towards Suva. To enter the bay, continue straight in on the leads.

A little over 20 miles further on is Lautoka, 'The Sugar City', and the main base for cruising in the Western Division. From here on the rains of Suva are long gone.

North Coast of Viti Levu

A yacht wishing to continue with an anticlockwise circumnavigation of Viti Levu from the area of Natovi or Naigani (Chapter 6) should plan her passage using charts BA448 and BA379 as far as Viti Levu Bay and then use the larger scale (1:50,000) BA387 and BA389 to Lautoka. Chart BA381 may be used instead of the latter two, but care should be exercised as not all navigational marks may be shown. The route should pose no problems if executed in good visibility as there are ample terrestrial features to use as marks ahead and astern. The recommended tracks originally shown on the BA charts are now being removed and planning now rests with the navigator. The coast and reefs are generally as charted, except that those beacons indicated on the charts as not having topmarks are sometimes missing. On the other hand there are some additional ones not charted. The remarks given in Chapter 3 are particularly relevant.

The distance from either Natovi or Naigani to Viti Levu Bay is about 30 miles and with the prevailing south-easterly winds is a comfortable and enjoyable day sail. There are a few bays during the latter half of the passage that appear to offer satisfactory anchorage in all except north-easterly winds, but they have not been visited by the author as they appear to possess little of interest.

Viti Levu Bay—(BA387, BA381):

Viti Levu Bay provides an ideal staging point to await good weather, before undertaking the more difficult passage through Navolau Passage around the north-eastern end of Viti Levu. The main village at the head of the bay is Nanukuloa.

One of the main points of interest accessible from Viti Levu Bay is the mural of the "Black Christ" in the church of the village of Naiserelagi, about one mile south of Nanukuloa. The painting is by the French artist Jean Charlot and is considered by some to be the finest non-Fijian work of art in Fiji.

There are few facilities at the village of Nanukuloa.

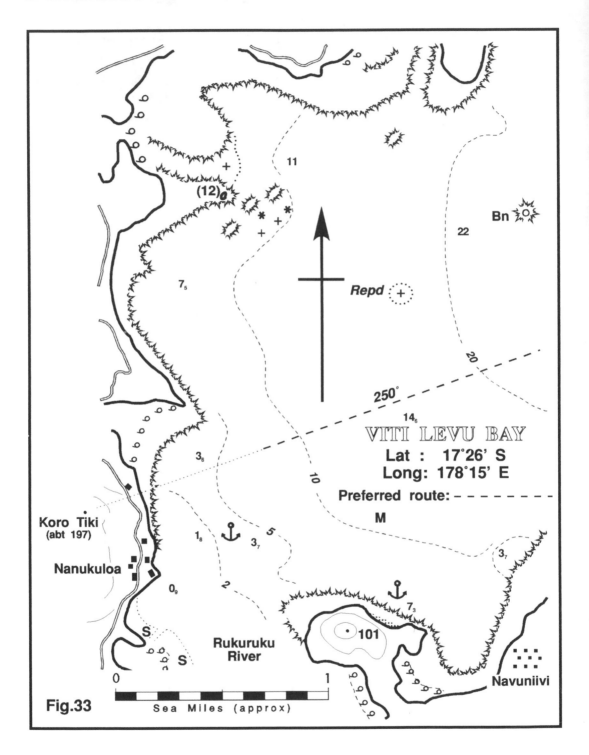

11

(12)

Bn

22

7₅

Repd +

250°

20

14₆

VITI LEVU BAY
Lat : 17°26' S
Long: 178°15' E

Preferred route: – – – – – – –

M

3₆

10

Koro Tiki
(abt 197)

1₈

5

3₇

3₇

Nanukuloa

0₉

2

·101

7₃

S

Rukuruku
River

S

Navuniivi

0

1

Fig.33

Sea Miles (approx)

The landing must be made over the black sand beach, either on the west bank of the river or in front of the "big house" in the village.

At the former you may see some local boats at anchor, but it is shallow and you may have to carry your dinghy closer to the shore at low water, or alternatively into deeper water if the tide has gone down during your absence. At the latter you would probably be expected to make a presentation of sevusevu. This would of course be obligatory if anchoring off the village for more than a few days and going ashore there regularly.

There is a small store from which, amongst other staples, bread can be obtained. There is a Post Office that also houses a public telephone. The main road that circles the island carries buses between Suva and Lautoka in both directions. The same buses also pass through the village of Ellington mentioned later.

Directions:

The entrance to Viti Levu Bay contains several shoals in its northern half, one of which, almost in the middle, is marked by a beacon. In 1992 the beacon was badly damaged and barely visible.

A small islet 12 metres high, in the north-west corner of the bay and a prominent "finger", Koro Tiki, about 197 metres high on the south-western shore, make excellent marks to plan a safe entry. Korotiki ahead on a bearing of 215° will lead south of all shoals. (View 50)

Korotiki bearing 235°

View 50.   **Approach to Viti Levu Bay**

The southern half of the bay appears very much as charted, with a gently shelving mud bottom. The Rukuruku River discharges into the bay and the water is not clear. In 1992, EUREKA anchored in about 2 metres, mud, with good holding 3.5 cables 052° from the village of Nanukuloa. A deeper and slightly more protected anchorage may be found in the south-eastern corner of the bay off the village of Navuniivi. There is a small yellow sand beach on the north side of the conspicuous peninsula (101m) which forms the eastern bank of the Rukuruku River.

Navolau Passage to Volivoli Point—(BA387, BA381):

The route around the north-eastern end of Viti Levu is not difficult and the recommended track is marked on chart BA387. The most restricted area, Navolau Passage, is adequately marked, but it is necessary to have a good fix to ensure you are on track when approaching from the South as the number of beacons that can be seen in the one area makes eyeballing the passage difficult. At low water, when the reefs are exposed, there are no problems. The recommended track will take a yacht south and west of Nananu-I-Cake, passing the remains of Ellington Wharf on Viti Levu, then heading generally westward past Volivoli Point and Malake for Lautoka. From here the inner route is well charted and marked.

There are several anchorages in this area of use to yachts.

Ellington Bay—(BA387(Plan)):

Although the wharf at Ellington, the name given to the small village on the main highway, has fallen into disuse, a concrete loading ramp is still used by the ferries linking Viti Levu with Vanua Levu. These ply daily between Ellington and Nabouwalu (page 91) through Nananu Passage. There is also a set of steps from which passengers embark in the local longboats that service the resorts on Nananu-I-Cake and Nananu-I-Ra. There is a buoy off the wharf, used by the ferries, which is generally vacant during the middle of the day. A yacht can secure to this for a short time.

There is a good anchorage in 8 metres, mud, in the bay that I have chosen to name Ellington Bay, about 700 metres west of the wharf. The entrance between the reefs can be clearly seen on the plan, and is made on a course of 202° with the south-western point of Nananu-I-Cake in transit with the centre of Yanuca (18) bearing 022° astern. (View 51)

Summit of Yanuca Ø LHE Nananu-i-Cake

Nananu-i-Ra   020°

View 51.   **Entering Ellington Anchorage looking Astern**

The bay provides a safe anchorage if one wishes to visit Rakiraki. There is a tap, with good water, inside the shed by the ramp. On my second visit to the area I found the shed locked, but another tap was available by a group of buildings close by in a fenced area bearing a sign "Site of Ellington Lodge". If this should be unavailable in the future, the staff at the Fiji Sugar Corporation sheds will probably oblige.

Rakiraki:

The real name for the town of Rakiraki is Vaileka. However, the name of the nearby village is that generally accepted. It is about 12 km. by road from the ramp at Ellington and the taxi fare is $6.50. Nearby is the Penang Sugar Mill. Rakiraki provides reasonable resupply facilities for yachts that wish to remain in the area. There is a small but active daily market, two supermarkets including MH's, a butcher who collects his meat from Fiji Meats on Wednesday (order the day before), and several banks including ANZ and Westpac but they are not open every day, details should be available in Suva. There are several buses daily to Lautoka and Suva, some of which can be caught on the main highway at Ellington.

Anchorages:

 There are several possible places to anchor on the west coast of the two islands immediately north of Ellington. There are several backpacker resorts, and one major resort, Mokusiga's, on Nananu-I-Ra, together with some rather opulent private homes at the southern end of the island. Nananu-I-Cake is privately owned. Most of the anchorages are in about 15 metres but one major advantage over Ellington Bay is the clarity of the water.

Mokusiga's Resort, situated on the middle west coast bay of Nananu-I-Ra, welcomes visitors. It has most of the usual resort facilities and you can dine in the restaurant. Their substantial jetty makes landing easy but the anchorage is somewhat restricted if wishing to anchor close by.

Shallower anchorages can be found southward of Volivoli Point. This area also provides ready access to a stone jetty at the south-eastern head of the bay, known as Malake Landing. There is a store close by on the main road, and the jetty provides an alternative landing for those wishing to visit Rakiraki.

Nananu Passage—(BA387, BA381):

Two miles north of Nananu-I-Ra lies Nananu Passage. About one quarter of a mile wide, and marked by leading beacons, it provides an easy exit from the inner reef waters of north-eastern Viti Levu for yachts wishing to make the passage to Vanua Levu or Yadua.

The chart shows several beacons on the outer reef on either side of the passage, but all were missing in 1992. There was, however, a large white cylindrical buoy marking the eastern reef that I believe had been placed there by Paterson's Ferries.

The rear lead, painted red, white, red vertical stripes, on Nananu-I-Ra is below the skyline but is quite conspicuous. The front lead, a white beacon on Cakau Savua, resembles a giant transistor standing on three legs and is more nearly in the centre of the reef than is charted. In 1992 the legs looked to be somewhat damaged. There is a black beacon, also damaged, close by. Care is needed to ensure that the white beacon is used as the forward (seaward) leading beacon .

The reefs on the western side are difficult to see and a yacht, once it has identified the white cylindrical buoy, should favour the eastern side of the passage. From here it is only 27 miles to Yadua. Once clear of the passage course may be set for either the eastern or western side of Yadua proceeding as described in Chapter 10.

Nananu to Lautoka—(BA387, BA389, BA381):

From the anchorages in the Nananu area it is only 53 miles to Lautoka and generally down wind. With an early start, a yacht should have no trouble in completing the passage in one day. Due to the rivers that empty into the inner route, the water throughout is somewhat murky. Nevertheless the route is well marked and with proper planning and attention to one's position, no problems will be met. The passage may be broken into shorter legs by choosing to anchor at any of several convenient places along the way. Toba Naloma, about half way, is well charted and shallow. A clean water alternative can be found on the barrier reef. EUREKA anchored in the indentation on the western side of Ve Drala, but the snorkelling was not all that spectacular. We did manage to catch a very large great trevally. Passage through Na Tobu Drauivi is not recommended unless conditions for reef spotting are excellent.

Nacilau Point Anchorage—(BA387):

A convenient anchorage, well protected by the reefs, can be had in the one mile long indentation in the reef close eastward of Nacilau Point (17° 22'S, 178° 01'E). There is a small loading ramp about 0.5 miles south-south-east of the point, into which a dinghy can get at all stages of the tide. The main highway (The Kings Road) passes within 100 metres of the landing, giving access to both Lautoka and Rakiraki. The small island of Nanuyakoto is privately owned and a house has recently been built upon it.

Vitogo Bay—(BA389, BA381):

Should a yacht not wish to go on to anchor off Lautoka at the end of the day, a convenient alternative is Vitogo Bay. The bay is clear of dangers and the entry is easy and may be made with the minimum of light. From the mouth of the bay continue in a south-easterly direction until the required depth is found. The bottom is mud and good holding.

Lautoka:

 As you approach Lautoka from the north, passing to the east of Bekana, you will immediately come upon the yachts anchored off Neisau Marina (Page 177).

Lautoka and Nadi Waters

Lautoka—(BA845, 1670):

Fiji's second major city and second largest port is Lautoka. It lies on the north-west coast of Viti Levu and is the main sugar-exporting port, the centre of cruise ship operations and the gateway to the Mamanauca and Yasawa island groups, in which the majority of Fiji's island resorts are located. Facilities required by a yacht are very good with the recently (1991) opened Niesau Marina situated at the eastern end of the town. The port is the nearest port of entry for vessels arriving from Vanuatu and New Caledonia. Yachts that have entered through Suva and intend to cruise in the Western Division will be required to clear into the area, and obtain permits for the outer islands at Lautoka. At some time during the stay a visit for stores and fuel is sure to occur. If departing Fiji to the westward the yacht will undoubtedly clear out of Lautoka.

The port of Lautoka lies some 22 miles inside the barrier reef which makes the adjacent waters such pleasant cruising. There are several passages through the reef, the best marked and recommended being Navula Passage to the south-west.

Navula Passage:

View 52.   **Momi Bay Leads - 077°**

The track in through the reef is marked by two leading beacons at the head of Momi Bay. Both are white beacon towers with Day-Glo orange stripes, and are lit. The leads in line bear 077°.

The seaward edges of the reef can be clearly identified by the breaking water, and a beacon marks the inner or north-eastern end of the southern reef. A substantial light marks the northern reef (Navula Reef).

During the first few hours after sunrise the leads can be difficult to see, and care and attention is needed. Once identified however, they are easily maintained. (View 52)

The tidal streams in the entrance can attain a rate of about 2 knots and there is a marked across track component. Due allowance must be made.

Once abeam the north-eastern end of the southern reef, course can be shaped to the north-north-east through Nadi Waters and on to Lautoka, or continued into Momi Bay.

Five miles north of Navula Passage are two further passages, Wilkes and Malolo passages. These are not recommended for entry from seaward as tidal streams are more complicated and fixing is difficult.

Mana Passage:

Nineteen miles north-west of Navula Passage lies an unnamed passage about 2 miles wide. As Mana, with its regular conical summit, provides an excellent lead bearing 082°, I have called this passage 'Mana Passage'.

If, on the voyage east from Vanuatu, a yacht is unable to lay Navula Passage, she will find Mana Passage an acceptable alternative and a saving of several hours hard work to windward into the prevailing south-easterly. When within about 5 miles of the barrier reef, little difficulty will be found in fixing the vessel using Monu, Mana and Malolo islands. However, during the early stages of the approach, care is required in identifying the islands. Waya, the highest and most southerly of the Yasawas, is usually sighted early but is outside the northern border of chart BA845. The southern fall of the summit of Koroyantu (Mt. Evans.) (1200 m.), is also identifiable in good visibility, but both of these objects are too far away to give reliable position lines with a hand-bearing compass.

Once inside the reef course should be shaped to the southward of Mana, north of Malolo and Navini, between Levuka and Kadavu, and thence direct for Lautoka.

Directions:

From a position 262° - 5 miles from the summit of Mana (70m.), steer 082° on this lead, until Mociu (55m.) is in transit with the left-hand edge of Malolo (218m.) bearing 118°. Steer 118° until about 1 mile south of the eastern end of Mana, then alter course to 085° to pass north of Navini. If visibility is satisfactory the fuel installation at Vuda Point can be seen ahead. Maintain this course until Navini is in transit with the summit of Malolo bearing 130°, then alter course to 050° with this transit astern, to pass between Levuka and Kadavu. When the left hand edge of Levuka bears 254° - 2.1 miles, alter course for the Lautoka sugar sheds bearing 074°.

Anchorages—(BA1670):

Vio, which forms a natural breakwater to the west for the wharves of Lautoka, can be rounded either to the north or south. The normal anchorage for yachts is off the marina, however it is permitted to anchor to the north-east of the north-east end of Queen's Wharf.

Yachts do not have to anchor off in the quarantine anchorage but they must not go alongside the marina until they have carried out clearance formalities.

The general area preferred for yacht anchorage is shown in Fig.34.

If anchoring near Queens Wharf care must be taken not to anchor west of a line joining the inner dolphin and the eastern end of Bekana, or too close to the reef to the eastward of the anchorage.

Facilities:

Lautoka is a compact town and most requirements will be found within walking distance of the marina. There is a resident taxi at the marina and the fare to the market (or elsewhere in town) is $1.50.

The post office, situated at the western end of the commercial area, also provides international telephone facilities. Most major banks have branches in Lautoka, including ANZ, Barclays, Baroda, BNZ, Westpac and the National Bank of Fiji.

The major supermarket chains are well represented, with Morris Hedstrom boasting the first 'hypermarket' in Fiji. Motibhai, Patel and Four Square are amongst the others. The market, though smaller than that at Suva, has the same comprehensive range of produce and excellent competitive prices.

The major meat supplier in this area is Fiji Meats. They have a store near the markets and another opposite Kings Wharf. The latter is the major wholesale outlet but provides retail service also. Here they will package and freeze if required. Flake ice and fuel is also available at the fish co-op and wharf, across the road.

There is a major hospital in Lautoka.

Neisau Marina:

Neisau Marina is Fiji's first international marina complex. It commenced operations in mid 1991 and further development is ongoing.

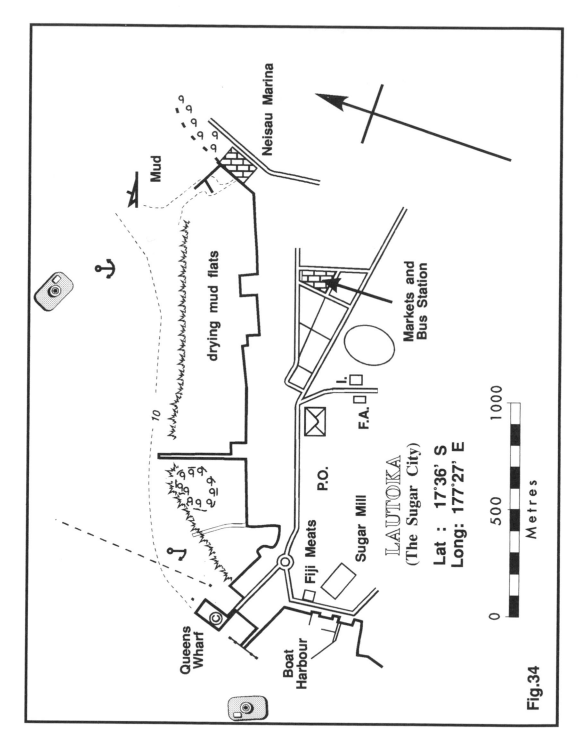

LAUTOKA
(The Sugar City)

Lat : 17°36' S
Long: 177°27' E

Fig.34

Never-the-less at the beginning of the 1992 cruising season it provided the following facilities:-

30 stern to berths with water and power.

63 tonne marine hoist.

Hardstand area for 25 yachts including long term. Laundromat (3 machines and dryers).

Showers and toilets.

Service wharf for embarkation/disembarkation of persons/stores (short period use only).

Petrol, Diesel and water at the wharf.

Sails may be repaired in the bar area

Full refit facilities.

Besides those of the marina other repair facilities, including fitting and turning, welding, electrical, refrigeration and engine repairs can be found in the several industrial areas in Lautoka. The main activity of these workshops is the maintenance of transport and agricultural machinery, but the tradesmen are innovative and can handle most boat problems.

The road between Lautoka and Suva is excellent and there is a bus service several times daily. Nadi International Airport is only about 20 kilometres distant.

Wharves:

 There are four wharves at Lautoka. Queens Wharf, the main commercial wharf, standing off the shore and connected to it by a short bridge has already been mentioned. Kings Wharf, to the south-east, is the old wharf, and is now part of the fishing boat and small craft harbour. Although charted as having dredged approaches of 2.2 metres, the note added to the chart indicating a depth of 0.9 metres is correct as EUREKA grounded in the approaches at half tide. Fuel is available together with ice from the nearby fisherman's coop. A charge of $5.00 per day or part thereof is levied for using the wharf. A yacht could anchor off and use her dinghy to visit Fiji Meats and obtain ice.

FSC wharf is a specialised bulk loading facility.

Queen's Wharf is extremely busy, and all four sides are in use by commercial or local vessels. The northern and western sides are used by commercial shipping. The eastern side is the preserve of the local cruise vessels, while the southern side is used by the Navy and other government vessels. With the advent of the marina it should no longer be necessary for a yacht to use Queens Wharf. Should it be necessary a skipper should always enquire if a berth is available before proceeding alongside, to avoid being forced to leave to make room for a tourist or other vessel.

Charges will be made.

Garbage:

Only in Lautoka was I specifically told garbage must not be thrown into the harbour. According to "general regulations for vessels" it should be retained on board until the vessel clears territorial waters. This is clearly impractical in a cruising yacht remaining in country for some time, and I was told it is acceptable for garbage of local origin to be placed in garbage containers ashore.

Saweni Bay—(BA1670):

A little under 4 miles south-west from Lautoka is Saweni Bay. After the noise and soot of Lautoka it is a beautiful place to get away from it all. Though small, the inner anchorage can accommodate about half a dozen yachts.

Saweni Bay is still within the port limits of the port of Lautoka and it is not necessary to clear customs to go there. The southern shore of the bay is a yellow sandy beach that backs on to a public picnic reserve at the eastern end and on to the Saweni Bay Hotel, a low-key family resort, at the western end. Between the two, a short distance inland from the beach, is the Saweni Beach Store that sells the essentials. These do include, milk, ice-cream, and bread. If you wish to be sure of the latter it is advisable to order the day before.

The manager of the hotel, Mr Chandra Prakesh, makes yachties welcome at the bar and in the pool. The bar is a popular spot for crews to congregate at about sunset. Yachts may obtain limited fresh water by container.

One advantage of Saweni bay is the bus that runs to Lautoka every two hours. The fare is 50 cents each way. The trip takes about half an hour, the bus terminating at the market. It is about 15 minutes walk to the main road bus stop.

Approach:

Saweni Bay itself is about 3/4 mile wide by about 3/4 mile deep, but it has at its head a snug inner anchorage inside the horns of a drying reef that fringes its eastern and western shores. Passage from Lautoka is straightforward, as will be seen from the chart.

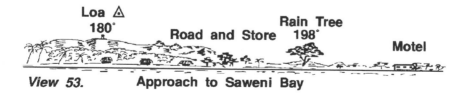

View 53.   **Approach to Saweni Bay**

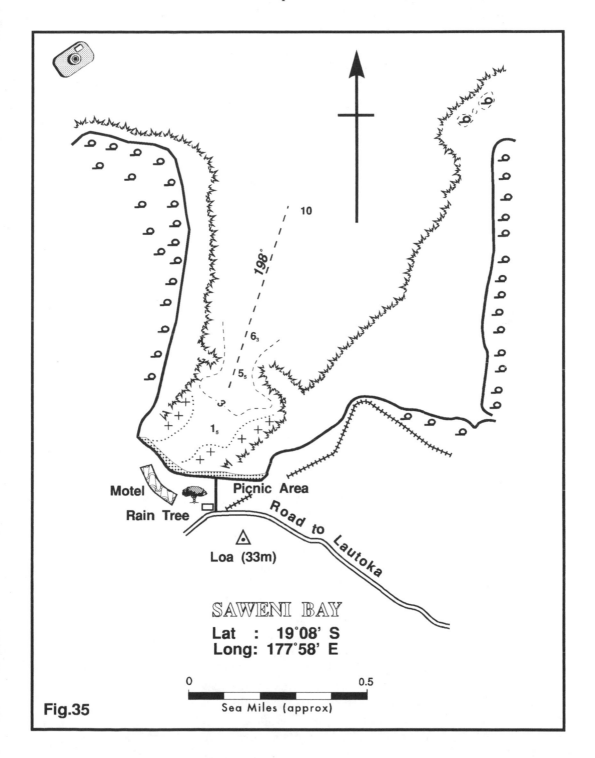

Motel

Rain Tree

Picnic Area

Road to Lautoka

Loa (33m)

SAWENI BAY
Lat : 19°08' S
Long: 177°58' E

0   0.5
Sea Miles (approx)

Fig.35

The final approach into the inner anchorage may be made steering either, 180° on Loa Trig.(33m.), or 198° on the prominent 'Rain Tree' between the hotel and the road. (View 53)

This will lead between the horns of the reef. Once inside, a yacht may anchor as convenient. (Fig.35)

Anchorage:

The anchorage in the inner anchorage is in 3 to 5 metres, sand and mud. Unfortunately the holding is not as good as one would expect. If the number of yachts necessitates a short scope on the anchor it may be necessary to use two anchors to ensure safety in a blow. The outer part of the bay has depths of about 7 metres and the holding in mud is very good.

Toba Ko Nadi (Nadi Bay)—(BA1670):

A further 8 miles south from Saweni Bay is Toba Ko Nadi (Nadi Bay), on the northern side of which is the Vuda Point fuel installation. There is a small boat harbour with sufficient water for a yacht alongside the breakwater jetty at half tide. Neither fuel nor water is available direct; fuel is delivered by tanker and water can be obtained in own containers.

I have been informed that a new marina complex will be completed at Vuna Point by mid-1994. Often, particularly in Fiji, such construction takes considerably longer than planned.

Regent Hotel:

On the southern side of the bay, at Denarau, is the Regent of Fiji resort hotel, with the Sheraton Hotel situated close westward. Construction of a "canal" resort is also proceeding to the eastward of the Regent.

Between the Regent and the Sheraton, and a little back from the beach is a bure that is the operating facility of South Sea Island Cruises. This is the area where yachts may land by dinghy keeping clear of the area that is immediately in front of the bure, as it is from this beach that passengers are ferried out to the Island Express and other ferries. Water can be obtained, own cans, at $2.00 per days' operations (i.e. if you have only a few cans you can make many trips). It is far less time consuming to borrow additional cans from others, as the hose reaches to the waters' edge. The closest stores are at Nadi, apart from the concessions at the hotel. You can dine at the hotel.

A bus runs to Nadi from the road about 500 metres inland from the landing, at roughly 90 minute intervals on the half hour, between 0900 and 1730. The fare is 45 cents. Taxis are readily available, fare $6.00.

At the head of the bay is Nadi International Airport. Two jetties are shown on chart BA 1670; the southernmost is in ruins but the one nearest to the runways has a small pontoon attached to it, and is the base for Turtle Airways which operates float planes to the resort islands. Close by this jetty is the Nadi Airport Golf Club (clubs may be hired) and the Nadi Motor Boat Club. The former is open daily until about 1900. It has a bar, (stubby— $1.70), manned by a most friendly barman who goes by the name of Gila, and you can ring for a cab if there is not one already there. The odd jerry can of water is not objected to.

The area is known as Newtown Beach and a small residential area, including several budget hotels, has been developed over the past few years. One of the hotels is on the beach front and has a pleasant poolside bar. It welcomes visitors. The area is serviced by a bus on a scheduled but irregular, basis. The current schedule has buses to Nadi at, 0730, 0830, 1130 and 1630. From Nadi they run at 0700, 0800, 1100, and 1600. The fare is 45 cents. The taxi fare is $6.00.

Although shopping would generally be done in Nadi, there is a small shop just in from the beach-front houses where fresh bread can be obtained. It is about 1.5 kilometres to the main highway running between Lautoka and Nadi, on which there is a 15-minute bus service. Fare to Lautoka 90 cents.

There is a laundry, Northern Press Laundry, just across the highway in Yenkat Lane off Northern Press Road. Newtown Beach is of course nearer to Nadi Airport than The Regent and the taxi fare is $8.00.

Directions:

The chart is quite clear and specific directions to the bay itself are unnecessary. There is now a beacon on the northern end of Malan Cay and a pole on the small drying reef about 0.3 miles north-west of the Turtle Airways jetty. Beacons also mark the channel to the south-west from the area between Yakuilau (used by the Regent) and Denarau.

Anchorages:

The anchorage off the Regent is between Yakuilau and Denarau. The resort boats will be seen, and there are invariably several yachts also in the area. Anchor near the other yachts to keep the area immediately west of the Regent free for the resort ferries. The depth is about 4 metres, mud, and the holding excellent. The anchorage is subject to slight tidal streams and at times due to wind, or wind and stream, a yacht may lie beam on to a slight south-westerly swell which can be annoying. This swell can also make the landing a bit damp, particularly if there is also an onshore breeze and it is low water.

The anchorage off Newtown Beach is rarely used by yachts, probably because no one has thought to investigate it. It is invariably calmer than the Regent, being completely free from swell. The dinghy trip ashore is marginally shorter than that at the Regent. The anchorage is in 3 to 4 metres, sand and mud, and the holding very good. The approach to the anchorage is straightforward on a course of 112° on the Turtle Airways hangar/jetty in transit with a prominent flat-topped hill, or butte, on the first range in from the coast.

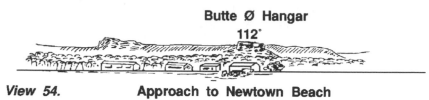

Butte Ø Hangar
112°

View 54.   **Approach to Newtown Beach**

Steer this transit until past the small drying reef, marked by the pole, and then anchor in the depth desired. Depending on the time of day and the amount of haze or smoke the butte may be hard to identify as it does not present a skyline mark until quite close to the shore. Care must be taken not to mistake the other much more conspicuous flat topped hill, which has a prominent "bump" on its northern fall that is part of the main range, and is about 10° to the left.

14

The Mamanuca Group

With the exception of Turtle Island Resort and Yasawa Island Lodge, all island resorts in the Lautoka/Nadi area are situated in the Mamanuca Group, or between the group and the mainland.

The Mamanuca Group is about 20 miles west of Lautoka in the generally sheltered Nadi Waters, and only half a day's sail from the major centres. For many it thus is the obvious spot to start cruising in the Western Division.

There are numerous anchorages in the group. Some are strictly day anchorages only, others are sometimes difficult or exposed to particular winds or swell, and there are two that are comfortable in all conditions. These are Musket Cove with its recently constructed marina, at Malolo Lailai, where yachts are most welcome; and Mana lagoon, which is somewhat restricted regarding the number of yachts that can anchor and the facilities available.

Malolo Lailai—(BA1670, 845):

Malolo Lailai is the southernmost of two islands, the other being Malolo, the largest island in the Mamanucas that are joined by drying reef and sand at low water. Plantation Island Resort and Musket Cove Resort, originally known as Dick's Place, are on Malolo Lailai. The island also has an airstrip and is serviced by frequent daily flights from Nadi Airport.

Musket Cove:

The Musket Cove Resort is the home of the Musket Cove Yacht Club and Marina.

The MCYC now has more than 800 members and all are blue water sailors. To be eligible for membership they have all sailed from foreign ports to Musket Cove. Life membership costs $1.00 for the skipper, and $5.00 for each crew member. A membership card is issued.

The Musket Cove Yacht Club:

> Address: Private Mail Bag NAPO352,
> Nadi Airport,
> Fiji Islands
> Phone: 679-662215/662878
> Fax: 679-662633

Amongst the many other facilities available to members, the MCYC has placed 20 moorings in the waters leading to the marina and the fuel dock and landing pontoon. On arrival at Malolo Lailai a yacht should contact "Musket Cove Dock" on VHF Ch.68 or 64, when advice will be given on which mooring to secure to. The moorings have a 2:1 scope and as the water is of the order of 18 metres deep, boats not intending to moor should anchor clear of the buoys. Shortly after arrival yachts will be provided with the MCYC "Welcome Pack" with details of the services provided. In summary these are as follows:-

The Yacht Club:

The Club House is located adjacent to "DICK'S PLACE".

Bar and Restaurant:

Members are welcome to use all Resort amenities. These are free with the exception of water skiing and game fishing. Dress rules apply for the Bar and Restaurant, shirts and shorts or sulu and similar for ladies. Swimwear is not acceptable.

Showers:

Showers and toilets are available at the dock or at the back of the Yacht Club.

Garbage:

Bins are provided at the dockside for tied bags of garbage. Bottles should be placed separately.

Mail:

In-coming mail is kept at the Dock Boat Shed. The out-going mail bag is in the Boutique, where stamps are available.

Phones and Faxes:

These services are available at the Dock Boat Shed. Pay phones are available. Faxes are charged at "resort" rates.

Shopping:

"The MUSKET COVE TRADER" is open 7 days a week and stocks a good range of provisions including frozen foods. Fresh bread, fruit and vegetables are flown in daily. Prices are approximately 25% higher than the mainland, but the saving in time and effort in a trip to Nadi or Lautoka (including Customs) may well outweigh this additional cost. Special items can be ordered if required. Island wear and toiletries are stocked in the "Boutique"

Laundry:

Two washing machines are available dockside. Laundry also can be sent to the mainland if required.

Crew Changes:

These can now be made at Musket Cove saving a trip to Lautoka.

Maintenance:

Limited boat repairs can be carried out. Outboard and general mechanics are available.

Fuel and Water:

Diesel and 50:1 Premix are available from pumps at the Fuel Dock. Super, Kerosene and LPG are also available by arrangement. Drinking water, which has to be imported from the mainland, is available free with a fuel "fill". On other occasions it is supplied at cost (2 cents per litre). Fuel is priced at the government approved "offshore" rate.

Special Events:

Two occasions that have become synonymous with the MCYC are the B.Y.O Sunday Night Barbecue and the Thursday night "Pig on the Spit" feast and Fijian Entertainment.

On shore barbeque facilities are available, free of charge, at any time, on Ratu Nemani Island off the dock.

It is not surprising that Musket Cove has become a Mecca for cruising yachts.

Annual Musket Cove to Port Vila Regatta:

Every year, usually about the second or third week in September, the number of boats gathering at Musket Cove increases dramatically in anticipation of the "Vila Race".

The race to Port Vila is the culmination of a week of festivities at Musket Cove that includes dinghy races, sailboard races, figurehead sail-past, picnic race to an offshore island and the Round Malolo Race. All events are fun races, and the unique handicapping system ensures that all have a chance at the most worthwhile prizes. The Coconut Cup for the Vila race is won on a lottery basis, and there is also a line honours cup, The P.I.T.C.O. Cup, for those in a hurry!

The timing of the Musket Cove to Port Vila Regatta is ideal for those yachts cruising on to Australia, and this ensures a good field that will undoubtedly grow with the years. To enable a better appreciation of the atmosphere of the Musket Cove fortnight, the following 'Rules of the Regatta 1992' are reproduced verbatim:

1. Each yacht must start from Musket Cove, Malolo Lailai, Fiji on or about September 12th, 1992 and finish at or near Vila, Vanuatu in the same year.

2. All vessels are requested to run their engines at least one hour per day.

3. This is a cruise event and not intended to be an ordeal. The rules of cruising apply; if the weather is poor at the intended start, the start will be delayed until the weather is good, or at least fair.

4. All boats to maintain a 24-hour watch.

5. All boats to have a 360 degree masthead light on during night hours.

6. All competitors to be at Dick's Bistro at 8.30 am for Customs and Immigration clearance. Please bring all relative papers. (Dick will provide a boat service for those who have no dinghy available).

7. Customs and Immigration will be at Port Vila.

8. The finishing line will be clearly marked; see finishing instructions.

9. Radio schedules NOT compulsory, but requested so we have some idea of how you are going.

10. Fishing is compulsory.

11. Apart from several prizes for various sections of the race, there will be a prize for the largest fish.

12. Each yacht must float at least 4" below her LWL.

13. Each yacht must carry fuel and/or spirituous liquor to the Race Committee's satisfaction, and the committee reserves the right to remove samples of either for analysis.

14. Use of light weather sails and drifters is strongly to be discouraged, and motoring is to be regarded as the usual means of propulsion in winds of less than 10 knots.

15. Line honours yacht will be automatically disqualified unless it can be proven that blatant cheating occurred.

16. Competitors are bound by the rules to keep overall placings in strictest confidence.

17. Penalties (and possible disqualification) will be incurred on yachts with any of the following:-

(a) Rod rigging

(b) Bloopers

(c) Matching oilskins

(d) Rating Certificate

(e) Sails less than 4 years old

(f) Trouble-free refrigeration system

(g) Sperry Topsiders or similar footwear.

(h) Bow thrusters

18. Handicap allowance will be given to yachts carrying 2 or more of

the following:-

(a) Ironing board

(b) Washing machine

(c) Pot plants

(d) Goose barnacles exceeding 2" in length

(e) More than 2 pairs of pyjamas per crew member

(f) Children

(g) Hand-drawn or photostatted charts or charts more than 15 years old.

(h) Homemade sextants, logs or outboards.

19. Each yacht will be awarded a divisional first place bulkhead plaque at the prize giving.

20. Small boats may start-up-to 3 days early if they wish but will miss the pig feast.

Although the regatta week is the highlight at Musket Cove, it is an excellent place for yachts at any time.

Malolo Lailai (Directions)—(Fig.36):

Following the hurricane season each year, extreme caution must be exercised when using beacons for quidance. Many are damaged and replacement takes some time. Some were still missing in June 1993. The approach to Musket Cove should only be made in full daylight when reefs can be clearly seen.

The normal direction of approach to Malolo Lailai is around the reef extending to the south-east of the island, and then around the south-western point, between it and the large detached reef about 0.5 miles south-west. The route is well beaconed and quite easy, although the chart BA1670 is not particularly helpful. The island can also be approached from the north-west after entering the northern reefs to the north of Qalito, on which Castaway Island Resort is found. The BA chart does not make this evident.

These directions refer to Fig 36, and take a yacht from south to north and inside the reefs fringing Qalito, Malolo, and Malolo Lailai.

Approaching from Lautoka, Nadi or Navula Passage, a vessel should steer for the south-eastern end of the reef extending from Malolo Lailai. The end of the reef is marked by a beacon with a white topmark, point up. There is also a large outcrop of rocks, with a height of about 0.9 metres, approximately 200 metres north-west of the beacon. After rounding or closing the beacon at a distance of about 100 metres, steer 275° to leave the beacon on the northern side of the isolated shoal about 0.5 miles west-south-west on the port hand, and the beacon close southward of the south-western point of Malolo Lailai on the starboard hand.

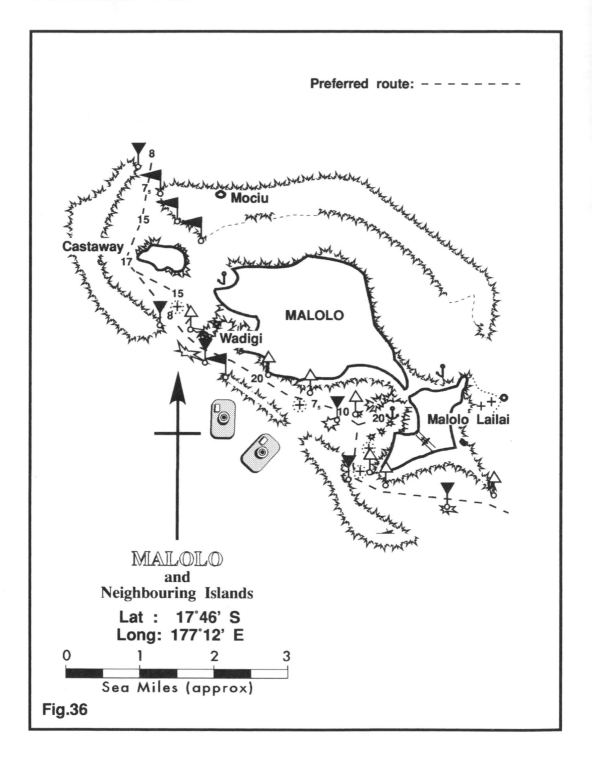

Preferred route: — — — — — —

Mociu

Castaway

MALOLO

Wadigi

Malolo Lailai

MALOLO
and
Neighbouring Islands
Lat : 17°46' S
Long: 177°12' E

0   1   2   3
Sea Miles (approx)

Fig.36

When abeam of the latter beacon, alter course to 323° to leave the beacon close west of the same point, about 50 metres to starboard. On passing this beacon, a depth of about 8 metres will be encountered.

When clear of the narrows, steer 000° until past Molly Reef, and then generally north-east for an anchorage in Musket Cove, Molly Reef and two other isolated reefs being left to starboard. All three reefs are surrounded by deep water but on first arrival it is better to avoid the 'slalom'.

Departing Musket Cove to the north-westward, leave Molly Reef to port and steer 301° with the main bar of Plantation Village astern, leaving the first two beacons to starboard and port respectively. Both are clearly marked with the relative topmark. This course is then maintained for a further 2 miles, during which time five more beacons will be passed. The first three have triangular topmarks and are left, in order, to starboard, to port and to starboard. The next two beacons have finger topmarks and mark an exit through the reef. Both are left to port if continuing past Wadigi.

The outer edge of the reef surrounding Wadigi is marked by two beacons, white, points up, which are left to starboard. On passing the second of these, course should be steered just open of the western end of Qalito, 320°, to leave the next beacon to port and an unmarked isolated shoal to starboard.

When rounding Qalito (Castaway Island Resort), keep about 100 metres offshore to avoid the boating area and the fringing reef. Having cleared the point, ease across to starboard until the point bears 189°, then place it astern steering 009° to pass two more beacons with finger topmarks, the first one to starboard and the last to port.

Having cleared the reef a yacht is clear to set course as required.

To make a circumnavigation or visit the north coast of Malolo, steer between Qalito and Malolo after having passed Wadigi. There are several beacons en route. At other times a yacht should favour the coast rather than the off-lying reefs.

If the south-easterlies are too persistent or too strong, or a change is wanted from Malolo Lailai, a sheltered anchorage may be found in the bay at the north-eastern end of Malolo, just around the point from Club Natasi Resort

Mana—(Fig.37):

The next anchorage that a yacht will encounter after those of the Malolo area is the lagoon on the south side of Mana. The anchorage is rather restricted due to the regular use of the lagoon by the Turtle Airways float planes.

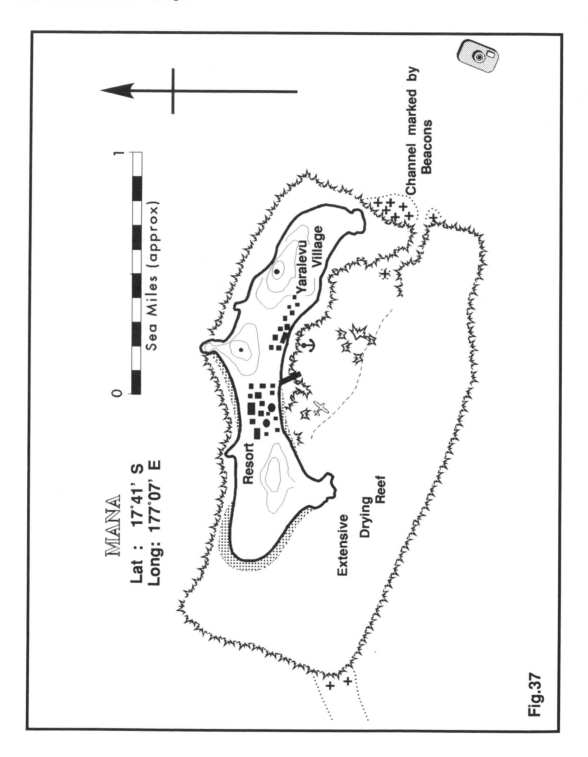

MANA

Lat : 17°41' S
Long: 177°07' E

Sea Miles (approx)

Resort

Yaralevu
Village

Channel marked by
Beacons

Extensive
Drying
Reef

Fig.37

It is possible that about 3 to 5 yachts could be accommodated in the lagoon, anchored to the east of the service jetty. In view of the increase in water sports activity over the last few years, yachts should not anchor west of the jetty.

Chart BA845 indicates that the reef on the southern side of Mana is continuous all the way from the shoreline. This is not so. The lagoon is extensive and deep and provides a very good anchorage within the restrictions mentioned above.

At Mana, yachts are welcome to make use of the bars, restaurants and other public facilities. The island is serviced by its own ferry six days a week. There is a store that carries some fresh provisions, including bread, but not all are received daily. There is a fair range of dry goods, and some frozen lines are carried on a haphazard basis. The owner of the store will, however order items, for delivery next day, if required. Prices are similar to Malolo Lailai which has a far greater range. The store is situated between the resort and the village, just behind the Gift Shop and Handicraft Centre, to the east of the jetty.

All water on Mana has to be imported and none is available to boats.

Directions:

The entrance to the lagoon is via a dogleg channel at the eastern end of the reef. The channel is extremely well marked, with beacons almost every 100 metres. It carries a least depth of about 5 metres at LAT.

The Mana lagoon, though lacking the camaraderie of Musket Cove, is a pleasant spot to spend a few days. Although well protected from the seas by the reef, it is open to the all winds with a southerly component. The holding is however adequate in fine sand.

About 5 miles north-west from Mana lies a group of islands known collectively as Mamanuca-I-Cake. This group includes the resort island of Matamanoa and the larger islands of Tavua, Tokoriki and Yanuya. The anchorages in the area tend to be exposed to one wind or another, but are suitable for overnight use in settled conditions. One other factor that can affect these and other anchorages further north is a residual swell which, though not large, is often present after bad weather. It is able to reach the islands as the outer barrier reef in this area tends to become more sunken, and finally ceases to exist altogether.

Yanuya:

Although the island itself has nothing to entice the yachtsman ashore, there are two anchorages on the north-east coast that provide a place to spend a night when sailing in the area. Both are open to the north and east but are generally comfortable in the prevailing south-east weather. The first, and the better of the two, is found close eastward of the village that is situated on the low sandy land joining the southernmost point, a large hill, with the remainder of the high ground to the north. The anchorage is in sand with some dead coral, in about 12 metres of water. The water is invariably clear and it is simple to place the anchor in a sandy spot to avoid fouling the coral. Holding is adequate providing sufficient chain is used.

The second anchorage is off the small beach just around the point north of Yanuya village. It is amongst coral and sand, with more chance of a foul anchor, and more prone to swell than the first.

A third anchorage, off the western side of the village, provides protection from the north-east, but is also subject to swell. The reef extends some way off shore on this side of the island.

The island of Tokoriki is part of the vanua of Yanuya. Although it was not visited, it is understood to have a good anchorage off the beach on its eastern coast. It now has a resort on the western shore.

Matamanoa:

There is a resort on the south side of this small island but it appears devoid of a good anchorage. The BA chart shows a clear passage to the south of the island, but this is not so. A passage does exist but it is encumbered with reefs and care is required for safe navigation.

About 7 miles further north from Yanuya is the northern- most sub-group of the Mamanucas, Mamanuca-I-Ra. This group contains a delightful anchorage enclosed by the three islands of Navadra, Vanua Levu and Vanua Lailai. It is protected from all winds except from the north, but unfortunately swell is sometimes present. I have chosen to call this anchorage Navadra Anchorage after the largest island of the group.

Navadra Anchorage—(Fig. 38):

The islands surrounding the anchorage are all uninhabited, although there are goats on Vanua Levu and probably on Navadra. There is a large reef awash in the middle of the entrance to the 'bay', but there is ample water on either side to permit access. The western side is, however, clearer than the east.

Directions:

The islands may be approached along either the eastern or western side, and are much as charted on chart F5. The best approach to the anchorage is to the west of the entrance reef, favouring the island side of the channel.

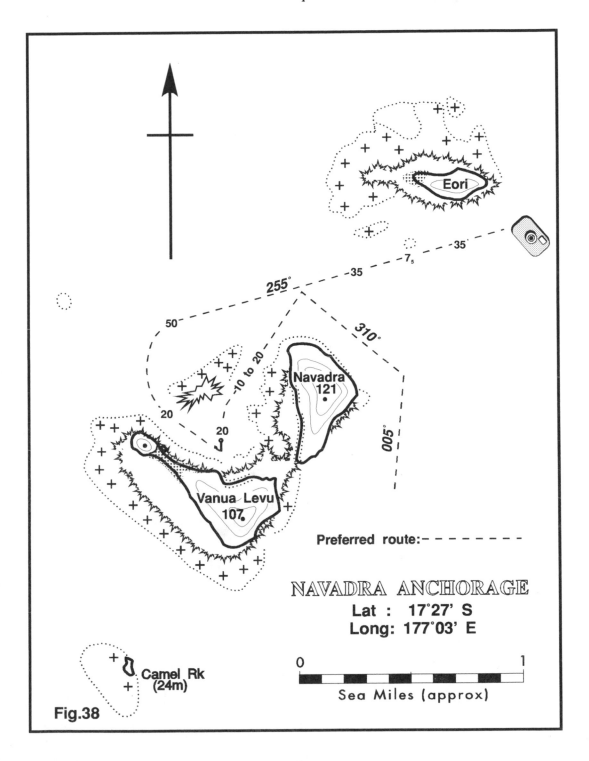

Navadra
121

255°

310°

005°

50

35

35

7₅

-10 to 20

20

20

Vanua Levu
107.

Eori

Preferred route:- - - - - - - -

NAVADRA ANCHORAGE
Lat : 17°27' S
Long: 177°03' E

0   1

Sea Miles (approx)

Camel Rk
(24m)

Fig.38

The best anchorage is to the north of a rocky headland in the centre of the north coast of Vanua Levu, which separates two beaches. The bottom here, though about 20 metres deep, is sand and the holding is good. Due to the nature of the area it is almost impossible to find an anchorage that is not too close to the reef, or foul with a coral bottom, that is not more than 18 metres. The beaches here are excellent, as is the diving and snorkelling. A residual swell, which appears to be present even in settled conditions, is more of a nuisance than a problem.

From Navadra Anchorage it is but 10 miles to Yalobi Bay on the southern side of Waya, and the first major island of the Yasawas. When making this passage the obvious route is to the east of Eori and Yamuto-ni-Dole. The waters are much as charted on F5, but one should not be tempted to venture westward unless visibility is good, as tidal streams can be strong and fixing is difficult.

Chart F5:

This chart, published by the Royal Fiji Military Forces Hydrographic Unit and only available in Fiji, is highly recommended for any yacht cruising in the Yasawa Group and to the north and west of Lautoka.

Although the standard of cartography is not as high as that of British or American charts, the information shown is the best available. In many places there are few or no soundings, for example around Waya, but the chart does show most reefs and shoals, or at least those which would threaten a yacht.

In good visibility, 'rock hopping' does have its advantages. It is often better to steer for a known shoal or reef, and when it is sighted then avoid it and move on to the next one. The philosophy here is that, as most of these shoals have been positioned from aerial photography, if only one has been plotted, then only one exists. In using aerial photographs as the primary method of deciding whether to visit an anchorage when compiling data for this book, I have usually found it to be so.

15

The Yasawa Group

Introduction:

The Yasawa Group lies to the north-west of Lautoka, at a distance of about 40 miles at its centre. The group lies in a north-east/south-west direction, from Waya in the south to Yasawa in the north, for a length of about 50 miles.

The group is the main cruising ground for most of the cruise vessels operating out of the Lautoka/Nadi area, including the Blue Lagoon vessels.

There is only two shore-based resorts in the Yasawas. Turtle Island Resort is situated on Nanuya Levu, is very exclusive, and the management does not wish yachts to call. I have not visited the equally exclusive Yasawa Island Lodge, but it is serviced by its own airstrip.It may provide an emergency means of flying to the mainland

In the last few years, several "backpackers' resorts" have been established by the landowners on Tavewa. These are low key affairs but may develop further in time.

Most of the villages in the Yasawas have some contact with tourists from the cruise ships, many being directly involved in the preparation of lovos, or the performance of mekes. There is a higher awareness of tourists, their behaviour and apparent affluence, more so than will be found in the Northern and Eastern Divisions. Because of this there is a degree of expectancy that gifts of cigarettes, or even beer, will be forthcoming. Though generally neither offensive nor blatant, it can be embarrassing. Requests for liquor should be resisted, and I have found that the early formal presentation of the sevusevu to the turaga enables a firm line to be taken without feeling inhospitable or awkward.

One less appealing development of this awareness is the practice of "charging" yachts to anchor off some villages. In a strictly legal sense, it is doubtful if such charges can be enforced providing crews do not proceed ashore, fish, or otherwise "use" village property. However any confrontation on this basis would achieve no useful purpose and it is preferable that yachts not wishing to accept such imposts stay clear of these places. Two villages known to be engaged in this practice in 1992 were Yasawairara and Malakati.

The major attractions of the Yasawas to the yachtsman are undoubtedly the fine, golden, sandy beaches, the plentiful sunshine, the clear ocean water on the off-lying reefs giving superb diving/snorkelling, and the many very good anchorages, several of which are protected from all directions.

Passage to the Yasawas may be made to arrive at Sawa-i-Lau in the north, Matacawalevu in the centre, or Waya in the south.

The most likely point of departure will be Lautoka, although the approach to Waya could well be made from the Mamanuca Group.

The shortest, most direct, and the least difficult route navigationally, is to Waya. Unfortunately this landfall then means that all further passages along the chain of islands are to the north and north-east, with the sun in its most unfavourable position during the preferred times of passage-making, in the morning and early afternoon.

Remember - leave early, arrive early!

The passage to Matacawalevu, via Kubo Passage, contains some difficult navigation for the first 15 miles, through the reefs north of Lautoka; although the route is regularly used by local boats.

The passage to Sawa-i-Lau requires a certain amount of tricky navigation but, providing that the weather and timing is right, can be made in reasonable safety. It has the advantage that, with the exception of the short hop to Yasawairara at the very top of the group, all other passages are then down sun.

Lautoka to Sawa-i-Lau.—(F5, BA389, BA381):

Although the total distance for this passage is only some 50 miles it is considered wise to undertake it in two legs to make best use of high or favourable sun conditions.

Departing from Lautoka, preferably a little before noon, the recommended track north about Viti Levu is followed as far as Malevu (17°28'S. 177°33'E.), when course is altered to port to pass through the deep and clear passage between Caku Udu Levu and Cakau Na Sasi.

On clearing the north-eastern end of Caku Udu Levu, course is then shaped to enable a positive sighting of the small reef close westward of Vatututotolu (17°11'S. 177°36'E.).

This reef is then left to port and the vessel proceeds into Bligh Water.

When executing this passage over two days, anchorage can be found in the vicinity of either Caku Udu Levu or Vatututotolu.

Because of the length of the position lines it is preferable to use horizontal sextant angles for fixing during this passage. BA381 will provide the most convenient fixing as far north as about 17°19'S. using marks on Viti Levu. F5 should be used thereafter. Three Sisters (Cakau Vatutolu) (17°14'S. 177°3 3'E.) is most useful during the 9-mile hop to Vatututotolu; it can be seen from a distance of about 3 miles except at high water springs.

Once into Bligh Water course is set to pass about one mile to the eastward of the reefs running northward, with the boat steering for the southern tip of Tivolei. The sheer south-west face of Sawa-i-Lau makes an excellent mark for gaining the entrance to Qio Passage. Water clarity is excellent, and an echo sounder gives timely warning of an overshoot!

Qio Passage is deep and the sides are steep to. The deep water is maintained until about one mile past the south-western 'wall' of reefs, when course is altered to 308° with the left hand fall of Sawa-i-Lau in transit with Taucake Trig.(233m.).

The final entry into Sawa-i-Lau Bay is made as follows:

When Yadravavatu (a small rocky outcrop) is in transit with the saddle in the twin hills on the northern end of Nacula, steer 293° along the transit. (View 55)

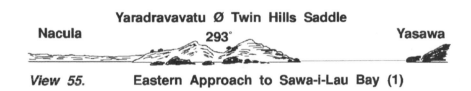

Yaradravavatu Ø Twin Hills Saddle

Nacula   293°   **Yasawa**

View 55.   **Eastern Approach to Sawa-i-Lau Bay (1)**

When Naidavedave (2m.) is in transit with the 'V' in the hills close eastward of Taucake, steer for it on a course of 327°. (View 56)

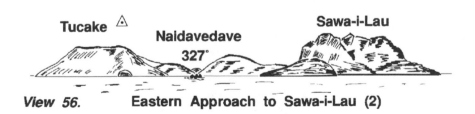

Tucake △   **Sawa-i-Lau**
              Naidavedave
                  327°

View 56.   **Eastern Approach to Sawa-i-Lau (2)**

When Neikavu Rock is in transit with the saddle in the twin hills used earlier, steer this line, 285°, until Yarawa bears 013°, and Yadravaqele 193°. Course may be altered to any convenient anchorage shown in Fig.39.

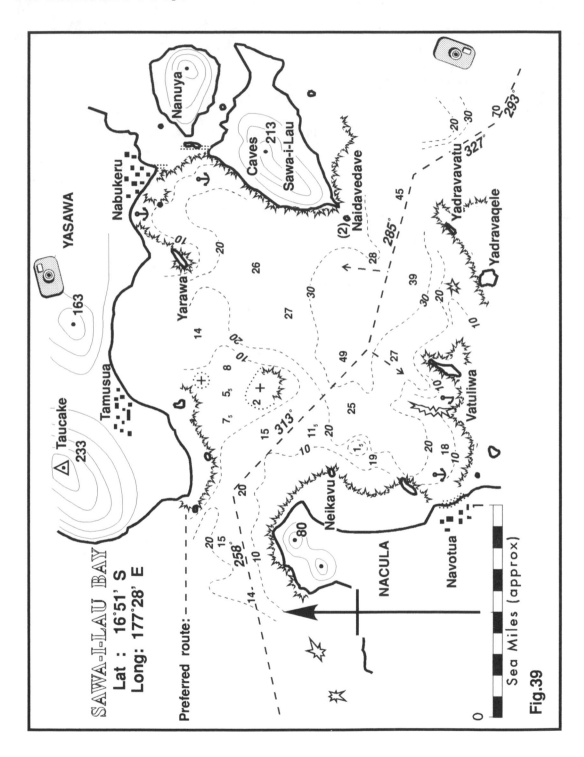

SAWA-I-LAU BAY

Lat : 16°51' S
Long: 177°28' E

Preferred route: - - - -

Fig.39

Sea Miles (approx)

0

YASAWA

Nanuya

Caves · 213

Sawa-i-Lau

Nabukeru

Taucake △ 233

Tamusua

· 163

Yarawa

Naidavedave (2)●

Yadravavatu

Yadravaqele

30
70
293
327
20
285°
45

39
30
20
10

27

49

27

Vatuliwa

25

18
20
10

19

Neikavu

· 80

NACULA

Navotua

258°
15
20
14
10

313°
15
258°
20
7
5₅
2
8
10
02
14
26
27
10
20
20

10
11₅
20
1₅

Yasawa:

The main attractions of Yasawa are the caves in Sawa-i-Lau and the beautiful long, sweeping sandy beaches as exemplified by those to the south of the village of Yasawairara at the northern end of the island.

There is also the quiet and sheltered harbour of Nadala Bay (Land Harbour), which is excellently charted on BA381.

Sawa-i-Lau Bay—(Fig.39):

There are three villages on the shores of the bay. Nabukeru, which operates the barbecue area north of Sawa-i-Lau; Tamusua, which owns Nadala Bay and Sawa-i-Lau, and hence the caves; and Navotua, which owns Vatuliwa and the adjacent islets.

The main tourist attraction of the area is the caves, but there is also good swimming and diving. During strong south-easterlies a degree of swell enters the bay; the best anchorage is then in the north-east tucked in behind Sawa-i-Lau.

Nadala Bay (Land Harbour)—(BA381(Plan)):

Passage to Nadala Bay is free of danger, keeping about 1/4 to 1/2 mile offshore around the south-western end of Yasawa. Anchorage can be found close to Bamboo Islet in the area charted as 2 to 3 fathoms, which is sand and free from coral.

Vawa, which is uninhabited, has a fine beach. It is fringed by reef, but there is a clear dinghy passage to Savusavuivawa Point, even at low water.

Yasawairara—(Fig.40):

This village is the seat of the Tui Yasawa. It is also one of the villages levying charges. In 1992 these were reported to be $20 per night to anchor, and sometimes even a landing fee.

Safe passage from Nadala Bay to Yasawairara can be made, in depths of from 23 to 38 metres, along a track with the gap between Yawini and Yasawa ahead, and Tucake astern, 038°-218°. This track is maintained until the large rocky headland in the middle of the village bears 085° when it is placed ahead. The conspicuous tin roof of the village church will be seen close eastward of the headland. Anchorage can be found in about 8 metres close to the headland in a large clear area of sand. Some effect of residual ocean swell may be felt, although it is not bad. This anchorage is least affected by the prevailing winds.

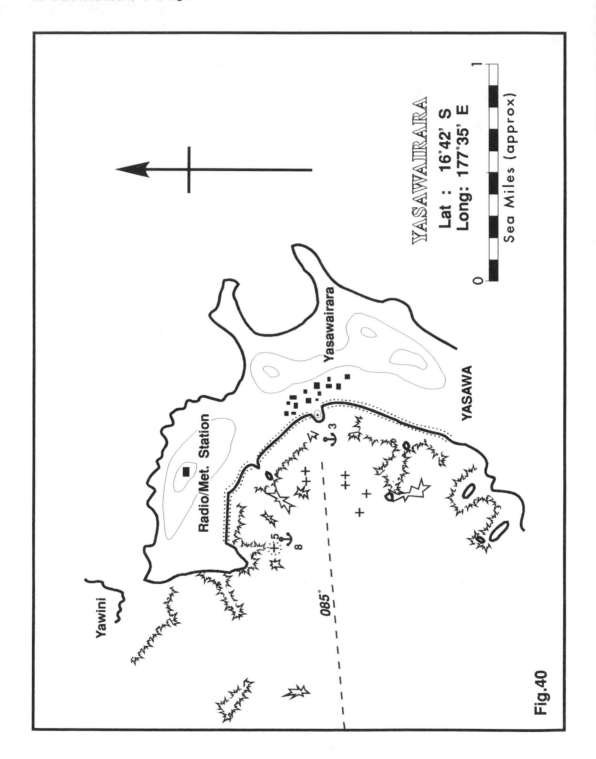

YASAWAIRARA

Lat : 16°42' S
Long: 177°35' E

Sea Miles (approx)

Yasawairara

YASAWA

Radio/Met. Station

Yawini

085°

Fig.40

An alternative anchorage can be found free from swell below the radio/met station, in about 6 metres, but with rocky outcrops rising to about 4 metres. The general bottom is sand and ample area can be found to anchor clear of the rocky outcrops. The holding in both areas is good.

Yasawa to Matacawalevu:

The passage between Yasawa and the northern end of Matacawalevu is generally made along the north-western shore of Nacula. The route along the south-eastern shore, though clearer and deeper, requires a passage through the strait between Nacula and Nanuya-sewa, which is not marked by beacons; or additional sailing to enter through Kubo Passage, south of Nanuya-levu. The former would provide little difficulty providing it is carried out in the forenoon.

Directions:

Having cleared either Sawa-i-Lau or Nadala Bays (see later), the preferred route is a course of 238° with Taucake Trig (233m.) astern, bearing 058° (View 57), to pass between Cokonibau Reef and the reefs to seaward.

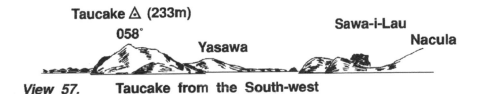

Taucake △ (233m)

058°

Yasawa

Sawa-i-Lau

Nacula

View 57.   **Taucake from the South-west**

Depths along this track are between 32 and 40 metres until near Yaromo. Shortly after passing Cokonibau Reef, and when the grassy summit of Tavewa (Valenisiga Trig) bears 193° (View 58), course is altered to steer for this summit and to pass between Mataniwai Reef and the reefs to seaward.

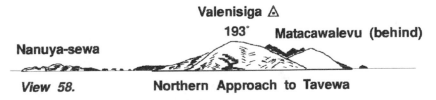

Valenisiga △

193°   Matacawalevu (behind)

Nanuya-sewa

View 58.   **Northern Approach to Tavewa**

Mataniwai Reef is marked on its northern end with a beacon (black triangle point down) which indicates that it should be left to seaward. This inside route carries slightly deeper water but lacks a positive lead, and

203

requires a little more eyeballing.

Having passed Mataniwai Reef, and with the summit of Tavewa 0.9 miles distant, course is altered to 175° with the summit of Nanuya-sewa ahead. When abeam the southern tip of Tavewa the first of the beacons marking the channel into Nanuya-sewa anchorage, also known as Blue Lagoon, will be encountered. These beacons were replaced in August of 1985 and were in good order. When transiting the east/west section of the narrows, depths of 4.5 metres will be encountered at low water.

Departure from Sawa-i-Lau Bay:

Proceed from the chosen anchorage to join the track of 313°, with the centre of the gap between Yadravavatu and Yadravaqele bearing 133° astern. (View 59)

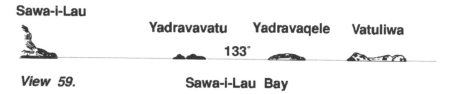

Sawa-i-Lau

Yadravavatu   Yadravaqele   Vatuliwa

133°

View 59.   **Sawa-i-Lau Bay**

This course is maintained until Yarawa is middled in the gap between Nanuya and Yasawa, bearing 078°, when course is altered to 258° and the transit maintained. (View 60)

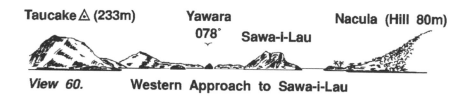

Taucake △ (233m)   **Yawara**   **Nacula (Hill 80m)**

078°   **Sawa-i-Lau**

View 60.   **Western Approach to Sawa-i-Lau**

Strong tidal streams may be experienced at springs. This track is maintained until Taucake bears 058°, when the main route is joined. (View 57)

Departure from Nadala Bay:

Proceed north-westward, leaving Vawa to starboard, until the left hand edge of Nanuya-i-ra (at the top of Yasawa) is in transit with Muaikubuwe Point on Vawa, bearing 035°. Steer 215° to maintain this transit until Taucake Trig bears 058°, when the main route is joined.

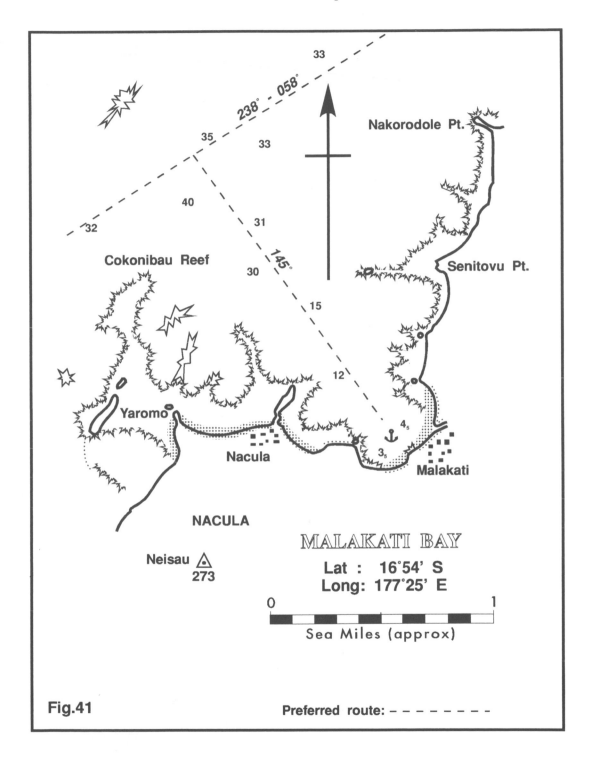

33

238° - 058°

35

33

Nakorodole Pt.

40

31

145°

32

Cokonibau Reef

30

Senitovu Pt.

15

12

Yaromo

4₅

Nacula

3₅

Malakati

NACULA

MALAKATI BAY

Neisau △
273

Lat : 16°54' S
Long: 177°25' E

0   1

Sea Miles (approx)

Fig.41

Preferred route: – – – – – – – –

Malakati Bay—(Fig.41):

This bay, which lies about half way down the north-western shore of Nacula, is clear of coral and provides a good anchorage in sand.

Unfortunately, it is one of the villages levying a charge for anchoring.

In this case the village will present a "meke", lasting about 30 minutes, to visiting yachts at a cost of $30 per yacht.

Attendance, or at least the payment, is obligatory!

There is a fine sandy beach and a fresh water creek runs into the bay near the village. However, water may not always be available. The reefs around the approaches to the bay seem to trap any swell from the north-west. The approach to the bay was examined on two tracks, 10 degrees apart, and the water between was seen to be clear and deep. A general approach course of 145° for the centre of the beach at the head of the bay provides easy access to the anchorage. (View 61)

Senitovu Pt.   Nacula Village

View 61.   **Malakati Bay from the Northwest**

Nalova Bay:

A popular spot with Blue Lagoon vessels, presumably when Nanuya-sewa is too crowded, is Nalova Bay, also on Nacula, about half a mile north of its south-western point. Again, a fine beach, but it is wide open to the north-west and has little for the yachtsman except as a day anchorage.

Alternative Track Inside Mataniwai:

From the track, 206° on the summit of Tavewa, alter course to 185° for the summit of Nanuya-sewa, when Yaromo is approximately abeam to port, to leave Mataniwai Reef beacon to seaward. When Naisau Trig (273m) bears 090°, alter course to 195° to rejoin the track with the summit of Nanuya-sewa ahead 175°, then follow the previous directions.

Nanuya-sewa (Sese) Anchorage—(Fig.42):

This is undoubtedly one of the most protected anchorages in the cruising area to the north-west of Lautoka. It gives easy access to Sese Village, Tavewa and Nanuya-sewa and the surrounding reefs and beaches.

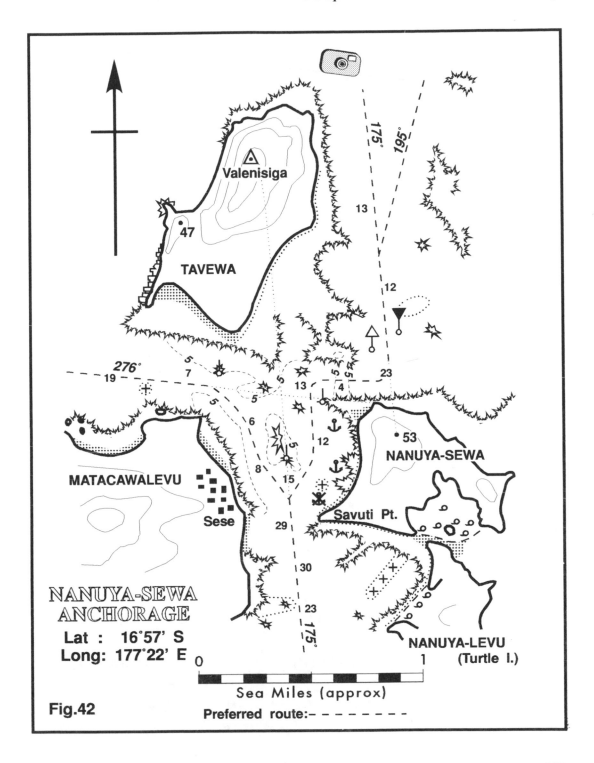

Valenisiga

47

TAVEWA

175°

195°

13

12

276°

19

7

5

23

5

5

13

4

5

6

12

5

15

8

MATACAWALEVU

53

NANUYA-SEWA

Sese

29

Savuti Pt.

30

NANUYA-SEWA
ANCHORAGE
Lat : 16°57' S
Long: 177°22' E

23

175°

NANUYA-LEVU
(Turtle I.)

Fig.42

0

1

Sea Miles (approx)

Preferred route:– – – – – – – –

By arrangement with the local village Blue Lagoon Cruises have rented an area on the western shore of Nanuya-sewa and have set up an entertainment area for their cruise vessels.

The cruise vessels require all the southern half of the western beach and the water adjacent to it, as they anchor their ships close inshore and run lines to the palms. Yachts should keep clear of this area.

The best anchorage, clear of the Blue Lagoon ships but still close to the beach, is between the horns of the reef at the centre of the beach, in about 12 metres, on a sand bottom. With a bit of a squeeze this little area can accommodate three yachts.

There are two caretakers' bures on the beach to the north of the Blue Lagoon area. The northernmost of the two runs a small pig pen and, if necessary, rubbish may be left here after sorting, papers and combustibles being burnt. Water is not available from this island but can be obtained from Sese village.

It is worth noting that should a boat be unable to return to Lautoka for any reason, it is possible for a crew member to return by Blue Lagoon vessel as they regularly make Nanuya-sewa the last stop before returning to Lautoka. The passenger will be charged the equivalent of one day's fare. You will have to ensure that the departing crew member signs off at immigration in either Lautoka or at Nadi, if he or she goes directly to the airport.

Departure from Nanuya-sewa:

There are three exits from Nanuya-sewa anchorage: To the east or north-east as already described; to the south, through Kubo Passage; or to the west, between Tavewa and Matacawalevu.

Kubo Passage:

The initial course, from Savuti Point on Nanuya-sewa, is 175° for a position midway between the beacon on Namalo Rocks and that on the fringing reef south of Namatadra Point (Nanuyalevu), with the right-hand (or eastern) brow of the summit of Tavewa in transit with the beacon on the south end of Yamotu Ni Cagilaba the middle ground reef. (View 62)

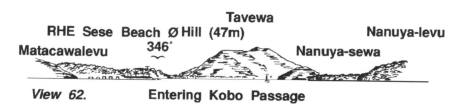

View 62.   **Entering Kobo Passage**

This course is held until midway between the beacons when it is altered to 166°, with the right-hand edge of Sese Village beach in transit with hill (47m.), on the south-western end of Tavewa, bearing 346°.

General depths of 25 to 30 metres will be carried throughout, except when passing between the reefs at Kubo Passage, when depths about 15 metres will be found. Kubo Passage has recently been marked with two small buoys, placed there by Blue Lagoon Cruises. The area is subject to tidal streams and, with a bottom consisting of fine sand and some mud, discoloration of the water is common particularly when there are moderate to strong winds.

Matacawalevu
Vatunibobo △   Tavewa   Nacula
                               Nanuya-levu

View 63.   **Approaching Kobo Passage from South-east**

Westward:

Proceed from the area of Savuti Point to the westward of Yamotu Ni Caqilaba Reef, steering generally mid-way between the reef and the coast north of Sese village for a pole on an isolated reef south of Tavewa. Alter course gradually as the pole is approached to leave it to starboard, and place the northern end of Nanuya-sewa astern bearing 096°, steering 276°. Hold this course until clear of Korosavuku Point. Depths of 7 to 17 metres will be found with the bottom clearly visible. The flood stream sets east and the ebb west in this passage.

Matacawalevu to Naviti:

 The next all-weather anchorage south from Nanuya-sewa is found at the northern end of Naviti in either Somosomo Bay or Gunu Bay, both of which are parts of a large, unnamed bay. Gunu Bay was not visited, but was reported as being slightly better than Somosomo Bay if any swell is entering from the north-west.

Passage to Somosomo Bay may be made down either side of Yageta, which lies between Matacawalevu and Naviti. During periods of strong south-easterly winds, the western route, though a little more difficult, is the most comfortable.

The eastern route is quite direct once a boat has cleared Kubo Passage. The reef east of Yaqeta is steep to and the entrance through Naivalavala Passage, into the waters north of Naviti, presents no problems.

West Coast Route:

Having cleared the passage between Tavewa and Matacawalevu, place the summit of Tavewa astern bearing 061° and steer 241° until about one mile west of Culo Reef when Ori, one of four small islands east of the north-eastern end of Naviti, will be in line with the western headland of Yaqeta, bearing 184°. (View 64)

View 64.   **Matacawalevu - West Coast**

This transit should then be steered for about two miles, until about abeam the northern end of Yaqeta. The transit will lead between two small reefs (Repd.1980), which do exist and are visible when close by.

Approaching the reefs, depths are about 50 to 60 metres. They then shoal gradually when passing between them, the least depth being 21 metres, before deepening again to about 35 metres on the other side.

As the boat draws abeam of the north end of Yaqeta the left-hand edge of Matacawalevu and Senakaga will close together bearing about 029°, with Koroiki showing open of Senakaga. (View 65)

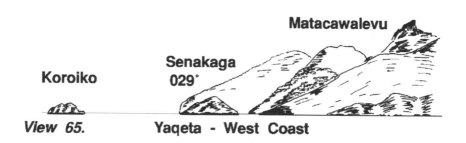

View 65.   **Yaqeta - West Coast**

This transit should be put astern steering 209°, which will lead between a number of reefs off the west coast of Yaqeta. When about 1.8 miles west of the southern point of the island course can be altered to 193° to enter Somosomo Bay, steering for Hill (182m.) in transit with the left-hand edge of Somosomo village. (View 66)

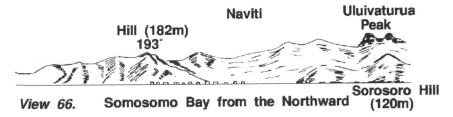

View 66. **Somosomo Bay from the Northward**

Alternatively, for passage west of Naviti, steer 230° for the transit of Vakaweitaci Point and the left hand edge of Nanuyanikucuve. (View 67)

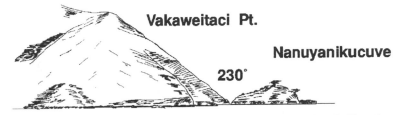

View 67. **Vakaweitaci Pt. from North of Drui Reef**

Course 193° may be held all the way into Somosomo Bay. It will pass about 300 metres to the east of Drui Reef.

Although the water appears deep, a yacht may wish to cast to port as the reef is being passed.

A 9-metre pinnacle, of very small extent, lies on this track midway between Drui Reef and Narewa Point. It is difficult to find but may offer rewarding diving.

Somosomo Anchorage:

Once in Somosomo Bay proper, leave Vomo Reef to starboard and anchor to the south of it in about 10 metres sand. The holding is good.

Although fringed by reef, there are some excellent beaches on the eastern shore of Somosomo Bay and to the northward.

Naviti:

The largest island of the Yasawa Group, Naviti has a number of anchorages that are worthy of a visit. Gunu Bay and Somosomo Bay, described above, are the best all-weather anchorages but there are others, particularly on the west coast, which offer good swimming and good beaches. Soso Bay, in the south, is a good anchorage in all but a southerly.

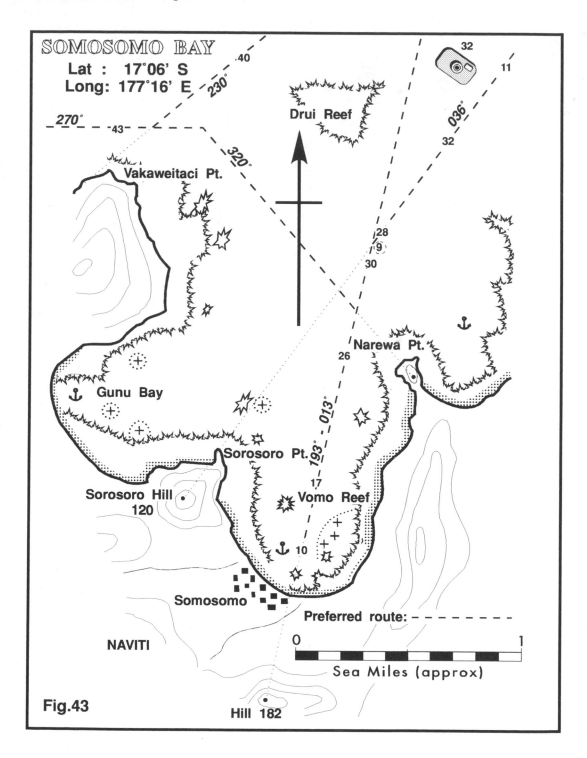

SOMOSOMO BAY
Lat : 17°06' S
Long: 177°16' E

Drui Reef

Vakaweitaci Pt.

Narewa Pt.

Gunu Bay

Sorosoro Pt.

Sorosoro Hill
120

Vomo Reef

Somosomo

NAVITI

Preferred route: - - - - - - - -

0   1

Sea Miles (approx)

Fig.43

Hill 182

The village at the head of the bay is renowned for its church which is beautifully decorated with wooden carvings. The ceiling is quite remarkable.

The passages and reefs between and around the four islands—Drawaqa, Nanuyabalavu, Naukacuvu, and Narara —to the south-west of Soso Bay provide excellent spots for swimming and diving, and in settled weather are satisfactory anchorages.

The east coast of Naviti is protected by a large reef. A yacht may therefore pass either side of the island, regardless of weather.

Somosomo Bay to Soso Bay:

Leave Vomo Reef close to port and steer 013° with Hill (182m.) astern, until Uluivaturua Peak is in transit with Sorosoro Hill (120m.), which has a clear grassy summit, bearing 216°.

Alter course to 036° with the transit astern for about 1.75 miles. When Ori just becomes visible from behind Nanuya-magutu Point, alter course to 135° for a further 1.7 miles then, with Uluikorolevu Trig. (also called Vatunibobo on 'Pickmere') on Matacawalevu astern, bearing 011°, steer 191°. (View 68)

Yaqeta   **Naisau △**   **Vatunibobo △**   **Nacula**
Matacawalevu

View 68.   **On the East Coast of Naviti - Looking North**

This course requires some care and adjustment may be necessary because of the distances involved. Nevertheless, the relationship of the Trig. to the skyline of Yaqeta in front of it provides a positive indication of drift once the correct line has been obtained.

This course leads between, and quite close to, several small reefs in the area near the southern end of the chain of small islands extending south-south-westward from Ori. Depths of 12.5 metres will be obtained and the bottom will be visible.

The course of 191° is maintained for a distance of about 2.8 miles until Vasukanavaci, which possesses (1992) a conspicuous lone palm tree, is abeam to starboard.

Course is then altered to 233° on a transit consisting of Tavuniko Point on Narara, Namasilevu Point, and Vuvui, all slightly open to port of one another. (View 69)

This course is held for almost 6 miles with the depth remaining at about 30 metres, except for about 15 metres 0.6 miles south-south-east of

Nalaqu, and an isolated 6.6 metres about one mile east of Nacilau Point.

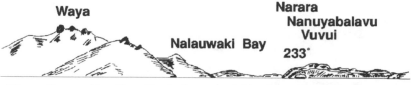

View 69.   On the East Coast of Naviti - Looking South

When south of Nacilau course can be altered gradually to remain about 1/2 mile off and to bring Soso village ahead bearing 000°. This course leads to the anchorage.

Soso Bay—(Fig.44):

A good anchorage over sand and mud, with excellent holding, will be found about 100 metres clear of the reefs off the village, in a depth of about 10 metres.

This anchorage is subject to wind waves in a southerly, but otherwise is a good base from which to visit the islands and bays close southward. Soso village relies on wells for water and none is available to yachts.

Naviti (West Coast):

On sailing from the anchorage in Somosomo Bay, leave Vomo Reef close to port and steer 013° with Hill (182m.) astern until Narewa Point bears 140°, then steer 320° with this point astern to pass between Drui Reef to starboard and Vakaweitaci Point to port.

As Vakaweitaci Point comes abeam, alter course to 270° with Nanuya-magutu Point astern bearing 090°.

After about one mile, when Enemauwau Point is just coming open to the east of Nanuyanikucuve, bearing 203°, alter course to 232° for another mile, until the main summit of Korokulu Point bears 185°, when course as again altered to bring this point ahead.

Steer 185° for about 0.7 mile, and when Vakawaitaci Point is just behind Nanuyanikucuve bearing 053°, steer 233° with this transit astern. (View 70)

Yaqeta
Vakaweitaci Pt. Ø Nanuyanikucuve   **Naviti**
Matacawalevu   053°

View 70.   Naviti - West Coast (1)

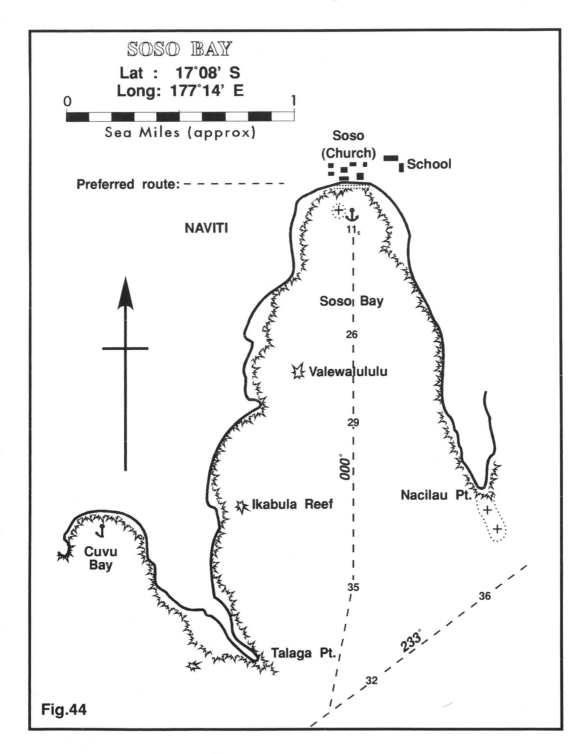

SOSO BAY
Lat : 17°08' S
Long: 177°14' E

0   1
Sea Miles (approx)

Soso
(Church)   ■ School

Preferred route: – – – – – –

NAVITI

11₅

Soso Bay

26

Valewalululu

29

000°

Ikabula Reef

Nacilau Pt.

Cuvu
Bay

35

36

233°

Talaga Pt.

32

Fig.44

215

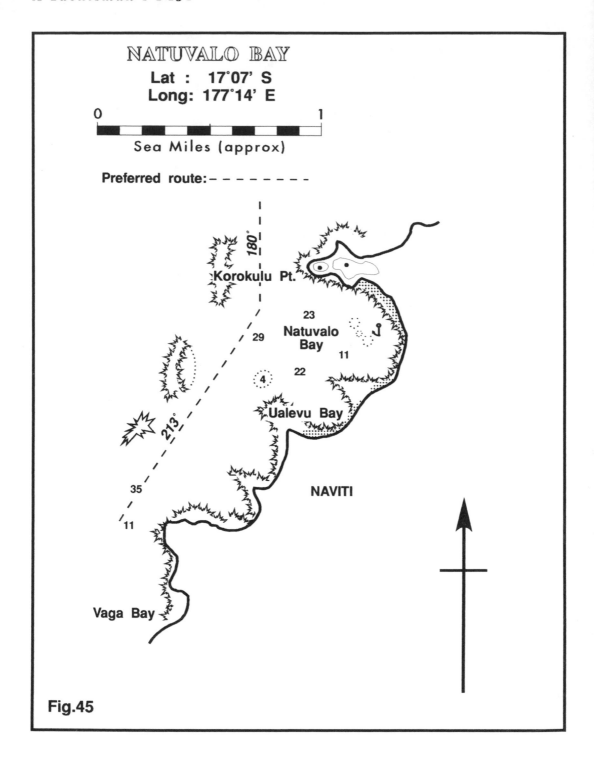

NATUVALO BAY
Lat : 17°07' S
Long: 177°14' E

0 — 1
Sea Miles (approx)

Preferred route: – – – – – – –

180°

Korokulu Pt.

23
Natuvalo
Bay

29

11

22

4

Ualevu Bay

213°

35

NAVITI

11

Vaga Bay

Fig.45

After another short leg of only 0.6 mile, alter course to 180° to pass between Korokulu Point and the reef 0.3 mile to the west. On passing Korokulu Point a yacht may choose to anchor in either Natuvalo or Ualevu Bays.

Natuvalo Bay—(Fig.45):

This bay provides a pleasant spot to anchor providing there has not been too much west in the weather, as this can result in some residual swell. The bay has a few isolated bures on the shore which are used as temporary dwellings by the villagers from Kese on the other side. There are several gardens on the hills backing the beach. The bottom is generally fine sand with some mud and a few isolated coral heads, which are useful for securing a stern anchor when it is necessary to hold the stern into any swell. Depths for anchoring are about 8 to 10 metres. In 1985 there was a fresh water shower standing alone in the foundations of a bure. Water was 'on tap' but neither its source nor its owner was found.

Naviti (West Coast)—(Continued):

From Natuvalo Bay steer a course of 213°, with Enemauwau Point and the left-hand edge of Nanuyanikucuve, 033° astern (View 71.),

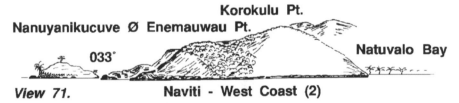

Nanuyanikucuve Ø Enemauwau Pt. **Korokulu Pt.**

033° **Natuvalo Bay**

View 71. **Naviti - West Coast (2)**

until abeam of Vaga Bay, when course is altered to 200° for the summit of Naukacuvu in transit with Salakolo Point on Nanuyabalavu. (View 72.)

Naukacuvu Ø Salakolo Pt.

Nanuyabalavu 200° **Waya**

Yaroiko Pt.

View 72. **Naviti - West Coast (3)**

This transit takes a yacht about 300 metres off Tavidi Point but the water is clear and deep. Once abeam Tokatokaunu Passage a yacht may continue to the south-west on a course of 210° for Yaroiko Point (View 73.),or steer south for an anchorage west of Drawaqa.

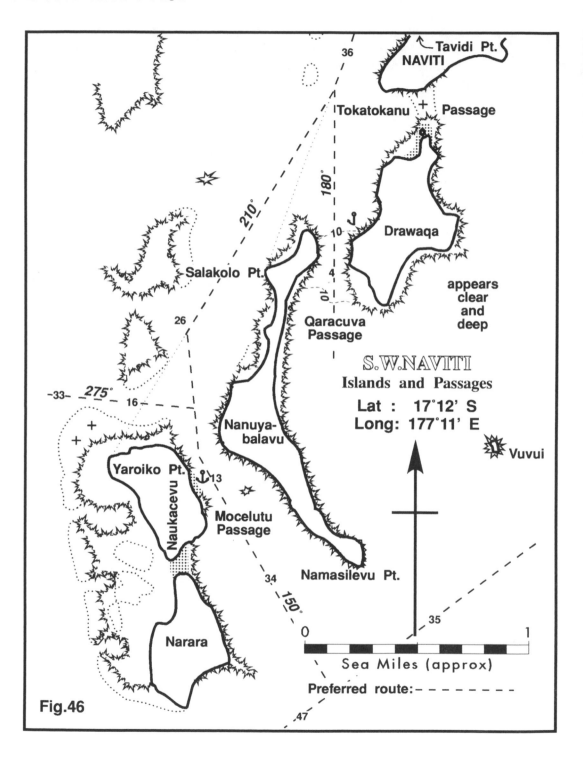

Tavidi Pt.
NAVITI

Tokatokanu + Passage

Drawaqa

appears
clear
and
deep

Salakolo Pt.

Qaracuva
Passage

S.W. NAVITI
Islands and Passages
Lat : 17°12' S
Long: 177°11' E

Vuvui

Nanuya-
balavu

Yaroiko Pt.

Naukacevu

Mocelutu
Passage

Namasilevu Pt.

Narara

0   1

Sea Miles (approx)

Preferred route: – – – – – –

Fig.46

If you feel like living dangerously, go through Qaracuva Passage and north-east to Cuvu or Soso Bays. Mocelutu Passage, just two miles further on, is clear and deep.

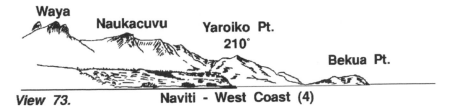

View 73.   **Naviti - West Coast (4)**

If proceeding south-westward, adjust course to keep about 1/2 mile off Nanuyabalavu after passing Salakolo Point. On approaching Mocelutu Passage you may choose to proceed directly to seaward through the gap in the reefs extending north from Naukacuvu, or pass through the passage. Pass through the reefs on a course of 275° with the summit of Nanuyabalavu astern, or keep to the centre of the pass between the islands and on into clear water.

Waya:

The largest of the southernmost islands of the Yasawa chain is the most rugged of the group, with numerous volcanic plugs rising to more than 500 metres. The scenery is most spectacular and the island is blessed with two large bays that provide reasonable anchorages for those wishing to remain for more than a day or two.

The better anchorage is Yalobi Bay, in the south, which is given added protection, on its eastern side, by two other smaller islands, Waya Lailai (shown as Wayasewa on chart F5) and Kuata. Here it is usually possible to select a part of the bay where the effect of swell is minimal, except when there has been bad south or south-westerly weather over several days.

The other anchorage is in the north at Nalauwaki Bay.

Waya is less than 30 miles from Lautoka and is often the first island in the Yasawas visited by yachts. The route passing west of Vomo presents no navigational complexities. The island is also easily approached from either Naviti in the north or the Mamanucas in the south.

Naviti to Waya:

The waters between Naviti and Waya's north coast appear clear of dangers, except for a shoal (Repd 1980) about one mile west of Narara, with depths of about 80 metres. Unless the weather has been bad from the north, the first anchorage will probably be in Nalauwaki Bay under the tall peaks in the north of the island.

Nalauwaki Bay—(Fig.47):

At the head of Nalauwaki Bay is a small indentation in the reef called Rurugu Bay. The indentation is caused by the outflow of fresh water from a creek draining the peaks and gullies behind. This creek has been dammed a short way in from the beach and provides the water supply for Nalauwaki village. Providing that water is spilling from the dam, the village will permit yachts to top up. The rocks below the dam are used as the village 'laundry'. Rurugu Bay was once called Watering Bay.

A good anchorage can be had over a sand bottom, in a depth of about 5 metres, at the mouth of Rurugu Bay.

Due to the open nature of the waters around Waya, a swell can be experienced in this anchorage and, although the wind is calm, a yacht may roll. The answer is, as always, the second anchor from the stern.

An alternative anchorage may be had off the sandy beach to the north-west of the village close in to the reef. If the swell is from the north-west, this will be more comfortable than Rurugu Bay, although a second anchor will still probably be needed.

Of interest at Nalauwaki are the goat herds. This end of the island is particularly rugged and, while there are gardens in the hills, the main 'cash crop' is goats. There are two large goat corrals on either side of the village. To prevent them eating out the sparse vegetation the goats are unpenned in the morning and, after several hours' grazing are repenned in the afternoon. Goats will often be seen foraging in the hills behind the village.

On the other side of the peninsula that lies north-west of Nalauwaki village is a beautiful bay, backed by a sandy beach. Likuliku Bay can be inspected by walking to the top of the ridge behind the goat corral. If the weather is good it is worth a visit by boat.

Waya (West Coast):

Sail from Rurugu Bay on a course of 000°, or from the alternative anchorage, so as to clear the reef to the north, and then place Rurugu Bay astern on a course of 000°.

Maintain this heading until Koromasoli Point bears 105°, then alter course to 285° with the point astern and steer 285°. (View 74)

This will lead north of the reefs extending north from Nacilau Point. If visibility is good it is possible to eyeball it between the reefs and the point on a course of about 270° with Koromasoli Point astern, then south-westward past Bekua Point.

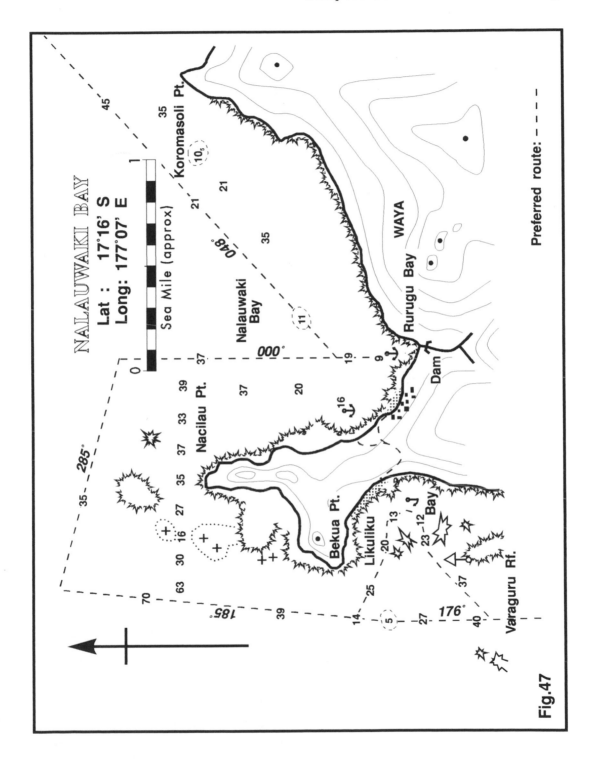

NALAUWAKI BAY

Lat : 17°16' S
Long: 177°07' E

Sea Mile (approx)

Koromasoli Pt.

WAYA

Rurugu Bay

Nalauwaki Bay

Dam

Nacilau Pt.

Bekua Pt.

Likuliku Bay

Varaguru Rf.

Preferred route: – – –

Fig.47

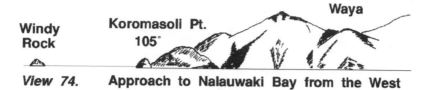

View 74.   Approach to Nalauwaki Bay from the West

From the position where Bekua Point is in transit with Vatunareba Trig. steer 185° until Likuliku Bay is abeam to port, and then adjust course to 176° to pass between the west coast of Waya and the reefs close offshore. Depending on the sea conditions, it is sometimes possible to see Yagusu Reef, south of Loto Point, ahead in the distance.

When abeam Likuliku Bay the boat may pass over a pinnacle with a depth of 5 metres in general depths of 12 to 14 metres. Once the pinnacle is passed depths remain at about 40 metres for the remainder of the passage down the west coast. It is on this leg that one will see what is probably the most spectacular scenery in the Yasawas, if not in Fiji.

A boat may enter Likuliku Bay passing to the north or south of the small reefs protecting it, and anchor as convenient in about 10 metres over sand. The best anchorage is probably in the south-east corner of the bay.

Another possible anchorage is behind Varaguru Reef, which carries a beacon at its northern end, close southward.

Continuing down the west coast there is little to do but enjoy the scenery until near Loto Point, a conspicuous cone that forms the south-western tip of Waya. Between Loto Point and Yagusu Reef, there are two sunken reefs. A yacht may pass either to the north of both on a course of 135°, steering midway between Waya Lailai and Kuata, or between the two on a course of 108°, steering for the highest point on Waya Lailai. (View 75.)

View 75.   Waya Lailai from the West

Both these sunken reefs appear to carry more than 2 metres of water but have not been sounded over.

On clearing Loto Point and the reefs, alter course to the east-north-east for the gap between Waya Lailai and Waya. Once into Yalobi Bay steer for the chosen anchorage.

222

Waya (East Coast):

From the anchorage in Nalauwaki Bay, steer 052° to clear Koromasoli Point. Depths of 10 metres may be encountered westward of the point. When north of the point, alter course to 103° to pass between Windy Rock and Waya. When Windy Rock bears 347° alter course to place it astern and steer 167° until Nabagi Point, the easternmost point of Waya, is abeam and then alter to 183° for Naqalia Point, the eastern point of Waya Lailai. There is a visible sunken reef about 1.5 miles east of the south-east point of Waya.

When approaching Naqalia Point, adjust course to pass about 500 metres off and, when the northern tip of Kuata bears 255°, steer 255° with the point ahead.

Steer this course until Viti Rock, off the southern end of Waya Lailai, is in line with the summit of the island, bearing 330°, then steer 279° through the centre of the passage between Waya Lailai and Kuata.

White Rock will be astern bearing 099°.

On clearing the passage, steer 354° for the high wooded peak above the western part of Yalobi village. This will lead between Ilo Reef and Waya Lailai (View 76.). Once in Yalobi Bay, anchor as required.

Vatunareba △ Wooded Peak Ø LHE Yalobi Village

354° School

View 76. Yalobi Bay from the South

Yalobi Bay—(Fig. 48):

Yalobi Bay is generally open to the south-west and after bad weather there can be some slight swell entering the bay. Nevertheless, a quiet anchorage can be found tucked up into the head of the bay off the west end of the village.

Yalobi village is the seat of the Tui Waya, who has many friends amongst yachtsmen. It is to him you should pay your respects.

The house of the Tui Waya, on the point between the village and the school, is easily recognised by the flagpole in the front garden.

As with Nalauwaki, the hills behind Yalobi ensure an adequate water supply, and permission to draw water from a tap at the school or the Tui's house will usually be granted. 1992 was a year of drought through much of Fiji, particularly the Western Division, and water was not available.

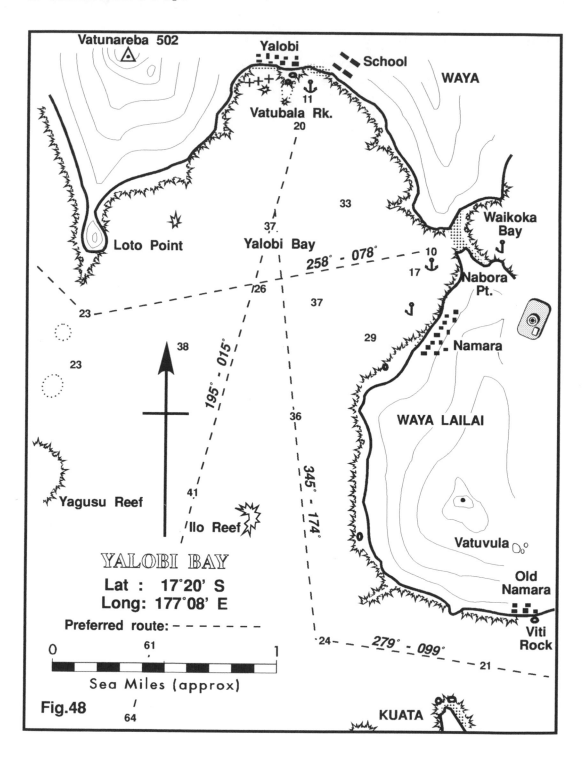

Vatunareba 502

Yalobi

School

WAYA

Loto Point

Yalobi Bay

Vatubala Rk.

11

20

33

37

258° - 078°

10

17

Waikoka Bay

Nabora Pt.

126

37

Namara

23

29

38

WAYA LAILAI

23

36

195° - 015°

345° - 174°

41

Yagusu Reef

Ilo Reef

Vatuvula

Old Namara

YALOBI BAY

Lat : 17°20' S

Long: 177°08' E

Preferred route: - - - - - -

24

279° - 099°

21

Viti Rock

0   61   1

Sea Miles (approx)

Fig.48

64

KUATA

In Fiji, the game of Rugby football is almost a religion. In the sub-district competition Waya fields a very good team. Their home ground is the football ground of the school, and a fine Saturday afternoon's entertainment can be had watching the game should one be scheduled for the time of your visit. Almost as entertaining on the day of a big match is the sight of hundreds of villagers from all over the island arriving by boat, usually crammed to the gunwales, or descending the track down the hills in a continuous file.

Waya, and Waya Lailai in particular, were badly damaged during the cyclones of 1985 but few signs of the damage remain today. The village of Namara on Waya Lailai was lucky to escape destruction by landslides from Vatuvula, the high hill that towers above it. Although the primary school and the village were resited on the north-west coast of the island near Naboro Point, it appears that much of the old village is still being used today.

Anchorages:

In settled weather there is a good anchorage off Naboro Point in 10 metres, sand, with satisfactory holding. The beach and swimming is good, however this spot is also popular with the Blue Lagoon Cruise vessels and it can become a bit crowded.

The water off Yalobi village provides several anchorages. There is one, and maybe two, in about 10 metres, fine sand and mud, with excellent holding, off the school to the east of Vatubala Rock. The others are to the west of the rock. These probably provide the quietest water, but are a bit more open to south-easterly winds. Depths here are a little deeper being about 15 to 20 metres.

It is reported that another anchorage can be obtained in Waikoka Bay on the north coast of Waya Lailai, during periods of westerly weather.

Lautoka to Waya—(BA845, F5):

The passage from Lautoka to Waya covers a distance of about 28 miles and, although a cautionary note will be found on chart BA845, the route described is through clear, deep water.

Unfortunately Waya, and Waya Lailai, both lie just outside the border of the British (and American) chart, just north of the island of Kuata. Chart F5 is, in any case almost essential if cruising the Yasawas. These directions refer to that chart.

Depart from Lautoka (do not forget to clear customs!), and steer north of Vio, Pinder Reefs and Tivoa to a position about 293° - 3 miles from Tivoa. Then shape a course of 328° directly for the summit of Waya Lailai, leaving Vomo and the islet and reefs north-west of it to starboard.

Both Waya Lailai and Kuata are steep to, and passage into Yalobi Bay may be made between the two. As the vessel closes Waya Lailai it will be possible to identify Viti Rock. Course may be adjusted to bring the rock in transit with the summit of Waya Lailai, bearing 330°.

When the centre of the passage between Waya Lailai and Kuata bears 279°, steer this course. White Rock will be seen astern bearing 099°. Do not cut the corner around Waya Lailai as the reef extends about 400 metres off the south-western shore. There is a drying rock a little way in from the edge.

On clearing the passage, steer 354° for the high wooded peak above the western part of Yalobi village, leaving Ilo Reef to port. Then anchor as described earlier in this chapter.

Waya to Lautoka:

By reversing the foregoing the passage back to Lautoka will be seen to present no problems, even though there may be some windward work. Providing that a yacht leaves Waya before about 0800, the passage can be completed easily in a day, and it should be possible to complete the obligatory customs formality well before close of business on the same day.

Even if going to windward the waters are reasonably clear, the fixing is simple, and it should be possible to enjoy the passage under sail without worry.

INDEX

Note: 1.   Places containing the following services or special attributes are also listed under the appropriate group heading:-

Airfields and Services, Anchorages, Buses and Taxis, Fuel, Hospitals, Hurricane-holes, Islands, Jetties and Wharves, Lights, Markets, Stores, Supermarkets, Resorts, Villages, and Water.

Note: 2.   A list is given, at the end of this index, of the **phonetic** spelling of place names found on British Admiralty and US Charts and US Sailing Directions, together with the spelling used below and in the book. Attention is also drawn to the section on **Orthography** on page x at the front of the book.

B

J

Jetties and Wharves:

K

L

Lights :

M

Markets:

List of Phonetic Fijian Names

The following list of the earlier phonetic spelling of Fijian names appears on most of the British Admiralty chart series including some that have been metricated. The most recent charts, from about 1987 onwards, have adopted the Fijian spelling and the phonetic names will in time disappear. Not all the names here given will necessarily be found on the latest charts. The Admiralty Pilot, since 1984, uses the Fijian spelling.

The US chart coverage of Fiji has been reduced to six. The names used both on the charts and in Pub.126, Sailing Directions (Enroute) (1988) for the Pacific Islands are the phonetic ones given below.

The phonetic names are given in *italics* with the modern day usage in normal print.

Kandavu	Kadavu	*Mamanutha*	Mamanuca
Kumbo	Kubo	*Mambualau*	Mabualau
Kumbulau	Kubulau	*Manggewa*	Maqewa
Lakemba	Lakeba	*Manunggiwa*	Manuqiwa
Lambassa	Labasa	*Matangi*	Matagi
Langalevu	Lagalevu	*Matathawalevu*	Matacawalevu
Langi	Lagi	*Mbakambaka*	Bakabaka
Lauthala	Laucala	*Mbala*	Bala
Lingau	Ligau	*Mbangasau*	Bagasau
Lovoninggai	Lovoniqai	*Mbavatu*	Bavatu
Lutunasombasomba	Lutunasobasoba	*Mbeka*	Beka
Makongai	Makogai	*Mbekana*	Bekana

Vonombia	Vonobia	*Yandravanggele*	Yadravaqele
Vunda	Vuda	*Yandravavatu*	Yadravavatu
Wailalambi	Wailalabi	*Yandua*	Yadua
Wandingi	Wadigi	*Yanggara*	Yaqara
Yalombi	Yalobi	*Yanggeta*	Yaqeta
Yandako	Yadako	*Yathalea*	Yacalea

List of Major Lights (1993)

Name	Lat S Long E	Description	Height metres	Range miles	Comments
KADAVU Cape Washington	19°06'.6 177°57'.8	Fl W 5s	63	11	White metal framework tower
Vanuatabu	19°01'.6 178°28'.8	Fl W 2s	50	15	Metal framework tower
Solo N Astrolabe Reef	18°38'.3 178°32'.2	LFl W 30s	29	10	Red metal tower, white bands
VITI LEVU Vatulele NW side	18°30'.5 177°37'.0	Fl W 10s	41	17	White concrete tower
Nasilai Reef	18°07'.9 178°41'.5	LFl(2)W 30s	14	12	White square tower, red bands
Suva Harbour Front ldg light	18°06'.4 178°24'.4	F R	40	14	Red square tower, white stripe
---------------- Rear ldg light	18°05'.8 178°24'.6	F R	103	19	Red square tower, white stripe
Beqa	18°24'.1 178°10'.2	Fl(3)W 12s	12	15	White metal tripod yellow band
Navo	18°06'.8 177°19'.7	Fl(2)W 12s	14	12	Red tripod tower
Navula Passage ----Reef S end	17°55'.4 177°13'.0	Fl W 5s	13	10	Concrete structure
Momi Bay Front ldg light	17°54'.9 177°16'.7	Q W	10	12	White and black tower
------------ Rear ldg light	17°54'.5 177°17'.7	Q W	63	20	White and black tower
Naikorokoro	17°39'.3 177°22.9	Fl(2)W 6s	13	10	White "box" on black piles
YASAWA GROUP Viwa	17°07'.7 176°55'.5	Fl(3)W 15s	17	12	White metal framework tower

Name	Lat S (W) Long E	Description	Height metres	Range miles	Comments
BLIGH WATER Yadua	16°49'.1 178°18'.1	Fl(2)W 15s	200	14	Red metal framework tower
Vatu-i-ra Channel	17°16'.0 178°33'.0	Fl W 2s	12	11	Black lattice tower on concrete pillar
Vatu-i-ra Channel West	17°16'.6 178°29'.2	Fl W 5s	12	11	Black lattice tower on concrete pillar
OVALAU N Ovalau	17°33'.9 178°51'.1	Fl(3)W 10s	12	11	Black framework tower on concrete
Levuka NaTubari Front ldg light	17°40'.8 178°50'.3	F G	15	7	Neon cross on church tower
------------------ Rear leading light	17°40'.8 178°50'.2	F G	30	11	Vertical neon on mast
Wakaya Reef	17°41'.4 179°04'.9	Fl(2)W 15s	23	19	White 8-sided tower, red bands
Batiki Irene Point	17°46'.2 179°08'.6	Fl W 4.5s	35	16	White 8-sided tower,concrete base
Makogai	17°27'.2 178°58.6	Fl W 7s	271	14	Red metal framework tower
Koro	17°23'.7 179°23'.0	Fl W 10s	59	18	White tower **TE 1989**
VANUA LEVU Point Reef (Savusavu)	16°49'.8 179°16'.2	Fl W 3s	8	10	White 6-sided concrete tower
Kia. N end	16°13'.3 179°06'.0	Fl W 5s	70	15	Metal tower
Udu Point	16°07'.4 W 179°57'.0	Fl(2)W 25s	49	17	White 6-sided concrete tower
TAVEUNI off Vuna Point	16°57'.9 179°52'.5	Fl W 8s	10	10	White concrete tower
Wailagilala, SW point	16°45'.0 W 179°06'.0	Fl W 5s	29	18	White round metal tower
Qelelevu, E end	16°05'.4 W 179°08'.8	Fl(2)W 12s	27	15	Framework tower **TE 1991**
LAU GROUP Totoya, SW point	19°00'.0 W 179°52'.0	Fl(3)W 10s	76	20	Framework tower
Vatoa	19°49'.7 W 178°13'.4	Fl W 5s	70	21	Framework tower

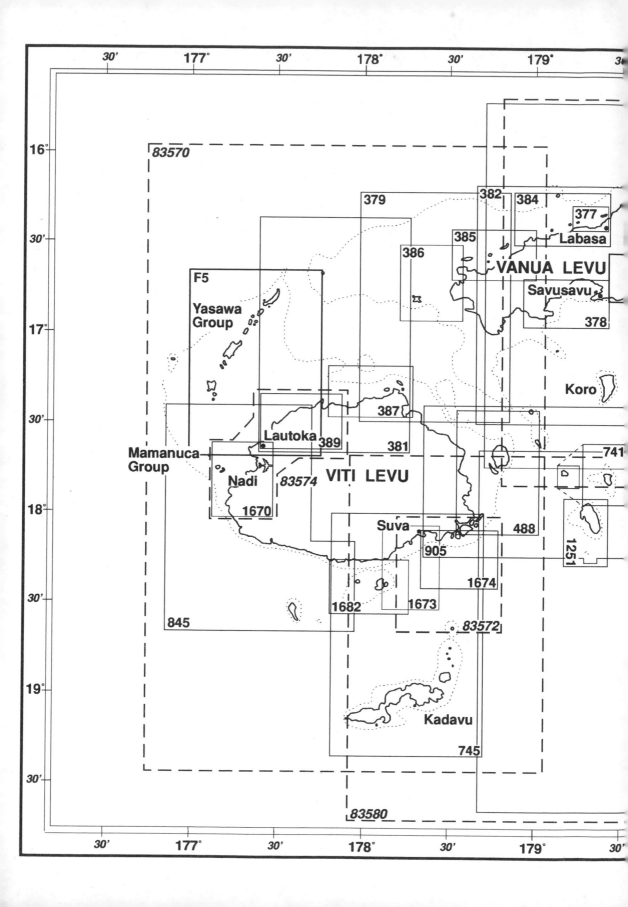